ESSENTIALS OF SUPERVISORY MANAGEMENT

About the Author

Lester R. Bittel has acquired an enormous amount of experience in a variety of fields and positions. He has worked in a number of manufacturing plants and managed more than one. As editor in chief of the leading industrial publication of its time, *Factory Management and Maintenance,* Mr. Bittel visited hundreds of plants and spoke with thousands of first-line supervisors and their bosses. As a management consultant, he has aided dozens of companies in developing and operating their supervisory training programs.

Mr. Bittel is the author of ten books, including *What Every Supervisor Should Know,* and many articles on various phases of industrial management, plant maintenance, personnel management, and human relations. Most recently he was the editor in chief of the *Encyclopedia of Professional Management.* He has been honored by the American Society of Mechanical Engineers as its Towne Lecturer, by the International Management Council for his contributions to supervisory and management education, and, five times, by the American Business Press for outstanding business journalism.

As a volunteer, Mr. Bittel was for 12 years the executive vice president of the Chilton Memorial Hospital, a board chairman of the Silver Bay Conference on Human Relations in Management, a vice president of the Society for the Advancement of Management, and a member of the public information committee of the National Safety Council.

ESSENTIALS OF SUPERVISORY MANAGEMENT

LESTER R. BITTEL
Professor
School of Business
James Madison University

Gregg Division
McGraw-Hill Book Company
New York • Atlanta • Dallas • St. Louis
San Francisco • Auckland • Bogotá • Düsseldorf
Johannesburg • London • Madrid • Mexico
Montreal • New Delhi • Panama • Paris
São Paulo • Singapore • Sydney • Tokyo • Toronto

Library of Congress Cataloging in Publication Data

Bittel, Lester R
  Essentials of supervisory management.

  Includes bibliographies and index.
  1. Supervision of employees. 2. Supervision of
employees—Case studies. I. Title.
HF5549.B518   658.3′02   80-13784
ISBN 0-07-005571-8

In short, to Muriel

Essentials of Supervisory Management

Copyright © 1981 by McGraw-Hill, Inc. All rights reserved. Printed in the United States of America. No part of this publication may be reproduced, stored in a retrieval system, or transmitted, in any form or by any means, electronic, mechanical, photocopying, recording, or otherwise, without the prior written permission of the publisher. Portions of this work are taken from Lester R. Bittel's *What Every Supervisor Should Know: The Basics of Supervisory Management, Fourth Edition,* © 1980.

1234567890 SMSM 8876543210

Sponsoring Editor: Gerald Gleason
Editing Supervisor: Karen Sekiguchi
Designer: Eileen Kramer
Art Supervisor: Howard Brotman
Production Supervisor: Priscilla Taguer

Technical Studio: Burmar Technical Corp.

Contents

Cases in Point	vi
Preface	vii
PART 1 MASTERING THE JOB OF SUPERVISORY MANAGEMENT	**1**
Chapter 1 **The Supervisory Management Job**	2
Chapter 2 **Problem Solving and Decision Making**	20
Chapter 3 **The Arts of Leadership**	34
Self-Check for Part 1	49
PART 2 PLANNING, ORGANIZING, AND CONTROLLING WORK	**53**
Chapter 4 **Making Plans and Carrying Out Policy**	54
Chapter 5 **Organizing an Effective Department**	68
Chapter 6 **Exercising Control of People and Processes**	87
Self-Check for Part 2	102
PART 3 MANAGING PEOPLE AT WORK	**105**
Chapter 7 **Individual Motivation**	106
Chapter 8 **Work Group Behavior**	118
Chapter 9 **Conflict and Cooperation**	131
Chapter 10 **Activating the Work Force by Communications**	148
Chapter 11 **Giving Orders and Instructions**	164
Self-Check for Part 3	177
PART 4 HANDLING SENSITIVE PROBLEMS	**181**
Chapter 12 **Counseling Problem People**	182
Chapter 13 **Handling Complaints and Avoiding Grievances**	200
Chapter 14 **How and When to Discipline**	214
Self-Check for Part 4	227
PART 5 IMPROVING EMPLOYEE PERFORMANCE	**231**
Chapter 15 **Appraisal of Employee Performance**	232
Chapter 16 **Training and Development of Employees**	248
Self-Check for Part 5	264
Appendix	267
Rankings for Solutions to Cases in Point	267
Key to Self-Checks	275
Index	**277**

Cases in Point

1. The Case of the Complaining Keypunch Operator — **15**
2. The Case of the Worst Job in the Department — **30**
3. The Case of the Nurses' New Supervisor — **46**
4. The Case of the Forgotten Price Change — **65**
5. The Case of the Backposted Overtime — **83**
6. The Case of the Overheated Copying Machine — **98**
7. The Case of the Conflicting Coffee Breaks — **115**
8. The Case of the Sixteen Drafters — **127**
9. The Case of the Unhappy Mixer Operator — **145**
10. The Case of the Changing Ledger Entries — **161**
11. The Case of the Refused Overtime — **174**
12. The Case of Mary Smith's Irrational Behavior — **197**
13. The Case of the Typist Who Got No Raise — **211**
14. The Case of the Sleeping Miner — **224**
15. The Case of the Revised Job Rating — **245**
16. The Case of the Lost Letter — **261**

Commentary and preferred rankings for the solutions to the Cases in Point appear in the Appendix.

Preface

Essentials of Supervisory Management is intended for the use of all those who wish to learn about, or improve their skills in, supervisory management. It is especially suitable for men and women already employed in commerce, government, or industry. You will find that its emphasis is on practicality and usefulness. Underlying theories and principles are explained, but maximum coverage is given to real-life, on-the-job applications. The 16 chapters of this text have been distilled from the author's landmark work, *What Every Supervisor Should Know, Fourth Edition*.

This book was conceived and designed to make reading and learning easy for you. Incorporated in its makeup are the following features to help maximize your own study efforts:

Key Concepts. Placed at the beginning of each chapter, Key Concepts should be read first because they summarize in five succinct statements the basic ideas covered in that chapter.

Questions and Answers. This is the main body of the text. The questions are arranged in a carefully selected sequence to advance one idea at a time from its fundamental stage to detailed suggestions for applying it in practice. On the other hand, you need not read every chapter from its beginning to end. Instead, you may choose to look for and read first those questions that apply most directly to your present work.

Review Questions. These follow immediately the end of the questions and answers. Check your ability to answer them. If you cannot, or are uncertain about your answers, go back to the text and reread the pertinent material. Only by doing this can you be sure that you fully understand the valuable principles and practices covered in the text.

Cases in Point. In each chapter, just after the Review Questions, there is a description of a real-life supervisory case history. A typical Case in Point tells about a particularly sticky on-the-job situation that requires solving by the supervisor in charge. Read the case. Then study the list of five alternative solutions at the end of the case. Choose the one approach that seems best to you, then the next most attractive, and so on, down to the one you like least. For each alternative solution enter a number from 1 to 5 in the space provided. After you have made your decisions, turn to the Appendix to see how the author ranked these alternatives. You may or may not agree with him, but you should be able to defend your choices if challenged by one of your associates.

Action Summary Checklists. At the very end of each chapter you will find a checklist designed for use on your job. Each list contains 15 items, which sum up the main ideas covered in the chapter. Look over the list. Under the *Action Needed* heading, check "yes" for any item that needs action from you. Check "no" if you already are using that idea on your job or if it does not apply to your present work. For each item that you have checked "yes" (needs action), make a notation of what you intend to do. When you have applied the idea, you can then mark down under the *Date Completed* heading the date it was done. Of course, just reading through the 15 items in the checklist will provide you with a detailed review and summary of the chapter's main ideas, too.

Self-Checks. At the end of each major part of the book you will find a set of questions to try out on yourself. These questions cover material outlined in the Key Concepts and Action Summary Checklist for the chapters in that part of the book. Questions are arranged in three formats: multiple choice, true and false, and fill-in-the-blank. After you have answered the questions, turn to the Appendix to find the correct answers. Here again, if you have chosen some wrong answers or have been uncertain about your choice, go back to that part of the text where the material was covered. Read it again before trying the Self-Check a second time.

Index. After you have finished reading the book, you may want to refer again to a particular idea or technique. Turn to the Index. Often a particular subject or term is listed as appearing on several different pages. By reading each page entry, you will broaden your grasp of that subject or term so that you may make the most of it when you next apply that idea on your job.

ACKNOWLEDGMENTS

I wish to acknowledge the valuable advice and counsel of the following individuals: Bernice Johnston, Children's Services Division of Salem, Oregon, for her thoughtful counsel on equal treatment of the sexes; Joseph T. Allmon of Riegel Textile Corp.; Ernest Balkany of Steelcraft Company; Albert Benglen of the International Management Council; Paul Deysher at AMP, Inc.; Frank Diehl of Sheller-Globe, Inc.; Robert Johnson of Blaw-Knox Division; Ronald E. Leigh of the National Management Association; Marie Leonard of Morton-Norwich Products, Inc.; Edward Martin of Hory-Georgetown Technical College; Patricia Moran of Veterans Administration Hospital in Downey, Illinois; George Piccoli of the New York Chamber of Commerce and Industry; Wallace Richardson, professor of industrial engineering at Lehigh University; and Ray Vogt of Pullman Standard Company.

PART 1
MASTERING THE JOB OF SUPERVISORY MANAGEMENT

Supervisory management requires the ability to get things done through other people. To master this job, supervisors must first fully understand the nature of the work expected of them and then master the science of decision making as well as the art of leadership.

Chapter 1 shows how supervisors can meet the demand for results and handle a heavy administrative burden while displaying a genuine sensitivity toward employee needs.

Chapter 2 outlines the techniques for successful problem solving and decision making, two activities that dominate the supervisor's role.

Chapter 3 presents various approaches to leadership in order that supervisors may develop their capability for securing cooperation and influencing the work force in meeting organizational goals and standards.

Chapter 1
The Supervisory Management Job

Key Concepts

- Supervisors are a vital and legal part of every management group; they add strength to an organization by serving as the keystone (or linking pin) between middle and executive levels of management and the employees who "put their hands on the work."

- Supervisors must bring to their work a unique combination of technical competence, individual energy, and ability to get along with and motivate others.

- The performance of supervisors will be judged by how well they manage the resources assigned to them (facilities and equipment, power and utilities, material and supplies, information, money, and human resources) and the results they get from the resources in the way of output, quality, and cost control.

- The supervisory management job generally requires three skills: technical, administrative, and human relations; of these the human relations skill is often the most demanding.

- It is essential for successful supervisors to balance their skills and efforts equally between that part of the work which is production- or task-oriented and that which is employee- or group-centered. Too much emphasis in a single direction is likely to be self-defeating.

Why does first-line supervision get so much attention?

First-line supervisors in industry and commerce represent just about the single most important force in our American economy. Over a million strong, they carry out a management tradition that dates back to the building of the pyramids, yet time has not simplified their work. First, the industrial revolution with its division of labor and, later, mass-production technique with its accelerated mechanization changed the supervisor's present-day role to one of bewildering and often frustrating complexity.

Today's supervisors (first-line supervisors, front-line supervisors, section or department managers — call them by any of their names) must be vigorous leaders of people, shrewd and effective planners of work, a source of technical know-how, and deft mediators between policy-setting management on the one hand and rank-and-file workers (and their union representatives) on the other. Small wonder that the cry goes up again and again: "We need better supervisors."

Recognition and acceptance of supervisors by top management have helped them to emerge finally as essential and integrated members of the management group and to assume all the responsibilities of full-fledged managers. The way hasn't been easy. Too often it has been painfully slow. Even today there are companies where the supervisor's status is shaky and insecure. But, on the whole, no single group of men and women has achieved and deserved such stature and attention in so short a time after so long a wait as have American supervisors.

Who is a supervisor?

A supervisor is anyone at the first level of management who has the responsibility for getting the hands-on-the-work employees to carry out the plans and policies of higher-level management.

Where did the term come from?

In earlier days the supervisor was the person in charge of a group of towrope pullers or ditch diggers. That person was literally the "fore man" because he was forward of the gang. His authority consisted mainly of chanting the "one, two, three, up" that set the pace for the rest of the workers. In Germany the supervisor is still called a *vorarbeiter,* "fore worker"; in England the term *charge hand* is used. Both terms suggest the lead-person origin.

The term *supervisor* has its roots in Latin, where it means "look over." It was originally applied to the master of a group of artisans. Less than 100 years ago it was not uncommon for masters in New England shops to have almost complete power over the work force. The masters could bid on jobs, hire their own crews, work them as hard as they pleased, and make their living out of the difference between their bid price and the labor costs.

Today the supervisor's job combines some of the talents of the fore man (or leader) and of the master (skilled administrative artisan).

Legally, what makes a supervisor a supervisor?

The federal laws of the United States provide two definitions of a supervisor:

1. *The Taft-Hartley Act of 1947* says that a supervisor is "any individual having authority, in the interest of the employer, to hire, transfer, suspend, lay off, recall, promote, discharge, assign, reward, or discipline other employees, or responsibility to direct them, or to adjust their grievances, or effectively to recommend such action, if in connection with the foregoing the exercise of such authority is not of a merely routine or clerical nature, but requires the use of independent judgment." The Taft-Hartley Act specifically prohibits supervisors from joining a union of production and clerical employees, although they may form a union composed exclusively of supervisors.
2. *The Fair Labor Standards Act of 1938* (or Minimum Wage Law) specifies that supervisors can spend no more than 20 percent of their time doing the same kind of work as the people they direct. It also stipulates that supervisors be paid a salary, regardless of how many hours they work. This latter provision makes some supervisors unhappy because it exempts them from the provision of the law that calls for overtime after a certain number of hours worked. Many employers voluntarily compensate supervisors for overtime in one way or another.

The significance of these two laws is to make supervisors, once and for all, a part of management.

Are supervisors permitted to do the same work as the people they supervise?

There is no law to stop it, but most companies with unions have a contract clause that prohibits supervisors from performing any work that union members would ordinarily do (except in clearly defined emergencies, in which the supervisors would do as they see fit).

Here's a point where most managements agree with unions. Few companies want supervisors to do the work their employees are hired to do. Supervisors are most valuable to their employers when they spend 100 percent of their time supervising. It makes little sense for a $300-a-week supervisor, for instance, to do the work of a $150-a-week employee.

Where do most supervisors come from?

Most supervisors rise from the ranks of the organization in which they serve. Typically they are long-service employees. They have greater experience, have held more different jobs in the organization, and have significantly more education than the men and women they supervise. Usually it is apparent that supervisors are chosen from among the best and the most experienced employees in the organization.[1]

What personal characteristics does higher management find most desirable in supervisors?

The job of supervision is so demanding that higher management tends to look for super people to fill the role. Most firms establish criteria against which supervisory candidates are judged. Here are some of the qualities most commonly sought.[2]

- Energy and good health
- Leadership potential
- Ability to get along with people
- Job know-how and technical competence
- Initiative
- Dedication and dependability
- Positive attitude toward management

Obviously, these are fine attributes to find in any person. Obviously, too, persons who measure up are hard to find. Fortunately, however, many of these attributes can be acquired or improved through supervisory training and development programs.

How can a newly appointed supervisor make the job of crossing over to the managerial ranks a less turbulent one?

A person who is made a supervisor crosses over from one style of thought to another. As an employee, an individual's concerns are with self-frustration in terms of pay and the work itself. As a manager, this same person is expected to place the organization's goals above all other job-related concerns. This means that a supervisor worries first about meeting quotas, quality, and cost standards; second about the employees who do the work; and last about himself or herself.

To make the task more difficult, the newly appointed supervisor usually has already made the long climb to the top of the employee ranks. Now the person must cross over to a new field of achievement — management, as shown in Figure 1-1. It will take a while to get a toehold at the supervisory level. For many, however, it will be the beginning of another long climb, this time to the top of the management heap.[3]

Such pressure from above and below makes many new supervisors feel uncomfortable. One Ford Motor Company assembly-

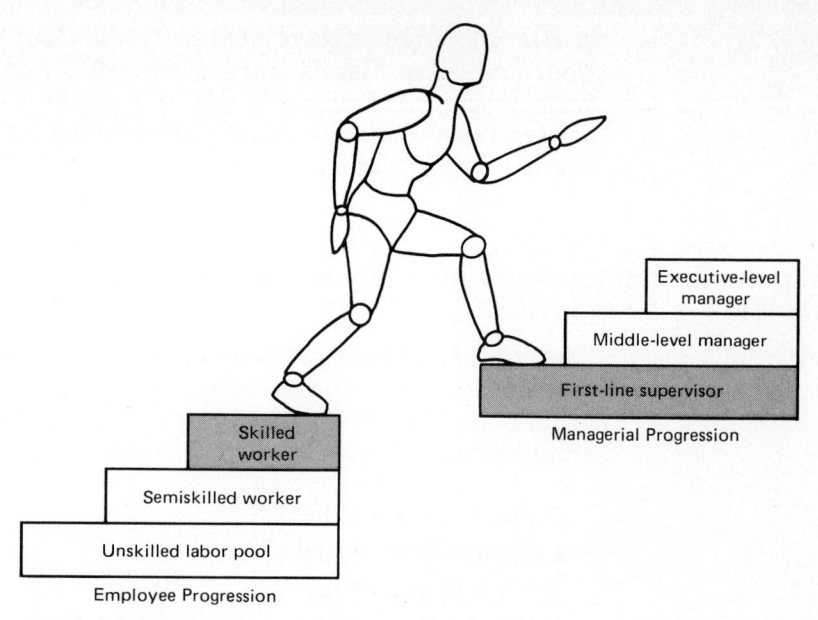

Figure 1-1. Crossing over from employee ranks to managerial ranks, from "top of the heap" to "bottom of the heap."

line supervisor, Ed Hendrix, put it this way: The supervisor "is a punching bag. You get your ears beat off from both sides of the fence."[4]

This need not be so, says Professor Keith Davis, one of the most astute observers of organizational relationships. Davis agrees that the supervisor takes pressure from both sides, but he likens the role to a keystone in the organizational arch. Says Davis: The keystone takes the pressure from both sides and uses this pressure to build a stronger arch. The sides can be held together only by the keystone, which strengthens, not weakens, the arch. The keystone position is the important role of supervisors in organizations.[5]

Experienced supervisors add this advice to the new person: Don't throw your weight around. Admit your need for help and seek it from other supervisors and your boss. Make a practice of coming in on time and sticking to your job for the full day; employees despise supervisors who push for productivity but who goof off themselves. Keep yourself physically prepared and mentally alert; the job will be more demanding than you expect. And don't indulge in petty pilfering of supplies or use of [company] equipment and time to do personal work; employees may try this themselves but they sure don't respect management people who do.[6]

When it comes to job responsibilities, what is expected from supervisors?

Responsibilities for most supervisors encompass four, and occasionally five, broad areas.

Responsibility to Management. Supervisors must, above all, dedicate themselves to the goals, plans, and policies of the organization. These are typically laid down by higher management. It is the primary task of supervisors to serve as a linking pin for management to make sure that these are carried out by the employees they supervise.

Responsibility to Employees. Employees expect their supervisors to provide direction and training; to protect them from unfair treatment; and to see that the workplace is clean, safe, uncluttered, properly equipped, well lighted, and adequately ventilated.

Responsibility to Staff Specialists. The relationship between supervision and staff departments is one of mutual support. Staff people are charged with providing supervisors with guidance and help as well as prescribing procedures to be followed and forms to be completed. Supervisors, in turn, aid the work of the staff departments by making good use of their advice and service by conforming to their requests.

Responsibility to Other Supervisors. Teamwork is essential in the supervisory ranks. There is a great deal of departmental interdependence. The goals and activities of one department must harmonize with those of other departments. This often requires the sacrifice of an immediate target for the greater good of the organization.

Responsibility to the Union. If there is a union in the company, union and management views are often in conflict, and supervisor and shop steward are often at loggerheads. It is the supervisor's responsibility, however, to keep these relationships objective, neither to "give away" the department nor to yield responsibility for the welfare of the organization and its employees.

How will supervisory performance be judged by higher management?

It will be judged by two general measures: (1) how well you manage the various resources made available to you to accomplish your assignments and (2) how good your results are. (See Figure 1-2.)

Management of Resources. These are all the things that, in effect, set you up in business as a supervisor.[7] They include:

Facilities and Equipment. A certain amount of floor space, desks, benches, tools, typewriters, and machinery. Your job is to keep these operating productively and to prevent their abuse.

Energy, Power, and Utilities. Heat, light, air conditioning, electricity, steam, water, and compressed air. Conservation is the principal measure of effectiveness here.

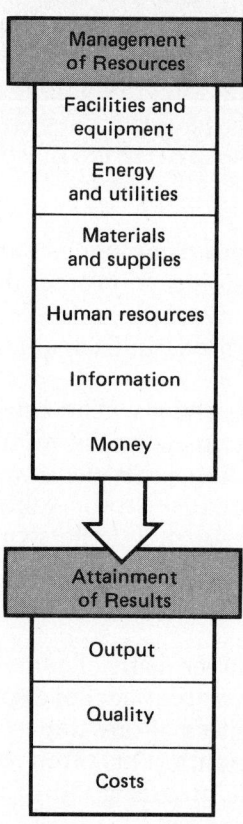

```
        ┌─────────────────┐
        │  Management     │
        │  of Resources   │
        ├─────────────────┤
        │ Facilities and  │
        │   equipment     │
        ├─────────────────┤
        │    Energy       │
        │  and utilities  │
        ├─────────────────┤
        │   Materials     │
        │  and supplies   │
        ├─────────────────┤
        │ Human resources │
        ├─────────────────┤
        │  Information    │
        ├─────────────────┤
        │     Money       │
        └─────────────────┘
                 ▼
        ┌─────────────────┐
        │  Attainment     │
        │  of Results     │
        ├─────────────────┤
        │    Output       │
        ├─────────────────┤
        │    Quality      │
        ├─────────────────┤
        │    Costs        │
        └─────────────────┘
```

Figure 1-2. Measurement of Supervisory Performance.

Materials and Supplies. Raw materials such as parts and assemblies used to make a product, and operating supplies like lubricants, stationery, typewriter ribbons, and wrapping paper. Getting the most from every scrap of material and holding waste to the minimum are prime measures here.

Human Resources. The work force in general and your employees in particular. Because you do little or nothing with your hands, your biggest job is to see that these people are productively engaged at all times.

Information. Facts made available by staff departments or found in operating manuals, specifications sheets, and blueprints. Your success often depends on how well you can use the data and know-how available to you through these sources.

Money. All the above can be measured by how much they cost, although the actual cash will rarely flow through your hands. Nevertheless, supervisors are expected to be prudent in decisions that affect expenditures and may have to justify these in terms of savings or other benefits.

Attainment of Results. It follows that if you manage each of your resources well, you should get the desired results.[8] Whatever your particular area of responsibility and whatever your organization, you can be sure you will be judged in the long run by how well you meet these three objectives:

Output, or Production. Specifically, your department will be expected to turn out a certain amount of work per day, per week, and per month. It will be expected that this will be done on time and that you will meet delivery schedules and project deadlines.

Quality and Workmanship. Output volume alone is not enough. You will also be judged by the quality of the work your employees perform, measured in terms of the number of product defects, service errors, or customer complaints.

Costs and Budget Control. Your output and quality efforts will always be restricted by the amount of money you can spend to carry them out. Universally, supervisors attest to the difficulty in living up to cost and budget restraints.

Of all that is expected of supervisors, which tasks loom largest?

They vary, of course, but one investigator took the time in 1971 to ask this question of 2,054 production supervisors.[9] The researcher found the following problems most immediately pressing and most persistently difficult:

	Percentage Mentioning Problem When First Appointed	Percentage Saying Problem Persistently Recurred
Handling employees with special problems	60	25
Maintaining a neat and orderly workplace	59	43
Dealing with crises or unexpected problems	54	Less than 10
Controlling costs	54	27
Meeting quality requirements	52	33
Learning how much authority you have	51	Less than 10
Handling complaints, grievances, or labor relations	50	Less than 10
Motivating employees	48	23
Meeting work deadlines or production requirements	47	26
Writing reports and handling paperwork	43	24

CHAPTER 1: THE SUPERVISORY MANAGEMENT JOB

Note how the anxiety over crises, authority sources, and grievances rather quickly dissipates while the concern for certain basic problems persists.

What does it really take to succeed as a supervisor?

No one knows for sure, but there are a number of qualities, or dimensions, of the supervisory job that experts look for. For example, the General Electric Company, at its Columbia, Maryland, facility, singles out seven important dimensions of the supervisory job: technical know-how, administrative skill, ability to develop a plan to meet department goals, ability to deal with the manager to whom you report, communications skills, ability to deal with people inside and outside the operating unit, and ability to deal effectively with people who report to you.[10] Other researchers also identify such success-related qualities as creativity, stress tolerance, initiative, independence, problem analysis, decisiveness, tenacity, flexibility, risk taking, and use of delegation.[11] Many firms, including American Telephone and Telegraph, attempt to measure these dimensions in supervisory candidates and base their selection on these qualities.

The best part is that many of these talents can be acquired by supervisors who learn from their experience and take advantage of developmental opportunities offered them by their employers.

In what way are the pressures on supervisors changing?

What started out as a mainly technical job at the turn of the century has gradually shifted to accommodate an increasingly demanding work force.[12] This trend will continue. In the 1980s pressure will be added by the general public for supervisors to accept greater responsibility for employment whether or not this employment contributes to profits. This means that supervisors will be expected to make work for their employees in slack times and motivate them to be more productive in active times.

Where do supervisors fit into the management process?

They are an essential part of it. Supervisors perform exactly the same managerial functions as do all other managers in their organization, up to and including the chief executive. Each specific task, every responsibility, all the various roles that supervisors are called on to perform are carried forward by the managerial process (Figure 1-3). This process, which is repeated over and over daily, weekly, and yearly, consists of five broad functions:

Planning. Setting goals and establishing plans and procedures to attain them.

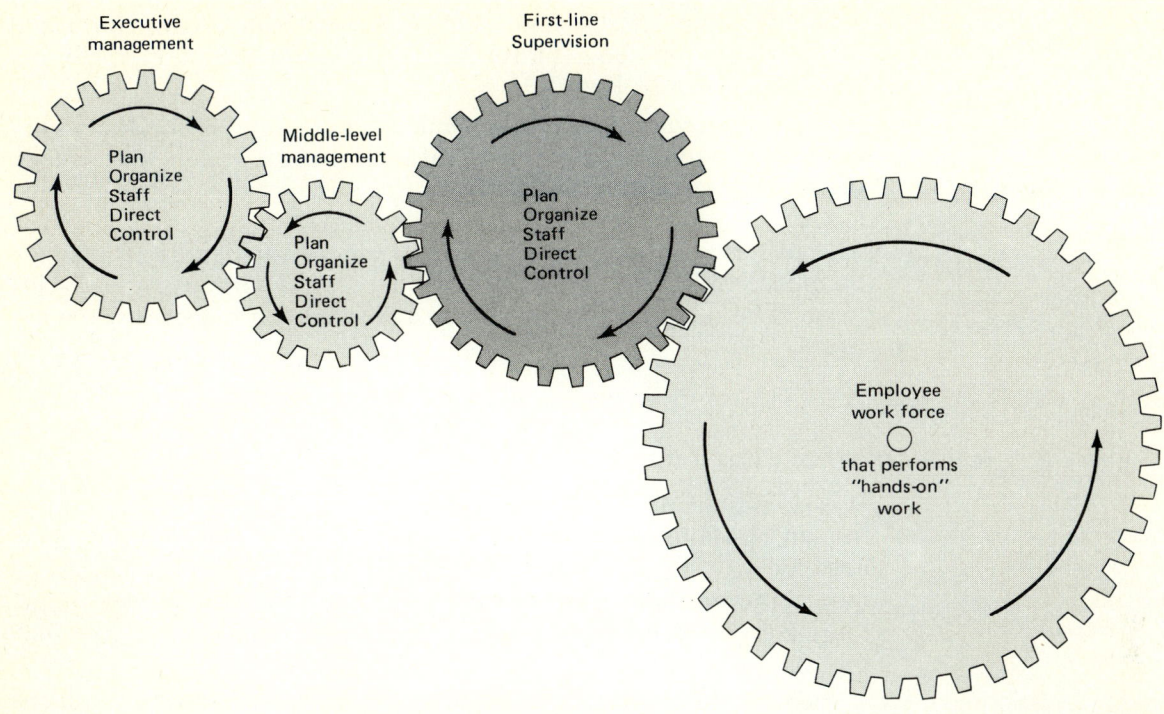

Figure 1-3. All managers take part in the managerial process: planning, organizing, staffing, directing, and controlling.

Organizing. Arranging jobs to be done in such a way as to make them more effective.

Staffing. Selecting and placing just the right number of people in the most appropriate jobs.

Directing. Motivating, communicating, and leading.

Controlling. Regulating the process, its costs, and the people who carry it out.

How do supervisory job roles differ from those of other levels of management?

They differ only in degree. Higher-level managers spend more time planning and less time directing, for example. Two people who studied this matter came up with three useful guidelines.[13] They first divided all the tasks and responsibilities we have listed so far in this text into three kinds of roles. Roles are the parts played by actors on a stage; they are also the real-life parts played by managers and supervisors in an organization. These three roles can be classified as those requiring:

Technical Skills: Job know-how, knowledge of the industry and its particular processes, machinery, and problems.

CHAPTER 1: THE SUPERVISORY MANAGEMENT JOB 11

Administrative Skills. Knowledge of the entire organization and how it is coordinated, its information and records system, its ability to plan and control work.

Human Relations Skills. Knowledge of human behavior, the ability to work effectively with individuals and groups—peers and superiors as well as subordinates.

The observers then concluded that supervisors' roles emphasize technical and human relation skills most and administrative skills least. This emphasis tends to be reversed for higher-level managers.

Supervisory balance: What does it mean?

It is a simplification of a valuable dictum: Pay as much attention to human relations as to technical and administrative matters. Said another way: Be as employee-centered in your interests as job- or task-centered. Said still another way: Spend as much time maintaining group cohesiveness, direction, and morale as you do pushing for productivity or task accomplishment.

This view has been borne out by a number of studies. Its principal basis, however, is in research carried out by Rensis Likert among clerical, sales, and manufacturing employees. He found that, on the average, employees who worked for supervisors who were job- or production-centered produced less than employees who worked for supervisors who were employee-centered.[14]

It would be dangerous to conclude from Likert's studies that being a nice guy is the answer to employee productivity. It isn't. As in sports, nice guys often finish last. The important conclusion the studies lead to is that supervisors who focus on job demands to the

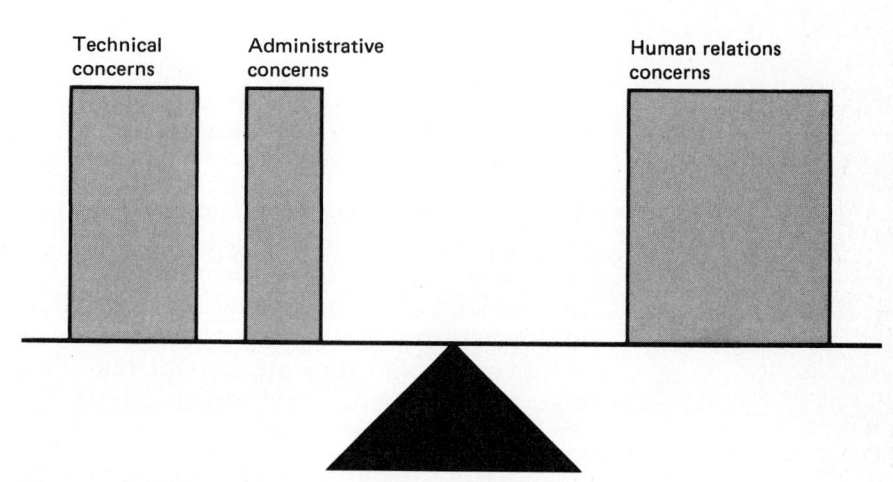

Figure 1-4. The Balance of Supervisory Concerns.

PART 1: MASTERING THE JOB OF SUPERVISORY MANAGEMENT

exclusion of their interest in the welfare and development of their people don't get the results they are looking for. Conversely, supervisors who bend over backward to make work easy for their employees don't get good results either. It takes a balance between the two approaches, as shown in Figure 1-4.

Being a supervisor can't be all good news. What are some of the drawbacks? What can a supervisor do to minimize them?

Generalizations about the negative side of supervision can be misleading because every job is different, companies and industries vary, and each individual is unique. It is usually true, however, that the advancements are limited: The managerial pyramid gets narrower at the top, and college-educated persons usually have an inside track. Often the pay isn't much better than that of the people you supervise; efforts to widen the gap often fail. The hours are long, and the human relations part of the job can be torturous. The supervisor is typically torn between loyalties to management and to the work group. In some companies a supervisor's ideas for improving methods may be taken for granted instead of being rewarded via the suggestion box. In most instances a supervisor's security depends not on seniority or union membership but on the ability to produce results. Frequently the supervisor may not have all the resources needed to attain the results.

Why do so many supervisors keep on plugging? Because of the reward *not* found in the paycheck.[15] Supervisors keep supervising because of the challenge inherent in the work itself and the sense of accomplishment gained from doing a difficult job better than anyone else can. A few supervisors quit or step down, but most of them hang in. They may complain, but they persist hard and long enough to get results.[16]

How professional is the work of supervision?

It is becoming more professional every day. Two leading management organizations, made up primarily of first-line supervisors, are working hard to make it that way. The International Management Council (IMC), affiliated with the Young Men's Christian Association (YMCA), and the National Management Association (NMA) have pooled their resources to form the Institute of Certified Professional Managers (ICPM). The institute, working with the American College Testing Program (ACT), has devised and is administering professional certification tests. Certification is based on a combination of experience and examinations in three areas: (1) personal skills like knowledge of communications, government regulation, and time management; (2) administrative skills like planning, decision making, staffing, and controlling; and (3) human relation skills.

Why do supervisors fail?

When a person doesn't succeed as a supervisor, only an examination of the particular situation will pinpoint the real reason.[17] Sometimes the individual isn't at fault; the boss may never have provided the right kind of training and encouragement. But if you'd avoid failure, check yourself against these six supervisory pitfalls revealed by the National Management Association after a study of 86 companies:

1. Poor personal relations with workers or with management people. This rated highest on the list.
2. Individual shortcomings, such as lack of initiative and emotional instability.
3. Lack of understanding of the management point of view.
4. Unwillingness to spend the necessary time and effort to improve.
5. Lack of skill in planning and organizing work.
6. Inability to adjust to new and changing conditions.

If success is your target, look ahead to the pages that follow, and fit the advice to your own job.

Review Questions

1. Why would a company be likely to object if, as supervisor of the molding department, you spent most of your time setting up and operating the molding machines?
2. Name at least four groups within the organization toward which a supervisor has responsibilities, and briefly describe the nature of the responsibilities to each.
3. Outline the performance measures you might describe to a new supervisor by naming nine measures grouped into two categories.
4. Contrast the likely priorities of a production worker in a glass factory with those of the department's supervisor.
5. Many of the most serious concerns of a new supervisor dwindle in importance as experience grows. What are three or four issues that will remain of prime concern no matter how experienced a supervisor is?
6. How is supervisory management similar to higher-level management? How is it different?
7. When a supervisor is told to achieve supervisory balance, what is it that should be balanced? Why is it important to achieve this balance?
8. If you had to point to one key area that is most likely to produce failure for a supervisor, what would it be?

A Case in Point The Case of the Complaining Keypunch Operator

Ruth Smyth was the best all-around clerk that Gibralter Finance Company's data processing section ever had. She was a natural for promotion to supervisor when the time came. During Ruth's first few weeks as section supervisor, everything went well. She obviously knew the work flow from A to Z. Given this chance, she quickly cleared up long-standing bottlenecks and eliminated a number of duplications. Her experience and good judgment easily won the respect of the people who worked for her. On the other hand, Ruth was a stern and serious taskmaster. She was fair and courteous with her employees, but she showed little interest in them beyond their abilities to get their work done.

As Ruth settled into the job, however, she had an uneasy feeling that something wasn't quite right in her section. Her employees came to depend on her decisions in the slightest matters. If a problem arose, they were likely to sit at their machines waiting for orders from Ruth. At first Ruth felt flattered by this dependence, but this caused her work load gradually to build. Increasingly she found herself giving curt instructions and short answers to people in her work group.

One employee in particular, Woodie Beck, a keypunch operator, really irritated her. Regardless of what the assignment was, he found some fault with it. Additionally, Woodie regularly complained about his machine, his chair, the lighting, the temperature, or his co-workers. Ruth responded to each of Woodie's complaints or requests with some attempt to accommodate him or set the problem straight.

To make matters worse, the quality of Woodie's work, which had been unspectacular but acceptable, began to fall off. He made errors, and frequently his tapes had to be checked and repunched. When this deterioration continued, Ruth called Woodie into her office. "I've been very patient with your unending complaints and requests," Ruth said, "but lately your work has been far below what is considered satisfactory. If it continues, I'm going to recommend that you be suspended or discharged."

"I'm sorry about my work," said Woodie. "I've had all kinds of problems at home. My oldest son was expelled from high school for drug dealing a couple of months ago. Neither my wife nor I can seem to keep him out of trouble anymore. It's driving us both crazy."

"Family troubles are a bother, I know," said Ruth, "but you can't let them interfere with your work. What's important right now to you is the fact that the quality of your work is no longer acceptable here. If it continues, you will lose your job. My advice to you is to find some way to keep your concerns about your son from affecting your work. Otherwise, your problems will be even worse. I've been very fair with you, but you owe your first attention now to improving your work. Unless it improves, I'll have to put you on notice."

CHAPTER 1: THE SUPERVISORY MANAGEMENT JOB

What is your opinion of Ruth Smyth's approach to supervisory responsibilities? What would you advise her to do now? Five alternatives are listed below. Rank them in the order in which they appeal to you (1 most attractive, 5 least). You may add another approach in the space provided, if you wish. In any event, be prepared to justify your ranking.

_____ **A.** Ruth's approach is right. She should stick to her guns. Woodie must shape up now or face the prospect of dismissal.

_____ **B.** Ruth's approach is wrong. Woodie needs sympathy now, not threats. Ruth should make an exception for his poor performance.

_____ **C.** Ruth should suggest to her boss that the boss talk to Woodie and try to straighten him out.

_____ **D.** Ruth should moderate her approach to develop a greater understanding of how Woodie's problem affects his behavior, while still maintaining that company standards must be met.

_____ **E.** Ruth should let the situation ride for a while in hopes that Woodie's personal problems will eventually improve.

If you have another approach, write it here. _____
_____
_____
_____

Action Summary Checklist		Action Needed Yes No	Date Completed
	1. Made a commitment to no longer work with your "hands on" the job and to embrace fully the management viewpoint.	____ ____	_____
	2. Determined to maintain good health, work hard, set a good example for your employees, and continue to learn.	____ ____	_____
	3. Identified those individuals and groups to whom you now owe a responsibility: higher management (especially your boss), staff departments, associate supervisors, union representative (if your organization is unionized), and, most of all, your employee work group.	____ ____	_____

Action Summary Checklist (continued)

	Action Needed Yes No	Date Completed

4. Checked the resources that enable you to carry out your job responsibilities: facilities, equipment, tools, power, utilities, materials, supplies, and information (dollar value of all this). ____ ____ _____

5. Obtained the personnel particulars about your work force: personal data on each employee, such as age, length of service, work history, present job title and description, and pay rate. ____ ____ _____

6. Learned about current and upcoming production schedules and other output requirements and project deadlines. ____ ____ _____

7. Found out exactly what the quality requirements or specifications of your product or service are. ____ ____ _____

8. Pinned down the cost and expense limitations under which you will be expected to operate. ____ ____ _____

9. Accepted the fact that pressures on you will be many and varied, with changing worker attitudes the most pressing of all. ____ ____ _____

10. Given thought to how well your present abilities measure up to the demands for technical, administrative, and human relations skills—and what you might do to improve them. ____ ____ _____

11. Prepared to balance your supervisory efforts between task-centered and employee-centered concerns.

12. Reviewed the managerial process so that you can anticipate problems and decisions that require planning, organizing, staffing, directing, and controlling. ____ ____ _____

13. Accepted the fact that your supervisory role will often be ambiguous and will occasionally put you in the middle between higher management and your employees; that the

Action Summary Checklist (continued)

	Action Needed Yes No	Date Completed
hours will be long and the pay not always good; and that the rewards come mainly from a sense of personal accomplishment.	____ ____	_____
14. Kept your guard up against pitfalls for new supervisors: poor relationships with others in the organization, failure to plan ahead, confusion about your managerial role, lack of initiative, discouragement, and inability to meet changing conditions successfully.	____ ____	_____
15. Retained an attitude of doing the best you can today with a plan for developing your knowledge and skills so that you can do even better tomorrow.	____ ____	_____

References Cited in This Chapter

1. Herbert R. Northrup, Ronald M. Cowin, Laurence G. Vanden Plas, and William E. Fulmer, **The Objective Selection of Supervisors,** Manpower and Human Resources Studies No. 8, University of Pennsylvania. The Wharton School, Philadelphia, 1978, pp. 58–69.
2. Ibid., p. 77.
3. Carl A. Benson, "New Supervisors: From the Top of the Heap to the Bottom of the Heap," **Personnel Journal,** April 1978, p. 176.
4. Laurence O'Donnell, "On the Line: As a Ford Foreman, Ed Hendrix Finds He Is Man in the Middle," **Wall Street Journal,** July 25, 1973, p. 1.
5. Keith Davis, "The Supervisory Role," in M. Gene Newport (ed.), **Supervisory Management: Tools and Techniques,** West Publishing Company, St. Paul, Minn., 1976, p. 5.
6. **Foremen in Indiana Industries,** Manpower Report 70-2, Office of Manpower Studies, Purdue University, Lafayette, Ind., 1970, pp. 8–10.
7. William H. Cover, "Stepping Back to Basics: Defining Performance Expectations for Operations Supervisors," **Training and Development Journal,** November 1975, pp. 3–6.
8. Saul W. Gellerman, "Supervision: Substance and Style," **Harvard Business Review,** March–April 1976, pp. 89–99.
9. Robert H. Schappe, "The Production Foreman Today: His Needs and His Difficulties," **Personnel Journal,** July 1972, pp. 156–172.
10. "What's Ahead in Personnel," No. 181, **Industrial Relations News,** Enterprise Publications, Chicago, 1978, p. 3.
11. William C. Byham, "Assessment Centers," in Lester R. Bittel (ed.), **Encyclopedia of Professional Management,** McGraw-Hill Book Company, New York, 1977, pp. 55–58.

12. Northrup et al., **Objective Selection of Supervisors**, p. 7.
13. Basil S. Georgopolous and Floyd C. Mann, **The Community General Hospital**, The Macmillan Company, New York, 1962, p. 431.
14. Rensis Likert, **New Patterns of Management**, McGraw-Hill Book Company, New York, 1960.
15. Michael J. Abboud and Homer L. Richardson, "What Do Supervisors Want From Their Jobs?" **Personnel Journal**, June 1978, pp. 308–312.
16. Archie B. Carroll and Ted F. Anthony, "An Overview of the Supervisor's Job," **Personnel Journal**, March 1976, pp. 228–231, 249–250.
17. William E. Fulmer, "The Making of a Supervisor," **Personnel Journal**, March 1977, pp. 140–143, 151.

Chapter 2
Problem Solving and Decision Making

Key Concepts

- Important marks of effective supervision are (1) the ability to recognize the existence of a problem or the need for a decision and (2) the ability to identify opportunities for improvement as well as to anticipate potential trouble spots.

- Problems are characterized by a gap between what is expected to happen and what actually occurs. Gaps are usually caused by a change in procedures or conditions. Problems are solved by removing or correcting the cause of the change, which in turn closes the gap.

- Decision making, an inseparable part of the problem-solving process, is the phase in which solutions, ideas, and new courses of action are examined critically and then chosen on the basis of their chances for success or failure in meeting related objectives.

- Problem solving should always be approached systematically. Decision making utilizes intuition and creativity as well as logic, but is always more effective when based on firm objectives and adequate information.

- Problem solving and decision making are greatly aided by the use of mathematical techniques, which arrange and analyze numerical data in ways that maximize a supervisor's mental abilities and minimize personal bias.

If supervisors are hired to manage people and get out the work, why doesn't someone else handle problems and make decisions?

Because at its very core, management is a combination of problem solving and decision making. Staff specialists and higher-level managers may help you to deal with these two essentials, but in your bailiwick these are your babies. As you'll find out, the two are often inseparable. They are also like the chicken and the egg. You may first discover you have a problem to solve, and this will lead to the need for a decision. Or you may be asked to make a decision and then realize that it represents a problem to be solved.

If everything ran smoothly or by the book, there would be few problems and no decisions to make. If that were true, however, there would be no need for supervisors, either. Organizations of all kinds are beset by change, variety, and unanticipated calamities, large and small. These bring about problems and the need for solutions (decisions)—dozens every day in the lives of most supervisors. That's why skill at problem solving and decision making is the bedrock of supervisory effectiveness.

What, specifically, is a problem?

A problem is a puzzle, a mystery, an unsettled matter, a situation requiring a solution, or a plan or an issue involving uncertainty. Your work is full of them:

Problems That Have Already Happened. These may be merchandise that spoiled, costs that got out of line, employees who have quit, or shipments that were missed. These problems may need immediate solutions to correct what has taken place.

Problems That Lie Ahead. Examples are how to finish the Ajax project on time, when to put on a second shift, where to place the new press, whether to tell employees of an impending change in their work. These, too, require solutions now to devise effective plans and procedures.

Problems That You Want to Forestall. These lurk in the future. You'd like to take preventive action now so that they never arise and thus never need solutions.

How can you recognize a problem or a potential problem?

A problem exists when there is a gap between what you expect to happen and what actually happens. Your budget, for example, calls for 2,200 insurance policies to be processed this week; the count at 5 p.m. on Friday shows that you completed only 1,975, a gap of 225 policies (Figure 2-1). Or you expected to hold the total of employee absences in your department to 300 days this year; the total is 410, a gap of 110 days.

It is almost the same with potential problems. You know what you would like to have happen in the future: a project completed, a

CHAPTER 2: PROBLEM SOLVING AND DECISION MAKING

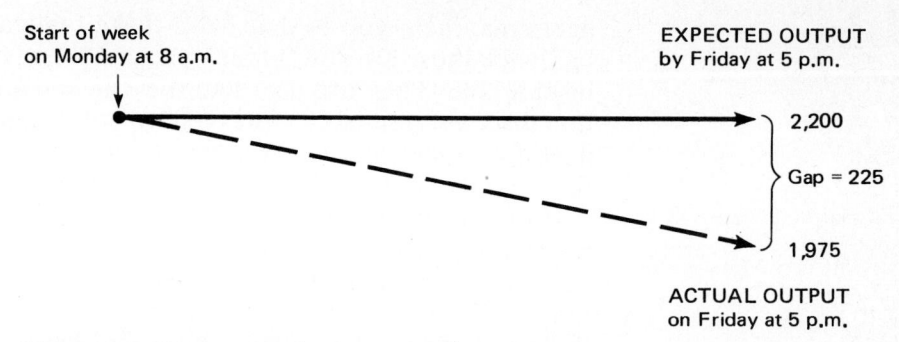

```
Start of week                          EXPECTED OUTPUT
on Monday at 8 a.m.                    by Friday at 5 p.m.
                                                      } 2,200
                                                      } Gap = 225
                                                      } 1,975
                                       ACTUAL OUTPUT
                                       on Friday at 5 p.m.
```

Figure 2-1. How a gap between "expected" and "actual" indicates presence of a problem.

perfect safety record, fewer than ten customer complaints. These are your plans. But when you look ahead at your procedures and the potential for mishaps, you think that your department will fall short of its targets—that there will be a gap.

How are problems solved?

By removing whatever has caused, or will cause, a gap between the expected or desired condition and the actual condition. That's the main idea, at least. Suppose, for example, that your hoped-for safety record of zero accidents is spoiled by three accidents on the punch press machine. You will want to find their cause (bypassing of the safety guard by the operators) and remove it (by designing a foolproof guard).

Finding and removing the cause or causes, however, is usually difficult and requires considerable examination and thought. There will be more discussion about the problem-solving process later.

What is the connection between problem solving and decision making?

The two processes are closely related. A decision is always needed to choose the problem's solution. In many ways problem solving *is* decision making. As you will see in a moment, any step along the way of planning, organizing, directing, controlling—and problem solving—that presents a choice of more than one course of action requires also that a decision be made. Take the safety record on the punch press again. A complete analysis of the problem might have suggested that the cause could be removed in three different ways: (1) using an automatic feeding device that would remove the need for a guard, (2) instituting an education and discipline program to instruct operators in the proper operation of the present guard, or (3) designing a foolproof guard system. The supervisor, as the decision maker, would have to choose among the three alternatives. The first might be judged too costly, the second not completely effective, and the third the best choice because it is relatively inexpensive and reliable.

How can you recognize the need for a decision?

Whenever there is more than one way of doing things, a decision is needed. Any kind of choice, alternative, or option calls for a decision. You might ask: If this is so, why are so many decision opportunities overlooked? The answer is that managers and supervisors alike get preoccupied with the status quo. In effect, they say: The way we are doing this is the only way. Such supervisors miss the point that there are always alternatives. There is always the choice to do something or not to do it, to speak or to remain silent, to correct or to let well enough alone. All too often a supervisor's decision is made by default. The supervisor does nothing. The tide of events carries the department along until a crisis occurs. In reality, however, doing nothing represented a choice. It was a decision not to change, not to plan for improvement, not to anticipate a potential problem.

Must the approach to problem solving be systematic?

Yes. There are few exceptions to the rule that the best results come from a systematic approach. Here is a fundamental procedure.

Step 1. State the Problem Clearly and Specifically. Stay away from a general statement like "We have a problem with quality." Instead, narrow it down and put figures on it if you can, like "Between the first of the month and today, the number of rejects found at final inspection has totaled 32, compared with our standard of 15."

Step 2. Collect All Information Relevant to the Problem. Don't go too far afield, but do find data that may shed light on process changes, materials used, equipment function, design specifications, or employee performance and assignments. Much of the data will not tell you anything except where the source of the problem is not. If your information shows, for example, that there has been no change in the way materials have arrived or machinery has been used, good! You can look elsewhere.

Step 3. List as Many Possible Causes for the Problem as You Can Think of. Remember, a problem is a gap between expected and actual conditions. Something must have occurred to cause that gap.

Most particularly, something must have been changed. Is an operator different from the old one? Was a power source less regular than before? Has there been a change, however slight, in the specifications?

Step 4. Select the Cause or Causes that Seem Most Likely. Do this by a process of elimination. To test a cause to see if it is a probable one, try seeing or thinking through what difference it would make if that factor were returned to its original state. For example, suppose a possible cause of rejects is that compressed air power is now only 75 psi instead of 90 psi. Try making the product with the pressure restored to 90 psi. If it makes no difference, then power irregularity is not a likely cause. Or perhaps you think that the new operator has misunderstood your instructions. Check this out. See if the operator is, in fact, following the instructions exactly. If not, what happens when your instructions are followed? If the rejects stop, then this is a likely cause. If the rejects persist, this is not a likely cause.

Step 5. Suggest as Many Solutions for Removing Causes as You Can. This is a good time for brainstorming. There is rarely only one way to solve a problem. If the cause of an employee's excessive absenteeism, for instance, is difficulty in getting up in the morning, this cause might be removed in a number of ways. You might change the employee's shift, insist on the purchase of an alarm clock, telephone a wake-up call yourself, or show where failure to get to work will threaten the job. The point is to make your list of alternative solutions as long as possible.

Step 6. Evaluate the Pros and Cons of Each Proposed Solution. Some solutions will be better than others. But what does better mean? Cheaper? Faster? Surer? More participative? More in line with company policy? To judge which solution is best, you'll have to have a set of criteria like the ones just listed. Evaluation requires you to make judgments based on facts. Consult the information gathered in step 2. Also consult anyone who can offer specialized opinions about the criteria you have chosen.

Step 7. Choose the Solution that You Think Is Best. Yes, this—like what you did in step 6—is the decision phase of problem solving. In effect, you will have weighed all the chances of success against the risks of failure. The strengths of your solution should exceed its weaknesses.

Step 8. Spell Out a Plan of Action to Carry Out Your Solution. Decisions require action and follow-up. Pin down exactly what will be done and how, who will do it, where, and when. How much money can be spent? What resources can be used? What is the deadline?

What approach is used for problems that involve the future rather than the past?

You must think forward rather than backward. What could change so as to cause a problem? An employee is retiring; you'd better have a trained replacement. The company has signed a contract with a new supplier; you'd better make sure the purchasing department relays the exact materials specifications to the vendor. Your plans call for ten new employees by the year's end; you'd better check with personnel to make sure these employees will, in fact, be available and fully trained when the new equipment is ready.

Analysis of a potential problem is essentially the same as basic, systematic problem solving. Its focus, however, is on step 3: listing possible causes. The main difference is that you must transfer what your experience has told you about past problems to estimates of what may possibly recur in the future. You must, of course, also use your imagination to anticipate new sources of problems—causes that have not occurred previously but which might in the future.

How systematic must the decision-making process be?

Unlike problem solving, there are good reasons to believe that decision making need not always be systematic or even logical. System helps up to a point, but when you are dealing with the future, hunches and intuition often pay off.

The systematic, or rational, approach to decision making takes place during steps 6 and 7 of problem solving: evaluating alternative solutions and selecting the best one based on the facts available. You can make this approach even more rational and more reliable by first setting goals that the decision must satisfy. For example, a problem-solving decision about cost cutting must be effective for at least six months and not involve employee separations. Or, if you are developing future plans, the decision may be required to fulfill the goal of assuring that production schedules are met without overtime.

This rational step of first setting a goal tends to make the quality of decisions better, even when they are ultimately made by hunch, because you know what your target is and what limitations will be placed on your choice of plans for implementation.

What is meant by mathematical decision making?

Mathematical decision making refers to the use of certain mathematical, statistical, or quantitative techniques to aid the decision maker. These are very valuable aids in many instances, but they are only aids. They do not make decisions. Numerical information is arranged so that it can be analyzed mathematically, but the executive, manager, or supervisor must make the final decision, based on interpretation of the results.

What is meant by cost-benefit analysis?

It is not unlike the closing steps in problem solving and decision making. This is the phase when you examine the pros and cons of each proposed solution. Cost-benefit analysis has become a popular technique for evaluating proposals in the public sector. Take a proposal for a local government to offer a child-care service to its residents. Cost-benefit analysis adds all the implementation costs and equates them with the value of the services to the community. Typically, the benefits of such nonprofit services are hard to quantify; that is, it is hard to place a dollar value on them. Accordingly, many cost-benefit analyses include quality judgments of benefits as well as dollar estimates.

Cost-benefit analysis is similar to *input-output analysis,* which tries to make sure that the cost and effort expended in carrying out a decision will at least be balanced by its outputs or results. In business, when outputs exceed inputs, the result is a profit. If there is an excess of benefits over costs in nonprofit organizations, the excess is called a surplus.

Some say that most decisions involve a trade-off. What is meant by that?

This is a way of saying that to attain your objective in one area, you must be prepared to give up something in another area. The department store maintenance supervisor who has only so much money to spend on new equipment may buy a powered floor sweeper and may have to forgo the purchase of a powered platform to facilitate ceiling maintenance. Housekeeping will improve on the floors; meanwhile, it may get worse on the ceilings. This is a trade-off in which someone must decide which goal is more important at the moment.

Are decisions based on intuition as good as those based on logic?

If it works out well, it won't make any difference how a decision was reached. Many decisions based on hunch have proved to be correct. They are harder to defend, however, when they go wrong. More important, any decision is likely to be better if its goals are clearly understood. The logical approach helps to strip away distractions and irrelevancies. Intuition often adds a valuable dimension by calling on some inner sense we don't clearly understand. Many authorities believe that the best decisions come from the dual approach—a combination of logic and hunch.

In seeking facts with which to solve a problem or make a decision, what should be the cutoff point?

Stop looking when the trouble and the cost of obtaining the extra information exceed its value. The rule is: The more critical and lasting the effect of a decision, the more you can afford to look for the last scrap of vital information. Don't spend two days hunting for background data on a purchasing decision, for example, if the item plays only an insignificant part in your process and will be used only once or twice. On the other hand, it might pay to defer a decision to hire a full-time employee until you have made a reference check.

Do guard against using the absence of information as an excuse for procrastination. Some decisions are especially hard to make and unpleasant to carry out. In these situations there is a temptation to put off an answer (yes, answers are decisions—or should be) by asking for more information. Rarely does the additional information add much to the quality of the decision.

One final comment on this question: Don't be too eager to rush into a decision, especially one involving people. Employees will often press hard for a quick answer and catch you with your guard down. They may imply, for example, that unless you arrange for a transfer next week, something drastic will happen to them. If you think that the urgency is forced, it makes good sense to wait a while. The situation may relax; the individual may find that the request for a transfer was only a passing inclination.

Do people approach decision situations differently?

Very much so. There are typically four kinds of decision makers:

Risk Seekers actively look for opportunities to make changes, to improve, to force action. Within limits, these persons make the best supervisors, especially in dynamic business enterprises where technology and the outside environment are fluid.

Risk Averters tend to stand pat, to presume that what is working now should not be changed without very sound reasons. These persons make good supervisors, too, especially in stable government organizations where it is important to have someone who can hold to a set and proved course.

Wishful Thinkers try to control the impossible or hope that good intentions will override harsh facts. These people don't make very good supervisors under any circumstances.

CHAPTER 2: PROBLEM SOLVING AND DECISION MAKING

Biased Thinkers have limited vision. They often act from prejudice or misinformation and should not be supervisors.

Of course, all of us have a little of each kind of decision maker in us, depending on the situation. For this reason many experts advise that the best, and the professional, approach to decision making is a contingency one. In effect, they say, use the technique and be the kind of person that best fits the problem at hand. Said another way, in times of great uncertainty, a standpat approach may be best. In times of great opportunity—when growth, for example, is taking place in your organization—you should look for chances to make changes.

What can be done to make your decisions more effective?

Besides starting with a specific goal in mind and laying a foundation of facts and systematic analysis, you can turn to a couple of other kinds of insurance.

Pick Your Spots. First, avoid decision making, if you can, where risks are high. Second, try to make decisions only where the potential for payoff is great. You can identify the second kind of opportunity by using ABC analysis. The ABC concept is based on an established economic fact: A vital few problems or opportunities for action account for the greatest loss or greatest gain. The majority of problems and opportunities are basically of little consequence. Economists call this the 20/80 syndrome. It means that 20 percent of your problems will account for 80 percent of your losses or profits. Then, to turn the idea around, 80 percent of your problems will account for only 20 percent of your losses or profits. In ABC analysis the vital few are called "A" items; the inconsequential many are "C" items; and those that fall somewhere in between are "B" items (Figure 2-2). If you were to take an inventory of items in your stockroom, for example, it is a sure bet that only a relatively few items would account for most of its value. A great many items, however, such as paper clips and erasers, would account for only a small portion of the inventory's total worth. Astute purchasing managers concentrate on the vital few items, not the trivial many. You should apply the same principle to your problems and decisions selection.

Maintain Your Perspective. Statistically, problems fall in what is called a normal distribution, and so do the results of most decisions. We say, "You win some and you lose some." That's really what a normal distribution tells us. If you make ten decisions, one or two will work out fine. One or two are likely to be bombs. The rest will fall somewhere in between. Knowing this, you should keep the following guidelines in mind when making decisions:

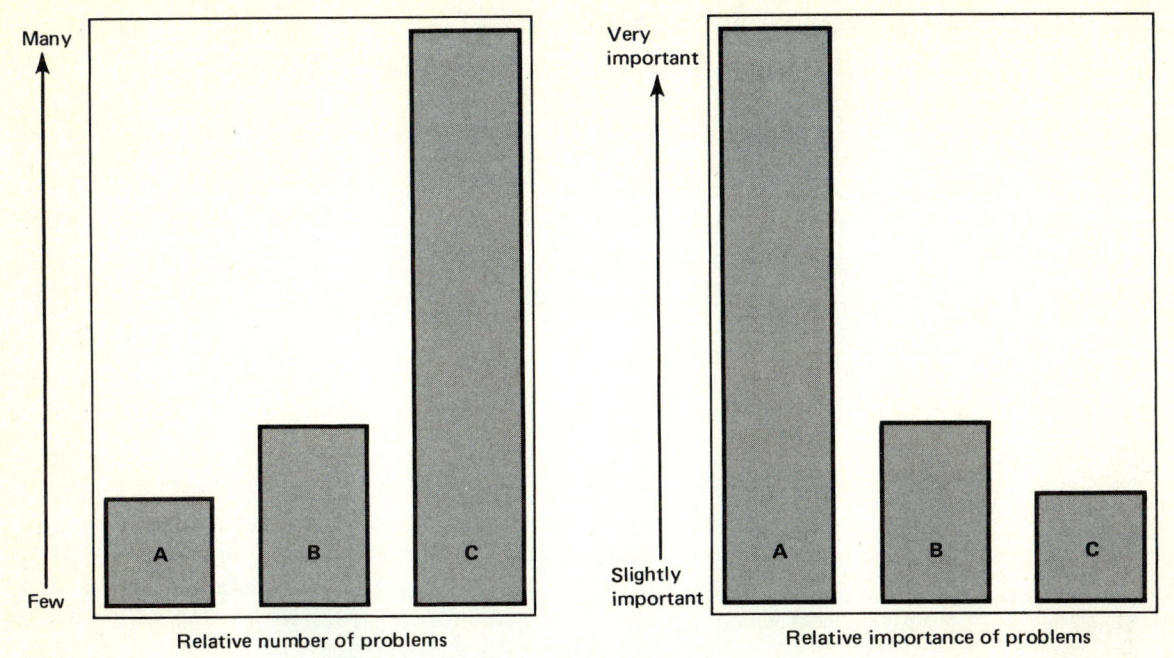

Figure 2-2. Distribution of Problems from Vital Few *(A)* to Trivial Many *(C)*.

1. Don't reach too high. Don't set your objectives at the very top; allow some room for mistakes.
2. Don't overcommit or overextend your resources on one problem; you may need them later for an unanticipated problem.
3. Always prepare a fallback position, a way to alter plans and attain at least part of the objective.

How good are group decisions?

They have their good points and bad points. Where a decision can be aided by shared views and mutual responsibilities—such as those affecting safety—committees have proved to be effective. Where action must focus to the benefit of a single area, group decisions may be weak and ineffective. For its participants the hidden objective of such group decisions often is to share the blame if anything goes wrong or to spread a scarce resource so that there are fewer complaints.

Generally speaking, decisions should be made by those charged with the responsibility to solve a particular problem. These decision makers may gain much, however, by seeking ideas and suggestions from others. But, in the main, they must make the final decisions themselves.

Just how good should you expect a decision to be?

The test of a good decision is: Did it meet the objectives set for it? Suppose, for example, the decision's goal was to prevent a recurrence of excessive turnover. At some point in the future, such as the end of the year, excessive turnover should have stopped. If so, the decision would be said to have satisfied its objectives.

How many of your decisions should be good ones? You probably make between 20 and 40 decisions a day. If more than 30 of them can be judged to be good, you've attained an excellent batting average.

Review Questions

1. Think of the last time something happened to you that you did not expect. What was the gap, or difference, between the "actual" and the "expected"? What sort of a problem did it cause?
2. If a furniture factory failed to produce as many finished chairs as were scheduled for the month, what possible causes would you look for?
3. What is the relationship between problem solving and decision making? If you must choose among three problems to try to solve, does that require a decision? Why?
4. If a fast-food restaurant kitchen ran out of hamburger patties several times a month, what are several things the supervisor might do to assure that there are enough on hand in the future? What are the pros and cons of each alternative action?
5. List some factors that could be used in applying a cost-benefit analysis to the question of whether it is worth the effort to regularly get to work on time.
6. What are some of the weaknesses of depending entirely on your hunches for a decision?
7. In a normal day you make dozens of decisions, some very important and others that are of little significance. List at least three vital decisions and at least ten trivial ones that you make daily.
8. What are some of the advantages and disadvantages of group problem solving or decision making?

A Case in Point

The Case of the Worst Job in the Department

Probably the most disagreeable job in Larry Cohn's department at the Shenandoah Guitar Factory is the operation of the shaper press. The shaper is used to form thin strips of mahogany into the gracefully curved sides of the guitar. First, the precut, flat strips—about 4 inches wide, 32 inches long, and $1/8$ inch thick—are soaked in a tank of hot water. Then the operator places six of them between the curved steel faces of the shaper. He touches a foot pedal and the opposing electrically heated faces come together with 150 pounds of pressure to shape the mahogany strips into sides for the guitar. Pressing takes about four minutes, and while this is going on, the operator takes finished shaped sides from a drying rack and transfers them to a cart for movement to the joining bench. All in all, the job is hot and sloppy. It is generally considered a nonskilled entry job in the plant. Accordingly, Larry is always having to train new operators. Their attendance is poor and many do not stay at the job long enough to move on to one of the more pleasant and more skilled jobs like purfling or joining.

Jason B., the current operator on this job, is about 22. English is a second language for him, and he dropped out of school in the ninth grade. Before coming to Shenandoah, he held a series of jobs as busboy, delivery man, gas station attendant, and most recently as presser's helper in a dry cleaning plant. Jason has been on this job only two and a half weeks, but already he is showing signs of dissatisfaction. Yesterday he was in a temper because of the needling he was getting from the joining bench, where the bench hands kept telling him that he was holding their work back. This morning, when Larry looked for him after the coffee break, he was not at his work station. While Larry was waiting for Jason to return, Larry looked around Jason's workplace and was dismayed to find that the housekeeping was so untidy. In one corner Larry discovered a pile of about 70 guitar sides that had been damaged because they had been incorrectly aligned in the shaper.

When Jason returned to the department, Larry was really uptight. "What's going on here?" he said. "You can't keep up with the boys on the joining bench, yet you treat yourself to a double coffee break!" Before Jason could reply, Larry jumped him again about the damaged parts. "Did you think you could hide those spoiled parts on me? We have an accurate count on everything that goes in and out of your operation, and by the week's end we'd know about those 70 'baddies' you've stashed away."

Jason's reaction was excited and his reply somewhat incoherent. "My stomach bothers me all week. I try to keep on the job, but the heat is no good. I never have a chance to rest between loads like others. Just rush, rush, rush! No one showed me how to start that load of sides with the new wood. They came out crooked, I don't know why. I work all alone here and I handle more parts than anyone else. This job is worse than the cleaning plant I worked. You can't find anyone but me to do this kind of job. And now you blame your troubles on me. I'll finish out the week because I need rent money, but I'll go on unemployment on Monday."

As Jason was blowing his stack, what he said seemed not unlike what others on the job had already told Larry. As simple as the job appeared, there was a knack to adjusting the molds to differing lots of wood stock. The job was hot and tiresome. Poor Jason's shop apron was already dripping with water and scorched from the shaper irons, and the pressure to keep abreast of the joining line was stiff. Jason is steadier than

CHAPTER 2: PROBLEM SOLVING AND DECISION MAKING

most people who have tried this job, and he seems like a hard worker. But Larry's job is to see that the operation keeps moving. Unless Larry gets 80 percent or better through that shaper, his own neck is on the line.

With all this in mind, which one or two of the following actions by Larry do you think might be most effective in keeping Jason on the job while also improving the utilization of the shaper? Five alternatives are listed below. Rank them in the order in which they appeal to you (1 most attractive, 5 least). You may add another approach in the space provided, if you wish. In any event, be prepared to justify your ranking.

_____**A.** Recommend that a second shaper be installed and another operator employed to assist Jason.

_____**B.** Recommend that the shaper operator's job be upgraded in consideration of its inherent difficulty, and thus given more appropriate status.

_____**C.** Recommend that the engineering department provide better ventilation for the shaper operation and also a more foolproof way of loading the press irons.

_____**D.** Suggest that Jason not pay attention to the pressure he gets from the joining bench, and that it will be all right for him to take a break any time he feels he needs it.

_____**E.** Accept the fact that the shaper operation is a good way to test the mettle of employees coming into the department. If they can take it, you keep them; if they can't, let them quit.

If you have another approach, write it here. _____

_____

_____

Action Summary Checklist		Action Needed Yes No	Date Completed
	1. Acceptance of a personal responsibility to seek out problem situations in your department and try to solve them.	____ ____	_____
	2. Regular check on actual results in your department to see if there is a gap between them and what you had expected to happen.	____ ____	_____
	3. Focus on a search for causes rather than quick or easy conclusions when attacking problems.	____ ____	_____

Action Summary Checklist (continued)

	Action Needed Yes / No	Date Completed

4. Understanding that solutions to problems require that you make firm decisions and carry them out.
5. Maintenance of good records, or knowledge of where they are kept, so that you can find adequate information when handling problems or decisions.
6. Careful evaluation of all alternative courses of action before committing yourself to a decision.
7. Keeping an eye and an ear to what might occur now or in the future to create problems in the weeks or months ahead.
8. Strong curb on your instincts and hunches until you've made a systematic analysis of a situation.
9. When possible, an effort to place a numerical or dollar value on the expenses of implementing a decision as well as the cost associated with the problem.
10. Goal to have the benefits of an action outweigh the cost or effort of putting the action into effect.
11. Neither too much haste nor too much delay in making decisions.
12. Guard against wishful or biased thinking when making choices.
13. Application of your available problem-solving time to those vital few areas where the payoff is likely to be large, as opposed to chasing after the trivial many.
14. Willingness to seek advice and counsel when you are faced with difficult problems and decisions.
15. Acceptance of the fact that a portion of your decisions may not prove to be correct, accompanied by a determination to keep on trying.

CHAPTER 2: PROBLEM SOLVING AND DECISION MAKING

Chapter 3
The Arts of Leadership

Key Concepts

- The techniques of leadership can be learned, provided the individual has the necessary strength of character and the energy this responsibility demands.

- The supervisor should strive to match leadership style and approach to the specific situation and to the individual personalities of subordinates. This requires command of a range of leadership skills.

- The success of leadership depends less on technique than on the creation of enthusiastic attachment and deep-seated trust between supervisor and supervised. This relationship can be fostered by modern views of human nature (such as Theory Y) and by balancing concerns for production with concerns for people.

- Leadership implies judgments, decisions, and actions, some of which inevitably result in mistakes; the successful leader presses on despite them.

- The responsibility of leadership places in the supervisor's hands a great moral trust, an accountability for his or her actions as they affect the lives and fortunes of others.

Is leadership the same as management?

Not exactly. Leadership is only one of the many functions a manager must provide for the work force. In addition a manager must plan, organize, communicate, and exercise control. Nevertheless, leadership is a basic requirement of all managers. It is especially important at the supervisory level, where the majority of personal contacts are made between management and employees.

What, exactly, is leadership?

Everyone will give you a different answer to this one. My definition is this: Leadership is the knack of getting other people to follow you and to do willingly the things you want them to do. Regardless of the fancy talk you'll hear about leadership, this definition pinpoints the real reason for the high premium on this scarce skill.

Are leaders always popular with the people they supervise?

The best leaders seem to combine the knack of leading and the knack of winning friends. But most leaders must be satisfied with respect and followers. Why? Because many of the decisions you must make as a leader will not always favor everybody. Sometimes they will please nobody. The chances are that you won't win any popularity contests among employees.

Why should you want to become a leader?

Although the job of leader is unbelievably difficult, the rewards are high. You'll find them in increased prestige and status among the people with whom you work, among your friends, and in your community. To many leaders the heady exhilaration of making decisions that prove to be correct is reward enough. To others it's mainly a sense of mission. To still others it's the satisfaction that power brings. You can have all these in varying degrees. You may even have more money, because leadership is a quality that business traditionally pay a high price for.

Are good leaders born or made?

Marshal Foch, the famous World War I leader, said of leadership: "These are natural gifts in a man of genius, in a born general; in the average man, such advantages may be secured by work and reflection." Foch's statement pretty much reflects the consensus: Some people are born leaders, but most leaders are good leaders because they have worked hard and thought hard to become so.

What are the ingredients for good leadership?

Men and women who prove to be successful leaders are characterized by such qualities as the following:

CHAPTER 3: THE ARTS OF LEADERSHIP

A Sense of Mission. This is a belief in your own ability to lead, a love for the work of leadership itself, and a devotion to the people and the organization you serve.

Self-Denial. This essential of leadership is too often played down. It means a willingness to forgo self-indulgences (like losing your temper) and the ability to bear the headaches the job entails.

High Character. People who become successful leaders usually are honest with themselves and with others, can face hard facts and unpleasant situations with courage, do not fear criticism or their own mistakes, and are sincere and dependable.

Job Competence. There's been too much talk about the insignificance of technical job skill to the supervisor. A person who knows the job he or she supervises has one of the best foundations for building good leadership.

Good Judgment. Common sense, the ability to separate the important from the unimportant, tact, and the wisdom to look into the future and plan for it are ingredients that make the best leaders.

Energy. Leadership at any level means rising early and working late. It leaves little time for relaxation or escape from problems. Good health, good nerves, and boundless energy make this tough job easier.

A word of caution, however: The "trait" approach to leadership can be misleading. Some natural leaders display few of these desirable characteristics. You have only to consider Hitler, Mussolini, and General George Patton to find some of these traits missing.

Is there only one way to lead people?

Here's where a lot of us have been fooled. Take this situation. Jane Smith supervises three material handlers. Each has become an absentee problem. Listen to how Jane deals with each person.

To Al: "It's time to get on the ball. I want to see you in here five days a week every week from now on. Otherwise, I'll put you up for discharge."

To Sid: "Your absences are getting to be a headache for me and the rest of us here. You'll have to see that your attendance improves. Let's you and me work out a way to overcome this problem."

To Terry: "Take a look at your absence record. Not pretty, is it? I'll leave it up to you to figure out some way to straighten it out."

Which method do you suppose works best? The answer is that all get good results. Al, Sid, and Terry are no longer attendance problems. What is the reason? There are three basic kinds of leadership because there are three basic kinds of people. To be a successful leader, you need to be able to master all three techniques.

What are the three traditional kinds of leadership called?

Autocratic Leadership (used with Al in the last question). Many people think this technique is old-fashioned, but it often works. The leader makes the decisions and demands obedience from the people supervised. The trouble is that the supervisor had better be right.

Democratic Leadership (used with Sid). This form is very popular today. The leader discusses, consults, draws ideas from the people supervised, and lets them help set policy. It makes for participation and strong teamwork. Some critics call this "compromise" leadership.

Free-Rein Leadership (used with Terry). This technique is the most difficult to use. The leader, who acts as an information center and exercises minimum control, depends on the employees' sense of responsibility and good judgment to get things done. The advocates of this approach also call it participative or integrative leadership.

Are the traditional approaches the only way to lead?

Not at all. Two somewhat related approaches have become popular in recent years.

Results-Centered Leadership is akin to the work-itself approach to motivation. Using this technique, the supervisor tries to focus on the job to be done and to minimize the personalities involved. In effect, the supervisor says to the employee, "This is the goal the organization expects you to reach each day. Now let's work together to see how your job can be set up so that you can make your quota."

Contingency or Situational Leadership maintains that leaders will be successful in a particular situation only if three factors are in balance. This approach, advanced by Professor Fred Fiedler and documented in many studies, asks the leader to examine (1) the extent of rapport or good feelings between the supervisor and those supervised, (2) the nature of the job to be done—in terms of how carefully procedures and specifications must be followed, and (3) the amount of real power invested in the supervisor by his or her superiors.

Surprisingly, the authoritarian approach, which uses heavy directing and controlling, is most effective in either very favorable or very unfavorable circumstances. That is, it works best when the relationships are either very good or very poor, the job methods are precisely defined, and the leader's true authority is either very strong or very weak. In the fuzzier, or middle, situations, the participative approach is likely to be most successful.

For example, an authoritarian approach works out best (1) where the supervisor has lots of real power, the process requires strong control, and rapport with employees is good; and (2) where just the opposite conditions prevail.

The participative approach is best where the supervisor's authority hasn't been clearly spelled out by the top management or acknowledged by the employees, where the process and procedures are somewhat flexible, and where the rapport between supervisor and employees is only middling good.

The contingency approach tends to explain why dictatorial supervisors can be effective in some situations and not in others. Similarly it helps to show where participative leadership may work best and to suggest where it might fail. An authoritarian approach looks good for assembly lines or for labor crews cleaning up. A participative approach seems favorable for jobs in which exact procedures are hard to set or for jobs that require creativity or initiative. These conclusions are contingent on the authoritarian leader's having either high or low position power and high or low rapport, and the participative leader's having moderate rapport and only so-so authority.

Which kind of leadership is best?

Many successful managers will tell you that democratic leadership is the best method to use. The fact is that although the democratic way may involve the least risk, you'll hamper your leadership role if you stick only to that one. You can play a round of golf with a driver, but you'll get a much better score if you use a wedge in a sand trap and a putter on the greens.

Suppose you have a problem of cutting down on scrap in your department. You may find it better to consult in a group meeting with all your workers to let them decide how they'll approach the problem (democratic leadership). Then the inspector, when informed of your plan, can adjust inspection techniques accordingly (free-rein). Merely tell the scrap collector how you want the waste sorted (autocratic). You see, you'd be using all three kinds of leadership to deal with the same problem.

Figure 3-1 illustrates what is called the continuum of leadership styles. At one extreme the supervisor relies on absolute authority; at the other, subordinates are allowed a great deal of freedom.

How much does personality have to do with leadership?

A good personality helps. Employees may react more easily to a supervisor who has a ready smile and who is warm and outgoing,

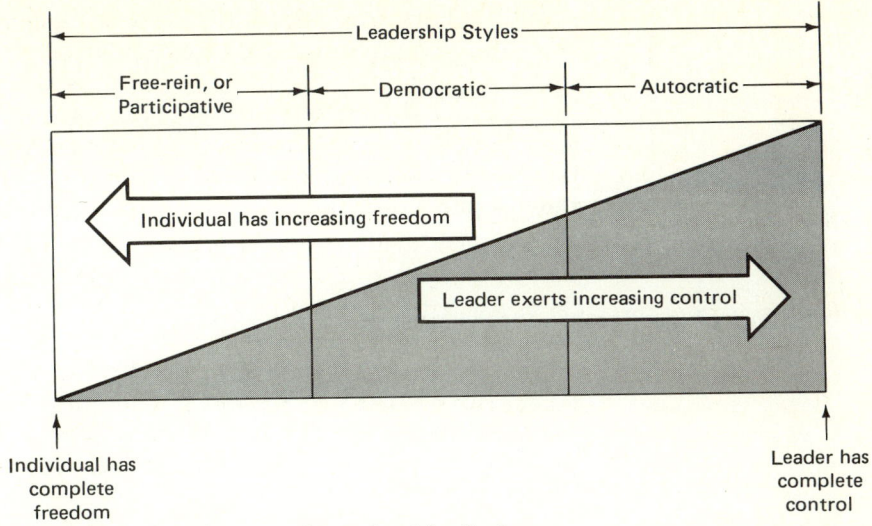

Figure 3-1. Continuum of Leadership Styles.

Reprinted by permission of the Harvard Business Review. *Adapted from the figure "Continuum of Leadership Behavior" from "How to Choose a Leadership Pattern," by Robert Tannenbaum and Warren H. Schmidt, May–June, 1973. Copyright © 1973 by the President and Fellows of Harvard College; all rights reserved.*

but personality must be more than skin-deep to be effective. Much more important is your real desire to understand and sympathize with the people who work for you. Fair play, interest in others, good decisions, and character will help make you a stronger leader than if you rely solely on personality.

Likewise, one kind of leadership may fit your personality better than the other two, and you may rely more on this form of leadership than on the others. But work hard to keep from depending on just one technique.

What do employee personalities have to do with the kind of leadership you exercise?

Noted author Auren Uris advises that you'll find the following connections between leadership methods and types of personality:

Aggressive, hostile persons do better under an autocratic leader. Their latent hostility must be firmly channeled to confine their work to constructive ends.

Aggressive, cooperative types will work better under democratic or free-rein leadership. Because their self-assertiveness takes constructive paths, they will head in the right direction when they're on their own.

Insecure types, who tend to depend on their superior, do better under the firmer hand of the autocratic leader.

CHAPTER 3: THE ARTS OF LEADERSHIP

Individuals, the solo players, are usually most productive under free-rein leadership, if they know the job well.

Uris calls this point of view "followership." It is based on a well-established fact that certain types of persons naturally follow certain kinds of leadership better than others. The trick is to match them when you can.

What kind of leadership works best in an emergency?

Autocratic leadership is fast. When an emergency arises—a live-steam hose breaks loose and is whipping about endangering lives—you wouldn't want to pussyfoot around consulting employees as to what to do. You'd probably shout, "Hey, cut the steam valve! Watch the safety!"

What kind of supervision gets the best results?

At first it may seem hard to believe that supervisors who place less emphasis on production goals actually get higher production from the employees they supervise. This is only one aspect of the picture of the successful supervisor drawn as a result of a landmark study in 1948 at the University of Michigan. Supervisors in high-production groups were characterized in the following ways:

Their own bosses gave them a freer hand than was given to supervisors in low-production groups.

They were more employee-centered and spent more time in supervising and less time on mechanical and paperwork details.

They encouraged employees to contribute their ideas on how best to get things done.

Note how close these findings come to describing free-rein, or participative, leadership. Rensis Likert, who had much to do with pursuing the Michigan studies, has come to believe that participative leadership (which he calls System 4) is the only form of leadership truly in tune with twentieth-century life. You may not be able to use it in every situation, but where you can, it brings the best results.

Must you always get participation?

No. If you plan your big targets by first asking for and considering the opinions of your employees, they'll understand that there isn't time to handle every decision that way. Participation is a long-range affair. If you show that you want and respect employees' opinions and that your decisions are affected by their opinions, you'll have achieved the goal of making employees feel they are part of a team. An occasional oversight or an infrequent decision made without their counsel won't destroy the feeling that generates cooperation.

By sowing the seeds of participation generously, you'll also find that you won't have to take over many of the minor decisions that occupy your attention otherwise. Employees who know from experience that their opinions are desired know in advance how the team (their team and yours) would act if the team had a chance to go into a huddle, and they'll act accordingly.

How do leaders win loyalty from their followers?

You win loyalty by being loyal to your employees—by supporting their best interests and defending their actions to others who would discredit them. "We may not have made a good showing this month," a supervisor who is loyal to the group will say, "but no one can say the staff wasn't in there trying."

Loyalty is also inspired when you show employees your own loyalty to your superiors. For instance, if you have to pass along an order from your superior, you will breed only contempt among your subordinates if you say, "Here's the new operating instruction from the central office. I don't think any more of it than you do. But it was sent down from the top, so we'll have to try to make sense out of it, even if they don't know what they're doing."

According to the Associated Press, Tom Lasorda, who was voted National League manager of the year while manager of the Los Angeles Dodgers baseball team in 1977, was judged to be extremely effective with his players "because he showed them respect, so they respected him in return."

Is good leadership simply good human relations?

You could say that, because to be a good leader, you must be a student of human nature. Not because you love everybody—probably you don't. But you must develop shrewd judgment in estimating people's intentions, knowledge, and interests. Even the roughest, toughest industrialists have been keen estimators of human capabilities and have been expert in getting the most from people who work for them.

How much book knowledge of behavioral sciences do you need to handle people well?

There is much that can be done by serious supervisors who wish to improve their relationships with people. While the availability of

CHAPTER 3: THE ARTS OF LEADERSHIP

scientific facts may be slight, the fault lies more with the individual than with the research effort. Individuals who take the time, or make the effort, can learn a lot about human behavior—their own as well as that of others. It will give them a feeling of humility, of course, but this humility need not destroy their confidence.

Leadership depends on many things. Demonstrated technical ability to plan and coordinate plans wins many followers. Drive, courage, and persistence build a good foundation for leadership, too. People will respond to the supervisor who expresses confidence in them. People will lean toward the supervisor whose behavior is consistent. The supervisor who searches hard for the people-oriented facts when making decisions, who as a result creates the impression of trying to be fair, gets approval, if not accolades, from subordinates. These are actions any supervisor can take without being a psychologist, a sociologist, an anthropologist, or a parlor psychiatrist.

Theory X, Theory Y. What's this all about?

To get along with people effectively, you must make a couple of fundamental decisions. First you must recognize your responsibility for managing human affairs at work, but you must always weigh your concern against the practical urgencies of technical and administrative matters.

Douglas McGregor, late professor of industrial management at the Massachusetts Institute of Technology, had much to offer supervisors in his thoughtful work, *The Human Side of Enterprise* (McGraw-Hill Book Company, New York, 1960). Most of today's management thinking was forged to meet the needs of a feudal society, reasoned McGregor. The world has changed, and new thinking is needed for top efficiency today. That's the core of this unique philosophy of pitting Theory X against Theory Y.

Theory X, the traditional framework for management thinking, is based on the following set of assumptions about human nature and human behavior:

1. The average human being has an inherent dislike of work and will avoid it if possible.
2. Because of this human characteristic of dislike of work, most people must be coerced, controlled, directed, or threatened with punishment to get them to put forth adequate effort toward the achievement of organizational objectives.
3. The average human being prefers to be directed, wishes to avoid responsibility, has relatively little ambition, and wants security above all.

Do these assumptions make up a scapegoat for purposes of scientific demolition? Unfortunately, no. While they are rarely stated so directly, the principles that consitute the bulk of current management action could have been derived only from assumptions such as those of Theory X.

Theory Y finds its roots in recently accumulated knowledge about human behavior. It is based on the following set of assumptions:

1. The expenditure of physical and mental effort in work is as natural as play or rest.
2. External control and the threat of punishment are not the only means for bringing about effort to achieve organizational objectives. Individuals will exercise self-control in the service of objectives to which they are committed.
3. Commitment to objectives depends on the rewards associated with their achievement. The most important rewards are those that satisfy needs for self-respect and personal improvement.
4. The average human being learns, under proper conditions, not only to accept but also to seek responsibility.
5. The capacity to exercise a relatively high degree of imagination, ingenuity, and creativity in the solution of organizational problems is widely, not narrowly, distributed in the population among both women and men.
6. Under the conditions of modern industrial life, the intellectual potentialities of the average human being are only partially realized.

What makes Theory Y so applicable today?

Under the assumptions of Theory Y, the work of the supervisor is to integrate the needs of employees with the needs of the department. Hard-nosed control rarely works out today. Here are McGregor's words:

> The industrial manager is dealing with adults who are only partially dependent. They can—and will—exercise remarkable ingenuity in defeating the purpose of external controls which they resent. However, they can—and do—learn to exercise self-direction and self-control under appropriate conditions. His task is to help them discover objectives consistent both with organizational requirements and with their own personal goals. And to do so in ways that will encourage genuine commitment to these objectives. Beyond this, his task is to help them achieve these objectives: to act as teacher, consultant, colleague, and only rarely as authoritative boss.

Where does the Managerial Grid fit in?

The Managerial Grid helps you to assess your particular leadership approach. The grid, devised by industrial psychologists Robert R.

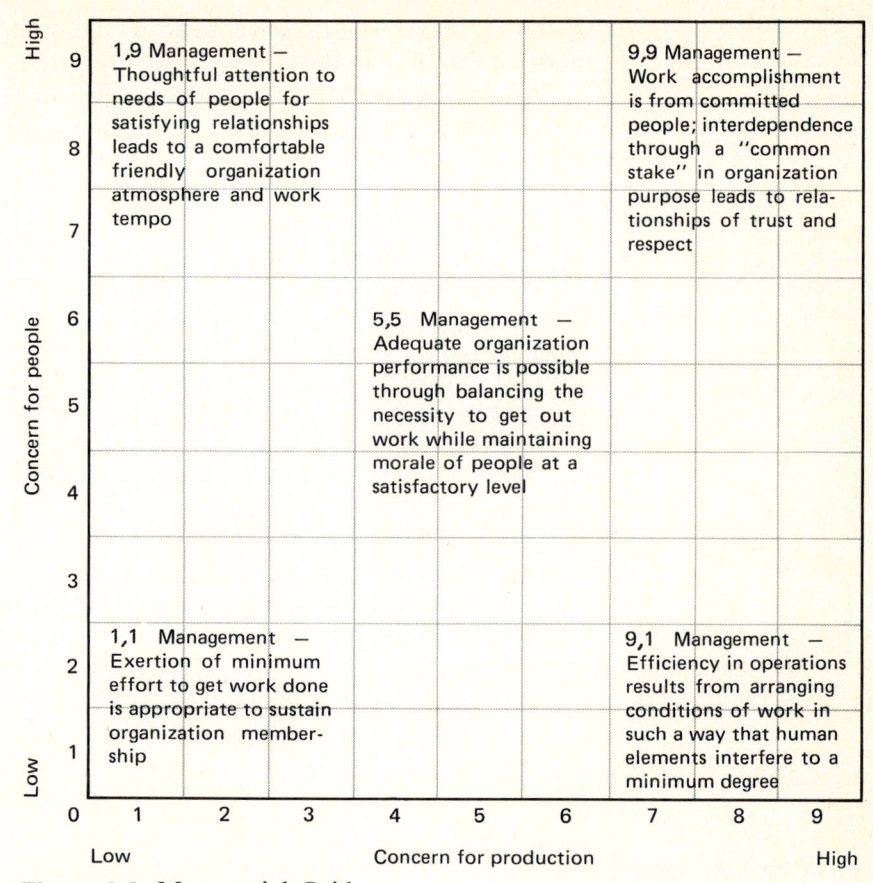

| | 9 | 1,9 Management — Thoughtful attention to needs of people for satisfying relationships leads to a comfortable friendly organization atmosphere and work tempo | | | | | | | | 9,9 Management — Work accomplishment is from committed people; interdependence through a "common stake" in organization purpose leads to relationships of trust and respect |

Figure 3-2. Managerial Grid.

The Managerial Grid figure from *The New Managerial Grid* by Robert R. Blake and Jane Srygley Mouton. Houston: Gulf Publishing Company, © 1964, p. 11. Reproduced by permission.

Blake and Jane S. Mouton, makes two measurements of a leader's approach: concern for production and concern for people. As shown in Figure 3-2, these two factors are typically plotted on a grid chart. The least concern for each factor is rated 1 and the highest, 9. To judge your own approach, first rate yourself according to your concern for people; say you believe it is fairly high—a score of 6. Next rate your emphasis on production or job results; say you rate that medium—a score of 5. You then find your place on the Managerial Grid by putting a mark on the chart 6 squares up and 5 squares across.

Blake, Mouton, and others have given nicknames to various places on the grid. The lower left-hand corner (1,1) could be called the creampuff, a supervisor who doesn't push for anything. The upper left-hand corner (1 for production, 9 for people) can be called the do-gooder, a person who watches out for people at the cost of overlooking production needs entirely. The lower right-hand corner (9 for production and 1 for people) is the hard-nose, a supervisor for whom production is all that counts. The supervisor near the middle of the chart (5 for both production and people) is the middle-of-the-roader, a person who makes a reasonable push for both concerns. In the eyes of many, all supervisors should strive to make their leadership performance score 9,9 (highest for both production and people) so that they might be called professionals.

Blake and Mouton believe that a 9,9 rating can be obtained only by a team approach. As we have seen, however, the team, or participative, approach doesn't work in every situation. Yet, it is a good one to choose if the conditions favor it.

Are there special tips for leaders?

Advice for leaders is free and plentiful. Most of it makes sense for the person who can put it into practice.

Be Predictable. People want to know where they stand with the boss—tomorrow as well as today. You might borrow a page from the books on child psychology. The experts have studied the maladjustments and the frustrations of kids. They suggest one good rule for handling them: Be consistent. If a child is praised for an act today and bawled out for the same act tomorrow—bingo, tears. If the child tries to help with the dishes, breaks one, and gets a scolding—watch out for tantrums. If you embarrass the child in front of others, look out—the cat may be painted green just to make it look ridiculous, too. It's the same thing for adults.

Put Yourself in the Employee's Place. Maybe you recall the last time you were at a ball game. Did you find yourself leaning with every pitch—trying to put body English on foul balls? Do the same thing with people. This mental shift can become a regular and desirable habit. It will help you understand, predict, and direct the responses of people.

Show Your Enthusiasm. If you sincerely like an idea, the way an employee did a job, or your next assignment, show this feeling to others in words and manner. It is a mistake for a supervisor to play it cool in relationships with employees. The personal atmosphere you create determines whether people will welcome you.

Be Interested in Employee's Welfare. Employees "want a supervisor or manager whom they can trust in time of need, to whom they can go when they need advice and about personal affairs," said Brehon Somervell, late president of the Koppers Company, Inc. It is a good outfit, indeed, when employees can "ask the boss."

Treat Employees Equally. Men and women insist on a leader's having a sense of fair play. They want to feel they are being given assignments entirely on their merits and that the boss won't play favorites. Not only is favoritism a sign of weak character, but it can also wreck an organization.

Review Questions

1. Why is leadership essential to effective supervision?
2. Compare autocratic leadership with democratic leadership.
3. Which kind of leadership is best in an emergency? Why?
4. If an employee tends to be aggressive but cooperative, which style of leadership might be most suitable to use? Why?
5. Provide examples of the use of a leadership style at three different points along the continuum of leadership styles.
6. If you had to choose between a supervisor who was predictable and consistent and one whose enthusiasm was contagious, which one would you rather work for? Why?
7. What might a supervisor do to move his or her placement on the Managerial Grid from 3, 7 to 7, 7? In what way is the Managerial Grid related to Theory X and Theory Y?
8. According to Fiedler's contingency model of leadership, what is likely to be the best approach in a situation where the supervisor has been newly appointed, relationships with the new group are standoffish, and the task to be performed requires great accuracy? Why?

A Case in Point

The Case of the Nurses' New Supervisor

This action took place on the general surgery floor of a small hospital in western New York State. For several months the hospital trustees had debated the feasibility of building an addition in order to move all critical-care facilities into a modern, fully equipped building. Just last month, however, the decision was made not to expand, but to modernize the present facilities. During the period of this decision making, the administrative organization of the hospital changed markedly. A new administrator from a large city hospital took over and brought a new nursing head and several new nursing supervisors.

The general surgery floor on this particular shift (3 p.m. to 11 p.m.) is staffed by eight old-time registered nurses, three licensed practical nurses, and two nurses' aides. Molly P., the new nursing supervisor for this shift, reported for the first time on Saturday night. She observed during the shift that there were several infractions of sterile procedures; that on two occasions practical nurses administered injections which, by law, must be handled by the registered nurses; and that there was a tendency for nurses to congregate at the nursing station for long periods of time. The first thing Molly did when she went on shift Tuesday night was to call the entire staff together. She said that they should know she expected all of them to adhere strictly to sterile procedures, that there must be no abrogation of RN responsibilities, and that coffee klatching at the nursing station must be kept to a minimum. To the best of Molly's knowledge, things improved on Wednesday and Thursday nights, but by the middle of the following week she sensed a return to the general laxness evident when she first took over.

Molly waited until the next Monday. That night she met with each of her staff individually in the quiet room. With each person she reiterated her determination to run a tight ship, medically, and then asked for cooperation. From most of the staff she got no meaningful replies. However, one of the older RNs looked her in the eye and said, "We've handled this floor in our own way for a number of years, and we've had no problems. Our record is as good as any in the hospital. We don't need your big-city ways here. And since the new addition won't be built, the chances are that you won't be here for long anyway."

If you were Molly, what would you do? Five alternative approaches are listed below. Rank them in the order in which they appeal to you (1 most attractive, 5 least). You may add another approach in the space provided, if you wish. In any event, be prepared to justify your rankings.

_____ **A.** Continue to insist on a high standard of performance while you take steps to weed out those of the staff who don't or won't measure up.

_____ **B.** Put off making changes until the staff is better unified under your leadership.

_____ **C.** Relax the rule about coffee klatching, but stick to the letter on the procedures for sterile practices and RN responsibilities.

_____ **D.** Hold fast to your demands for a medically tight ship, but work along with each person to find a way to persuade the worker of the value of operating this way.

_____ **E.** Get together with the other nursing supervisors to make certain that the procedures set down are uniform from floor to floor.

If you have another approach, write it here. _____
_____
_____

Action Summary Checklist		Action Needed Yes No	Date Completed
	1. Concern for personal leadership as part of your total management responsibility.	____ ____	_____

CHAPTER 3: THE ARTS OF LEADERSHIP

Action Summary Checklist (continued)

	Action Needed Yes No	Date Completed

2. Setting good examples of personal commitment and willingness to make sacrifices to help your team meet departmental objectives. ____ ____ _____
3. Maintenance of your health—physical and mental—so that you have the energy needed to handle the job actively. ____ ____ _____
4. Skill developed in applying all three kinds of traditional leadership approaches. ____ ____ _____
5. Proper focus on job objectives for yourself and each employee. ____ ____ _____
6. Balanced application of leadership techniques based on each particular situation. ____ ____ _____
7. Attempt to match your leadership style to the followership inclinations of each employee. ____ ____ _____
8. Willingness to be autocratic or hard-nosed when needed. ____ ____ _____
9. Concern for people equal to your concern for job results. ____ ____ _____
10. Regular self-study of human relations—formal as well as informal—to improve your leadership skills. ____ ____ _____
11. Demonstrated personal progress in the direction of point 9,9 on the Managerial Grid. ____ ____ _____
12. Determination through self-analysis of your own assumptions about employees as examples of either Theory X or Theory Y. ____ ____ _____
13. Ability to keep your head in the face of criticism, conflict, or routine job stress. ____ ____ _____
14. Consistency in the nature of your relationships with others for whose work you are accountable. ____ ____ _____
15. Conscious effort to treat employees equitably in similar situations: neither to play favorites nor to pick on those you don't particularly like. ____ ____ _____

Self-Check for Part 1

Test your comprehension of material in Chapters 1, 2, and 3. Correct answers are in the Appendix.

Multiple Choice Choose the responses that best completes each statement below. Write the letter of the response in the space provided.

1. Which of these is the best example of a good supervisor?
   a. Judy is a great technician and spends much of her time doing actual production work.
   b. Mike aspires to be an executive-level manager and doesn't spend any time on the department floor.
   c. Greg concentrates on the welfare and productivity of his employees and on linking his department with the goals and policies of higher managers.
   d. Jane stresses only the output her department is able to achieve.

   1. _____

2. The one role that is usually more important for executive-level managers than for supervisors is:
   a. Technical.
   b. Administrative.
   c. Scheduling.
   d. Human relations.

   2. _____

3. Which of these supervisors in an insurance company would probably get the best performance rating?
   a. John, who devotes all his energy to cutting costs.
   b. Carla, whose main relation with employees is telling them, "You've got to get more work done."
   c. Nancy, who strives for absolute highest quality at any cost.
   d. Ed, who gets results through careful management of resources.

   3. _____

4. A supervisor's first goal in managing human resources must be:

   4. _____

a. Keeping people productively engaged.
  b. Satisfying the personal desires of employees.
  c. Developing as large a staff as possible.
  d. Reducing employment whenever possible.
5. Keeping costs under control is: 5. ____
  a. Unimportant as long as output and quality are satisfactory.
  b. The job of accountants, not of supervisors.
  c. An automatic result of concentrating on output.
  d. A measure both of effectiveness in managing resources and of results.
6. A supervisor's efforts to keep morale high demonstrates: 6. ____
  a. An employee-centered approach.
  b. A task-centered approach.
  c. A production-centered approach.
  d. A job-centered approach.
7. A supervisor in a department that produces record jackets is serious about getting the best results and the highest productivity possible. The supervisor should, therefore: 7. ____
  a. Concentrate solely on pushing for more productivity.
  b. Limit supervisory efforts to human relations; productivity will always follow.
  c. Try to balance productivity concerns with human relations needs.
  d. Concentrate on getting the employees' esteem because that's the only way to get results.
8. Some supervisors carry out their leadership activities by the book. Others play it by ear. Both types can be successful provided they: 8. ____
  a. Perfect the techniques of leadership.
  b. Don't let anything stop them.
  c. Can generate mutual confidence with their subordinates.
  d. Stay in control of situations.
9. A supervisor whose leadership behavior is based on the contingency model has been made the head of a department, but has been given little real authority. The supervisor has little rapport with the workers, and the work itself is thoroughly routine with no prospect of change. What leadership style would you expect this supervisor to stress?   9. ____
  a. Authoritarian.

b. Participative.
   c. Free-rein.
   d. System 4.
10. Which one of these persons would be likely to function well and to feel comfortable under an autocratic leadership style?   10. _____
   a. Marcia, who is self-assertive but cooperative and constructive.
   b. Tom, who is insecure and somewhat dependent on his supervisor.
   c. Alice, who is a noncomformist but one of the best cutters in the business.
   d. Bob, who is self-confident and very competent and likes to make up his own mind.

True-False Indicate whether each of the following statements is true or false by writing *T* or *F* in the answer column.
11. One good way to identify a problem is to see if there is a difference between what was expected to happen and what actually did happen.   11. _____
12. Decision making cannot be separated from problem solving; it must be used to evaluate possible solutions and to choose the ultimate plan of action.   12. _____
13. To solve most problems, management must find a way to remove whatever it was that caused them in the first place.   13. _____
14. Change—in the past or in the future—leads to most problems. Accordingly, managers can do little to prevent problems from occurring.   14. _____
15. Power in leadership depends to some degree on the authority invested by higher management in a supervisor.   15. _____
16. In a real emergency most supervisors wisely adopted a participative approach.   16. _____
17. A supervisor who says, "You can't tell me that anyone likes working," reflects the Theory X point of view.   17. _____
18. Free-rein leadership often works quite well for individuals who know their job well.   18. _____
19. Theory Y includes the belief that human beings accept and even seek responsibility.   19. _____
20. The Managerial Grid describes leadership approaches by the way they combine concern for people with concern for production.   20. _____

Problem Anne Tandy is the supervisor of a keypunch operation in a data processing section of a federal agency. Ten operators report to her. Last week Anne and other supervisors received a directive from the agency commissioner. It read: "Effective June 1, all sections will be expected to reduce their staff by 10 percent. This should present no hardship because it is forecast that the data processing work load will be reduced by the same percentage. Please make plans accordingly." Anne looked over her personnel list and selected for transfer or termination the employee who was least productive. Anne said to herself, "I will notify Tom of this decision on June 1."

Make a list of at least three potential problems that might interfere with Anne's plans for reducing the work force. You may list more than three, if you wish.

a. _____

b. _____

c. _____

PART 2
PLANNING, ORGANIZING, AND CONTROLLING WORK

Supervisors are judged by their ability to manage their resources in such a way as to get the proper results in terms of departmental output, quality, and cost control. This requires a sound knowledge of planning principles, organizational structuring, and methods for controlling people as well as processes.

Chapter 4 outlines principles and techniques for planning and goal setting at the departmental level together with ways for establishing effective procedures.

Chapter 5 shows how to design an organizational structure that best suits a department's goals and resources.

Chapter 6 links planning concepts with controls so that supervisors can see how to maintain and enforce process and work force standards.

Chapter 4
Making Plans and Carrying Out Policy

Key Concepts

- Planning is the process of systematically working out what you and your work group will do in the future. Plans establish a hierarchy of goals—based on the needs of the organization and on the strengths and weaknesses of the work group—and specific procedures, regulations, and policies designed to achieve the goals.

- Objectives, or goals, for a work group should (1) support the goals of the overall organization and (2) be attainable, given the limitations and resources of the group. Objectives should be clearly and concretely stated. Supervisors usually deal with short-term objectives that span a few days, weeks, or months.

- Decisions and actions in every enterprise are guided by a body of operating principles that either have been set down in writing or have evolved informally (like common law) as a result of decisions made and actions taken by management under similar circumstances in the past.

- Company policies are dynamic, too, in that they are influenced by the decisions and actions of supervisors and managers as they cope daily with ever-changing situations and circumstances.

- In the eyes of employees the supervisor is inseparably identified with the policy of the employing organization, because it is at the supervisory level that philosophies and principles are translated into specific actions.

Why is so much emphasis placed on planning?

Because the resources that management applies must deal with the future, and the future is rarely the same as today. Planning is a tested way of coping with change. It helps to make certain that you have enough employees on hand to do the job, the right amount and kind of materials, and tuned-up machinery for use when you need it. Most important, planning prepares a road map, which enables a supervisor to move resources effectively.

Plans, planning, policies, goals: What is the difference?

If ever there is an area of management where the terms are mixed up, this is it. *Plans* come out of the *planning* process. Plans or programs are what you intend to do in the future. Before you can develop plans, however, you must set targets, which are called *goals, standards,* or *objectives*.

After you have set these goals (that is the simplest term to use), you establish general guidelines for reaching them. The guidelines are called *policies*. Only after policies have been set should you formulate plans.

As a final step, you may choose to lay down some *rules* and *regulations*. These will establish the limits (controls) within which employees are free to do the job their own way.

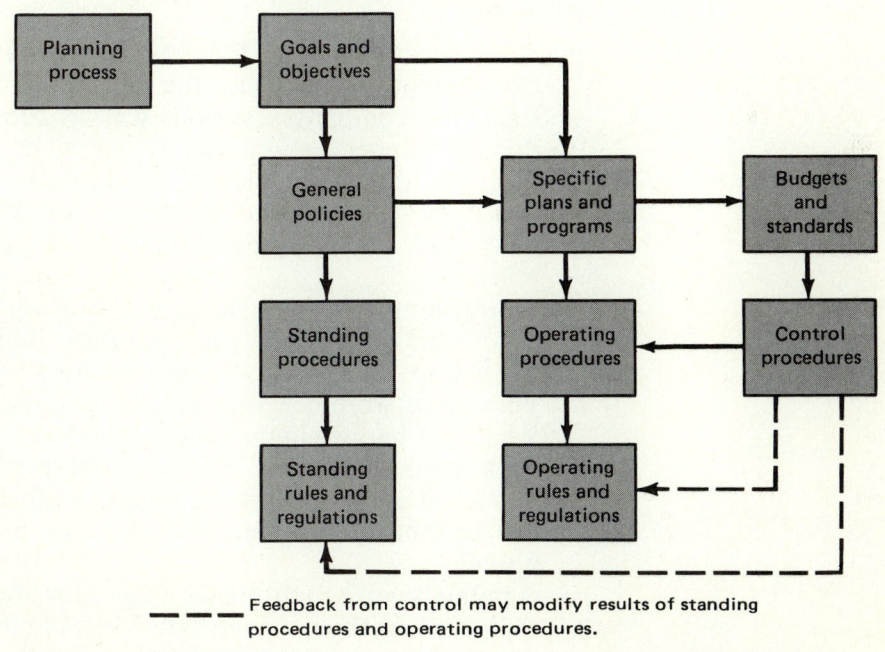

– – – – Feedback from control may modify results of standing procedures and operating procedures.

Figure 4-1. Relationship Between the Various Outputs of the Planning Process.

CHAPTER 4: MAKING PLANS AND CARRYING OUT POLICY

Take this example. You are thinking ahead—planning—about what your department will do during the annual spring cleaning. You make a list of things that you want to accomplish: filing cabinets cleared of obsolete material, shelving cleaned and rearranged, tools repaired and in tip-top shape. These are your goals. Next you establish some sort of policy. For example, cleaning will be done during normal working hours without overtime; discarding obsolete papers will conform to legal requirements; tool repairs may be done by your own maintenance department or by an outside machine shop. Next you lay out a master plan of how the housekeeping will be done, when, and by whom. If this plan is detailed as to its exact sequence, it would be called a *procedure*. You may want to set time limits for this procedure, which converts it to a *schedule*. If someone sets cost limits for this operation, these costs will form a *budget*. Finally, you set down some firm rules or regulations for your work crew. For example, only file clerks will make judgments about what paperwork will be discarded; before tools are sent outside for repair, employees must check with you; employees who clean shelving must wear protective gloves. Figure 4-1 illustrates common relationships between these terms.

What is the best way to approach the planning process?

Systematically. A number of factors contribute to good planning. You will get the best results if you follow them step by step:

1. Consider the goals of the entire organization, not just of your department. Think about the needs and wishes of customers, those the company serves as well as those "customers" your department serves internally.
2. Estimate the strengths and weaknesses of your department. Ask how they will help or hinder you in trying to meet company goals and in trying to serve external and internal customers.
3. Don't jump to conclusions at this early stage. Instead, keep your mind alert to new opportunities, such as ways to improve quality or lower costs. Don't restrict your thinking to what your goals were last year or how you met them. A forecast of what may happen in the future helps to keep you looking ahead.
4. Pick a reasonable set of goals. These should meet two standards: They (*a*) contribute to the organization's goals and (*b*) can be met by your department, given its strengths and weaknesses.
5. Arrange your department's goals in a hierarchy of objectives; that is, place the most important ones at the top of your list and the least important at the bottom.
6. Watch out for limitations. Think about restrictions that may be imposed on you by your company or by the need to coordinate

with, or serve, other departments. Your department cannot operate in a vacuum. It must base its plans on such realistic planning premises.
7. Develop your master plan. This should focus on your main objective. If, for example, the company's goal is higher-quality products or services, the master plan for your department should give this top priority.
8. Draw up supporting plans. This requires that you think about how each activity in your department can contribute to your master plan. Machinists may need more explicit blueprints. Assemblers may need brighter workplace lighting. Clerks may need a different order-entry procedure.
9. Put numbers and dates on everything you can. Plans work best when employees know how much is required of them or how many. Since plans are for the future—tomorrow, next week, or next month—times and dates are essential.
10. Pin down assignments. Plans are for people. Responsibility for carrying out each part of a plan or procedure should be assigned to a particular individual.
11. Explain the plan to all concerned. Plans should be shared. Their rationales should be explained and their goals justified. Employees who know *why* are more likely to cooperate.
12. Review your plans regularly. Circumstances and restrictions change. Your plans should be examined periodically to see whether they should be changed, too.

How strictly must the planning process be followed?

Experts say that nothing should be attempted without prior planning. There should be few exceptions to this rule of primacy. There is flexibility, however, in how a supervisor goes about planning. Nevertheless, thought should be given to each of the steps outlined above.

In what way are plans or programs usually classified?

They are usually classified according to their duration and purpose.

Long-range plans are typically set by higher management and are expected to be in operation from two to five years.

Short-range plans are those that supervisors are most concerned with and are usually based on operations of one year or less. At the departmental level, short-range plans may be in effect for a day, a week, a month, or a quarter of a year.

Standing plans include just about any activity that goes on without much change from year to year. Standing plans cover general employment practices, health and safety matters, purchasing procedures, routine discipline, and the like.

Single-use plans are used only once before they must be revised. Departmental budgets and operating schedules are examples. They will be good only for a week or a month until new ones are issued.

Generally speaking, then, supervisors will follow short-range, single-use plans for day-to-day operations; but they will also be guided by many standing plans that implement routine, relatively unchanging goals and policies.

When should supervisors plan and how often?

Before starting anything new or different. Planning should take place before a new day, a new week, a new product or service, or the introduction of different materials or machinery. As a matter of routine, a supervisor should make new plans each night for the next day, each Friday for the next week, and the last week in the month for the next month.

Which areas should be targets for a supervisor's planning process?

Just about anything qualifies. Any kind of change should trigger new plans. Every area within the supervisor's responsibility is a candidate for planning. For starters, here is a list of a dozen prime candidates:

Use of facilities and equipment—departmental layout and working conditions, equipment utilization and maintenance.

Use and care of materials and supplies—purchases, inventory levels, storage.

Conservation of energy and power—electricity, steam, water, and compressed air usage; waste disposal; fire protection.

Cash and credit management—petty cash, billing, collections.

Work force management—forecasting requirements, safety and health care, sanitation, communications, absences and turnover, employee training and development.

Information collection and processing—tallies and logbooks, recordkeeping, order processing.

Time conservation—startups, shutdowns, personal time.

Schedules—routing, delivery performance, shortages.

Quality management—inspection and control techniques, rework methods, scrap reduction, employee training and motivation.

Cost reduction and control—cost estimating, correction of variances, work simplifications, and methods improvement.

Productivity—work simplification and methods improvement.

Self-improvement—planning, organizing, communicating, public speaking, business writing, leading conferences.

How do controls relate to plans?

Controls are like like limit switches that keep plans in line. When a plan is moving directly toward its goal, the track is kept clear and the supervisor need apply no control. But when a plan strays from its target, the supervisor must take corrective action to bring it back in line. When planning a department's goals, the supervisor must also plan its control limits. (See Chapter 6 for details.)

What is a good way to double-check your plans and projects?

Try using the five-point planning chart illustrated in Figure 4-2.

What spells out objectives in terms of specifications for output, quality, and costs.

Where sets the location for the assignment (its workplace) and the place where the product or service must be delivered (the adjoining department, the shipping dock, the home office).

When records your time estimates for the work to be performed and, most important, specifies starting and finishing times and dates.

How verifies short- and long-range methods, procedures, and job sequences.

Who designates the individual responsible for the assignment and specifies that person's authority and extent of control over the resources needed (tools, machinery, additional labor, materials).

Figure 4-2 **Five-Point Planning Check Chart**

What	Objectives	Specifications
		Cost/price limits
Where	Locale	Delivery point
When	Time elapsed	Starting date
		Completion date
How	Tactics	Methods Procedure Sequence
	Strategy	
Who	Responsibility	Authority Control Assignment

CHAPTER 4: MAKING PLANS AND CARRYING OUT POLICY

What is meant by company policy?

Company policies are broad rules or guides for action. At their best these rules are a statement of the company's objectives and its basic principles for doing business. They are intended as a guide for supervisors and managers in getting their jobs done. Many policies give supervisors the opportunity to use their own best judgment in carrying them out. Others are supported by firm rules, which supervisors must observe if they are to run their departments in harmony with the rest of the organization.

Does policy apply only at high-levels?

Although policy is generally set by managers high up in the company organization, it can be no more than a collection of high-sounding words unless the supervisor translates the words into action on the firing line.

Take an example of a disciplinary policy. Here's how it might sound as it works its way down from the front office to first-line action by the supervisor.

Company president: "Our policy is to exercise fair and reasonable controls to regulate the conduct of our employees."

Vice president: "The policy on attendance in this company is that habitual absenteeism will be penalized."

Department manager: "Here are the rules governing absences. It's up to you supervisors to keep an eye on absences and to discharge any employee absent or late more than three times in three months."

Supervisor: "Sorry. I'm going to have to lay you off for three days. You know the rules. You put me in a bad spot when you take time off on your own without warning or getting approval."

Note that no real action takes place until the supervisor puts the words of the policy into effect.

What sort of matters does policy cover?

A company may have a policy to cover almost every important phase of its business—from regulating its method of purchasing materials to stipulating how employees may submit suggestions. As a supervisor you will probably be most concerned with policies that affect (1) employees and (2) the practices of your department.

Employee policies most commonly formalized are those affecting wages and salaries, holidays and vacations, leaves of absence, termination of employment, safety, medical and health insurance and hospitalization, service awards, and retirement and pensions.

Department practices most often reduced to policy are requisitioning of supplies, preparation of records, timekeeping, safeguarding classified materials, cost-control measures, quality standards, maintenance and repair, and acquisition of new machinery and equipment.

These listings are not all-inclusive. Some companies have more, others fewer policies.

Is policy always in writing?

Far from it. Many rigid policies have never been put down in black and white, and many firm policies have never been repeated by an executive. But employees and supervisors alike recognize that matters affected by such policies must be handled in a certain manner and usually do so.

The existence of so much unwritten policy has led many authorities to the conclusion that all policy is better put into writing so that it may be explained, discussed, and understood. Nevertheless, many companies don't subscribe to this way of thinking, and their policies remain implied rather than spelled out.

Is policy just a matter of do's and don'ts?

One of the great misunderstandings about policy is the belief that it's always negative, like "don't do that" or "do it this way or you'll get in trouble."

Policy can also be positive, encouraging, and uplifting. Just examine the written policy of a nationally respected company as expressed in a booklet published by its board of directors:

Importance of the Individual. We believe the actions of business should recognize human feelings and the importance of the individual and should ensure each person's treatment as an individual.

Common Interest. We believe that employees, their unions, and management are bound together by a common interest—the ability of their unit to operate successfully—and that opportunity and security for the individual depend on this success.

Open Communications. We believe that the sharing of ideas, information, and feeling is essential as a means of expression and as the route to better understanding and sounder decisions.

Local Decisions. We believe that people closest to the problems affecting themselves develop the most satisfactory solutions when given the authority to solve such matters at the point where they arise.

High Moral Standards. We believe that the soundest basis for judging the "rightness" of an action involving people is the test of its morality and its effect on basic human rights.

Words? Yes. Policy? Definitely. And as an official guide to action committed in print by the top officers of the organization, these statements are an excellent example of the positive side of policy.

Should a supervisor change policy?

No. That's a very dangerous thing to do. Policies are set to guide action. It's a supervisor's responsibility to act within policy limits.

Supervisors can influence a policy change, however, by making their thoughts and observations known to the boss, the personnel department, and the top management. After all, supervisors are in the best position to perceive employees' reactions to policy—favorable or otherwise. You do your boss and your company a service when you accurately report employees' reactions, and that's the time to offer your suggestions for improving or modifying the policy.

Do supervisors ever set policy?

In a way, supervisors always set policy at the departmental level. Supervisory application of policy is their interpretation of how the broader company policy should be carried out for employees. It's important for you to recognize that company policy usually allows you discretion at your level—even though this discretion may be limited.

Suppose your company has a policy that forbids bookmaking on the premises. Anyone caught will be fired. You can carry out that policy many ways. You can bait a trap, hide behind a post, and fire the first person you catch. Or you can quietly size up the most likely violator and warn that there won't be a second chance. You can put a notice on the bulletin board calling employees' attention, generally, to the policy. Or you can hold a group meeting and announce how you will deal with bookmakers. You can choose to regard only taking horse-racing bets as bookmaking, or include professionally run baseball, basketball, and football pools. Or you can rule out any kind of gambling. Whatever you decide, so long as you carry out the intentions (and the letter where it's spelled out) of the company policy, you are setting your own policy.

How responsible will employees hold you for company policy?

If you have done a good job of convincing employees that you fully represent the management of their company, your actions and company policy will be one and the same thing in their eyes. Naturally you will sometimes have to carry out policy that you don't fully agree with—policy that may be unpopular with you or with your employees. Resist the temptation to apologize for your actions or to criticize the policy to employees. When you do, you weaken your position.

If you have to reprimand an employee, don't say, "I'd like to give you a break, but that's company policy." Or when sparking a cleanup campaign, don't say, "The manager wants you to get your area in order." Handle such matters positively. Give the policy your own personal touch, but don't sell the company down the river or you're likely to be caught in the current yourself.

How can you prevent your policy interpretations from backfiring?

Try to protect your actions in policy matters by asking yourself questions before making decisions:

Is policy involved here? What is the procedure? What is the rule?

Am I sure of the facts? Do I know all the circumstances?

How did I handle a similar matter in the past?

Who can give me advice on this problem? Should I ask for it?

Would my boss want to talk this over with me first?

Does this problem involve the union? If so, should I see the union steward or should I check with the labor relations people first?

What is a supervisor's policy manual?

Many companies have actually taken their general company policies and written down interpretations as a specific guide to supervisor action. Those written guides for supervisors are usually placed in a loose-leaf folder and called a Supervisor's Manual. Supervisors use these manuals as references whenever a policy question comes up that they aren't certain about handling. If your company has such a manual and it's up to date, it's an invaluable aid in handling your job.

What do employees want to know about policy?

Employees are rarely concerned with nice phrases. General statements of policy will mean little to them. But they do have a keen and critical interest in the specific and concrete aspects of policy whenever it affects them.

If your company's policy is to "treat employees equitably in disciplinary affairs," this will probably be unclear to them. You can help a lot if you rephrase the broad statements of policy (which may necessarily be generalized) into language that every employee understands. In this case, "We intend to give everyone a fair and square deal if a rule is broken."

CHAPTER 4: MAKING PLANS AND CARRYING OUT POLICY

But even such a clear summary of a regulation still doesn't answer for an employee: "What does this mean to me?" You'll have to be still more specific: "If more than three out of every hundred pieces you turn out don't measure up to standards, I'll give you a warning the first time. The second time, you'll be given time off without pay. If it continues, you may be discharged." You wouldn't get far with policy, for instance, if you say to the employee, "If the quality of your production is substandard, we may have to take disciplinary action." The employee may very well ask, "What's quality? What's my production? What's substandard? What's disciplinary action?"

What kinds of goals are typically set for supervisors?

Objectives or goals—especially at the supervisory level—are usually targets that you or your department must aim for in order to (1) put policy into practice and (2) specifically assist the firm in making a reasonable profit or in living up to its service commitments. Typically, the goals for your department are short-range. These goals pin down your cost, quality, and performance targets for next week, next month, or next year. Frequently these goals are quantitative (with numbers on them) rather than merely qualitative (described by words such as improve, maintain, good, better). Typical performance goals for a first-line supervisor are shown in Table 4-1. In many companies the manner in which you and your depart-

TABLE 4-1.
Typical Performance Goals for a First-line Supervisor

Area of Measurement	Last Year's Record	Next Year's Goals
1. Ratio of jobs completed on schedule to total jobs worked	85% average, 92% highest, 65% lowest in June	90% average, minimum acceptable 75%
2. Percentage of job costs held within 3% of standard costs	91% average, 95% highest, 75% lowest in June	90% average, bring up low figure to 87% or better
3. Rejects and rework	Less than 1% rejects Rework averages 7%	Keep rejects to less than 1%, but cut rework to 3%
4. Labor stability	Two quits, one discharge	No quits of employees with over three years service
5. Absences, latenesses	5% absences, 7% latenesses	5% absences, 2% latenesses
6. Overtime	Only on jobs okayed by sales department	Only on jobs okayed by sales department
7. Accidents	No lost-time accidents; 37 calls to dispensary for minor ailments	No lost-time accidents reduce number of dispensary visits

ment attain your goals determines what kind of raise you'll get or how good a job you can be groomed for.

Review Questions

1. Give an example from your work or personal life of a time when prior planning would have made things work out better than they did.
2. How are plans and controls related?
3. Contrast the way in which policy affects top management decisions and the supervisor's actions.
4. What are some of the things typically covered by company policies?
5. When would it be wise for a supervisor to check with the boss before carrying out a particular policy?
6. Give an example of how a supervisor's decision in a particular instance might be influenced by more than one policy.
7. One company's policy manual stated: "It is our intention to listen with an open mind to employees' complaints." What supplementary information might a supervisor add to that statement when explaining it to the employees?
8. Which do you think is more important to a company in the long run: the policies it sets or the actions its supervisors take? Why?

A Case in Point

The Case of the Forgotten Price Change

The written policy of a major supermarket chain is posted in all its stores. It reads as follows:

Our policy is always to:
　Do what is honest, fair, sincere, and in the best interests of every customer.
　Extend friendly, satisfying service to everyone.
　Give every customer the most good food for the money.
　Assure accurate weight every time—16 ounces to each pound.
　Give accurate count and full measure.
　Charge the correct price.
　Refund, cheerfully, customers' money if for any reason any purchase is not satisfactory.

In a supermarket located in a ghetto in a northeastern state, the following was reported to have happened. The store manager received notice from the district superintendent that the price charged for a certain brand of coffee was to be reduced from $2.98 per pound to $2.68 per pound on the Monday preceding Thanksgiving. Routinely (for the manager received dozens of such notices each week), the supermarket manager told the head stock clerk to insert a price change notice in the shelves, to restamp existing stock with the new price, and to make a notation on the registers at the checkout counters. On the Wednesday before Thanksgiving the district office received a telephone call from a customer who complained that this particular store was charging $2.98 for the coffee, although another store had it at a lower price. The district superintendent called the store manager to verify this. The store manager quickly checked the shelves and discovered that the head stock clerk had simply forgotten to carry out instructions. The store manager called back the district superintendent to report what had happened, but commented, "No harm's been done. If customers say they've been overcharged, we'll refund their money. And, besides, not many people down here know the difference anyway."

How would you evaluate the store manager's actions? Five alternative opinions are listed below. Rank them in the order in which they appeal to you (1 most attractive, 5 least). You may add another opinion in the space provided, if you wish. In any event, be prepared to justify your rankings.

_____**A.** The store manager had sincerely tried to see that the company's policy was carried out and should not be held responsible for the error.

_____**B.** The store manager should have made absolutely certain that the instructions had been followed to the letter.

_____**C.** The head stock clerk was the weakest link in the chain for carrying out the company's policy.

_____**D.** Both the store manager and the head stock clerk were weak links in carrying out the company's policies.

_____**E.** The store manager's expressed viewpoint did not properly reflect the intention of the company's policy.

If you have another opinion, write it here. _____
_____
_____

Action Summary Checklist		Action Needed Yes No	Date Completed
	1. Time set aside for planning: 5 minutes daily/15 minutes weekly/1 hour monthly.	___ ___	_____
	2. Nothing new nor any changes attempted without prior planning.	___ ___	_____
	3. Goals based on a realistic look at departmental strengths and weaknesses and company-imposed restrictions.	___ ___	_____

Action Summary Checklist (continued)

| | Action Needed Yes / No | Date Completed |

4. Departmental goals arranged in order of priority.
5. Plans, procedures, and regulations that fit into chosen goals.
6. Plans flexible enough to permit change when needed.
7. Control limits and control procedures established to enable you to monitor departmental progress toward goals.
8. Knowledge of your company's general policies, especially as they relate to personnel matters.
9. Up-to-date knowledge of procedures that affect operating practices.
10. Provision of feedback to your superiors about difficulties in policy implementation or the need for policy change.
11. Acceptance of company policies as your policies so far as employees are concerned.
12. Prudence in checking company policy implications before taking trend-setting action at the departmental level.
13. Willingness to explain and interpret policies, procedures, and regulations to employees in language they understand.
14. Commitment to goals that the company has set and to those you have set for your own operations.
15. Continuing alert for the need to plan new goals and to establish up-to-date procedures.

Chapter 5
Organizing an Effective Department

Key Concepts

- First-line supervisors represent the cutting edge of most organizational structures. They ultimately direct the specific actions that derive from the policies and strategies conceived in the upper echelons of the structure.

- Charts and descriptions of organizational structures, while valuable as starting points, never fully define or stabilize the complexities of informal relationships at all levels, which may take precedence over the formally prescribed ones.

- While formal channels for discharging responsibility and authority must be respected in most instances, it is usually wise for supervisors to modify their decisions and actions in accordance with the organizational relationships observed by their peers and superiors.

- Better-than-average supervisors know how to appeal for, and put to use, the specialized advice and guidance available from staff departments.

- The ability of supervisors to divide their work effectively among subordinates—to delegate—is probably the single most important factor in managerial success or failure.

What is an organization?

An organization is a grouping of people so that they can work effectively toward a goal that members of the group want to achieve.

The goal of a business organization is primarily profits for stockholders and wages and salaries for managers, supervisors, and employees. There are other important goals, too, like supplying goods and services to the general population or producing military materials for our defense in time of war. Members of the organization all aim for other satisfactions, too, such as the sense of fellowship, accomplishment, and prestige.

Why organize?

We'd have nothing but havoc without it. We take organization for granted because we have lived so long with it at home, in houses of worship, and at school. Little we do together would be effective if we didn't agree among ourselves who should do what. Because business organizations are under tremendous pressures to be effective, their organization tends to be more formal and rigid.

After the Dallas Cowboys won the professional football Super Bowl in 1978, one sportswriter made the comment that the victory wasn't the real accomplishment. "The thing that sets the Cowboys apart from other strong National Football League teams," said Phil Elderkin of the *Christian Science Monitor,* "is their ability as an organization. From the front office to the playing field, everything is done with calculated precision."

Are all organizations formal?

No. In many of our activities, even in complex companies, some people just naturally take over responsibilities and exercise authority without anyone's ever spelling it out. Chances are that in a group of 15 employees who you might imagine are all at the same level, you'll discover some sort of informal organization. It may be that the person who sweeps the floors actually swings weight in that group. Acting as staff assistant may be the lift-truck driver, who is the informant. The rest of the group may either work hard or stage a slowdown at a nod from the floor-sweeper. No one gave the authority, but it is there as surely as if the company president had published a special order giving a title.

So be alert to informal organization—among the employees you supervise, in the supervisory group itself, and in the entire management structure.

Which comes first, the organization or the work to be done?

If there were no work to do, there would be no reason for having an organization. So don't make the mistake of being organization-happy and trying to set up an elaborate organization just for the sake of having one. The best organization is a simple one that puts people together so that the job at hand gets done better, more quickly, more cheaply than any other way.

In business the job at hand in an industrial plant, for example, is very big and complex. The number of people involved is large, and their different skills are many. Some authorities say that organizations must manage four key resources:

Work Force. The people who manage others, as well as those who do the work.

Machines. The machinery, buildings, and equipment that enable the work force to produce the goods and services.

Material. The raw materials and other goods that go into the product or are used to refine it.

Money. The dollars and cents that provide the machines and materials for people to manage and work with.

Your job, too, involves management of these four resources. Your place in the company's organization should be designed to help you do that management job better. But recognize that the big organization can't be tailor-made to the last inch to suit all your preferences. Within the framework of your own department, however, it's up to you to see that your organization is tailor-made for the work as well as it possibly can be.

What is the purpose of organization charts?

To help you understand organizational relationships. Such charts are really pictures of how one job or department fits with others. Each box, or rectangle, encloses an activity or a department. Those boxes on the same horizontal level on the chart tend to have the same degree of authority or power and to have closely related work. Departments in boxes on the next higher level have greater authority; those at lower levels have less authority. Clusters of boxes that enclose departments performing closely related functions (such as shaping, fabricating, assembly and finishing in a manufacturing plant) are typically connected in a vertical chain to the head manager of that particular function (such as the production manager).

Boxes containing line departments tend to descend from the top of the chart to the bottom (where supervisors' departments typically are located) in vertical chains. Boxes that enclose staff departments tend to branch out to either side of the main flow of authority from top to bottom.

Organization charts can be drawn any way that shows relationships best, even in circles; but for practical purposes most charting is done in the manner just described and illustrated in Figure 5-1. One caution: Organization structures and staffing change constantly; organization charts therefore go out of date very quickly.

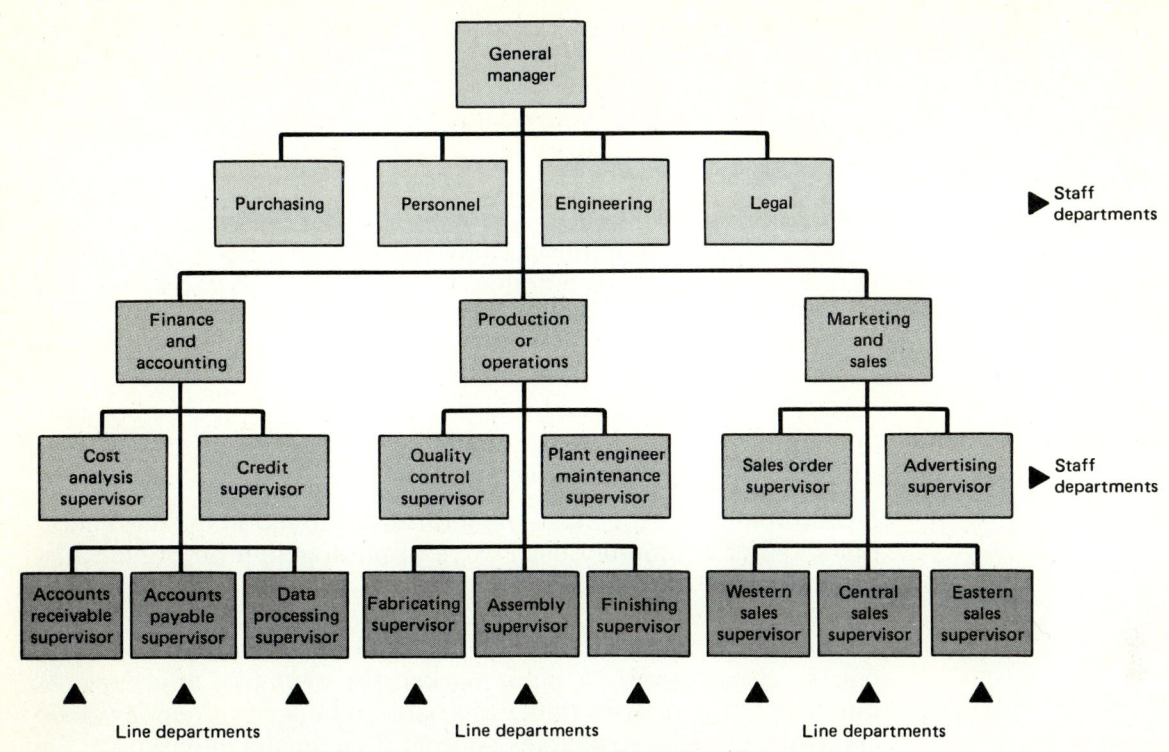

Figure 5-1. Line-and-Staff Organization in a Manufacturing Company.

What is the difference between line and staff?

An organization works best when it gets many related jobs done effectively with the minimum of friction. This requires coordination and determination of what to do and how to do it. Those managers and supervisors whose main job is to see that things get done are usually considered members of the line organization. Other management people who help them decide what to do and how to do it, assist in coordinating the efforts of all, or provide service are usually called staff people. (See Figure 5-1.)

In manufacturing companies, production departments, sales departments, and occasionally purchasing departments are the most common line activities. The production supervisor or first-line supervisor is likely to be a member of the line organization.

Departments that help the line departments control quality and maintain adequate records are typically staff activities. Industrial engineering, maintenance, research, accounting, and industrial and personnel relations are some other examples of typical staff activities.

In service organizations such as banks and insurance firms, the line organization may represent the primary "action" operations (like deposits and withdrawals and recordkeeping, or premium collections and claim settlements) and the staff organization such support activities as computer and actuarial departments.

CHAPTER 5: ORGANIZING AN EFFECTIVE DEPARTMENT

In hotels and motels, line may be everything connected with the operation of a geographic unit; staff, such activities as advertising, accounting, and legal.

In transport companies the line department may be fleet operations; the staff, equipment repair and maintenance.

In a hospital, medical and nursing may represent the line groups, with laboratory, culinary, and housekeeping the staff.

It may help you to think of line people as the doers, staff people as the advisers. Each function—line or staff—is important in its own way, even though there has often been rivalry between line and staff for credit and recognition.

Is the line-and-staff structure the only way to organize?

No, although it is the most common and is found in most organizations. Other commonly used ways to put together an organization are these:

Functional. Each group of related activities is collected under one functional head. A supermarket, for example, may have six functional supervisors under the store manager: groceries, dairy and frozen foods, vegetables and produce, meats, stockroom, and checkout. Most line-and-staff organizations tend to be somewhat functional in concept, however, and it may often be hard to make the distinction.

Divisional or Product. All functions needed to make a particular product, for example, are gathered under one highly placed manager. If a firm manufactures tractors for farmers, road graders for construction contractors, and lawn mowers for home use, it might "divisionalize" to make and sell each major product in its product line.

Geographic. A firm may divide some (such as sales) or all of its activities according to the geographic region where these take place.

Customer. A company may also choose to group together some or all of its activities according to the customers it serves, such as farmers, contractors, or homeowners. This kind of organization is closely related to the product organization.

Project or Task Force. This form is commonly used in research and development organizations and engineering firms for one-of-a-kind projects or contracts. It allows a project manager to call on the time and skills of personnel—for a limited period of time—from various functional specialties. When the project is completed, the specialized personnel return to their home units to await assignment to another project. Because project managers can exercise their authority horizontally across the basic organization, while the specialists receive permanent authority from their functional

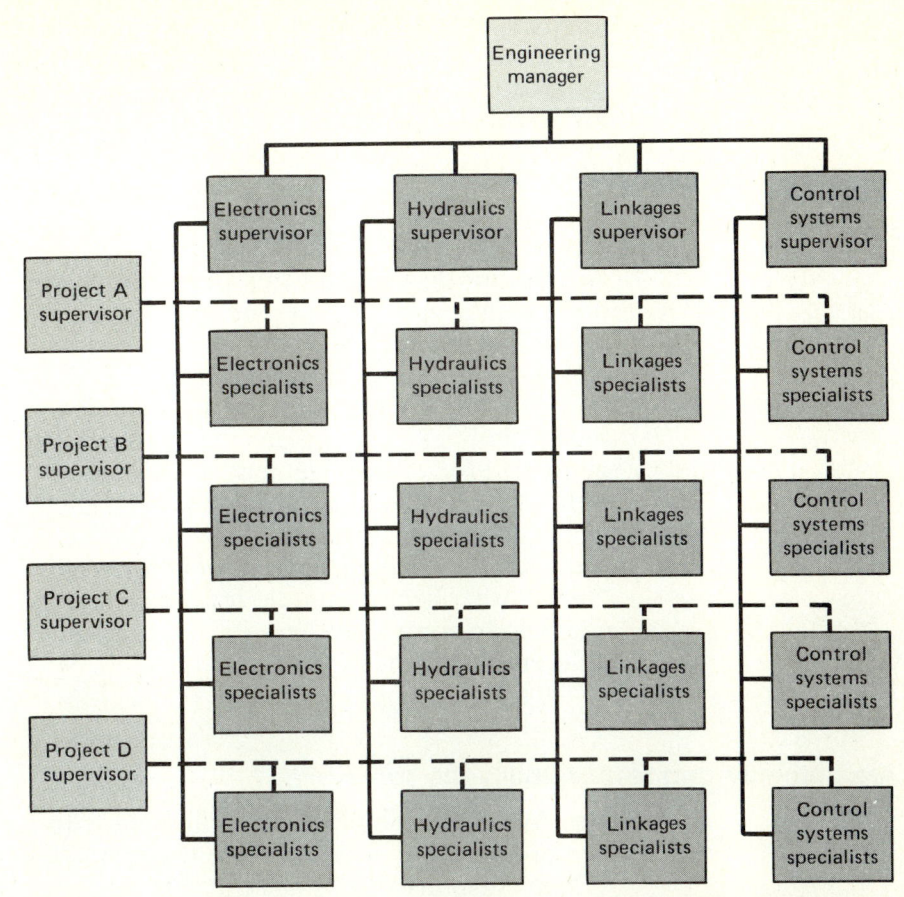

Figure 5-2. Example of Project or Task Force (Matrix) Organization Design.

bosses above them vertically on the chart (Figure 5-2), this form is called a matrix organization.

Regardless of organization type, always remember that the purpose of the organization structure is to make your department's work more nearly fit together with the work of other departments.

What is the distinction between a centralized and a decentralized organization?

A centralized organization tends to have many levels of management; to concentrate its facilities in one location; to perform certain functions such as engineering, labor negotiations, computer operations, and purchasing from a single source; and to gather together its power and authority at headquarters.

A decentralized organization tends to have the opposite charac-

CHAPTER 5: ORGANIZING AN EFFECTIVE DEPARTMENT

teristics, especially when a company is divided into distinctly separate units with varying degrees of independence. These units may be set up by product lines, by geography, or by methods of marketing and distribution.

How wide can a manager's span of control be?

Authorities disagree on this point, but it is a good rule of thumb that no manager or supervisor should have the responsibility for more than six separate activities. The more specialized and complex the activities, the shorter the span of control. The more uniform and less complicated the activities (as with many supervisory responsibilities), the greater the span can be. Sometimes the span of control (or of management) is defined by the number of people rather than by the number of activities. If such is the case, it is not unusual for a supervisor to have a span of 30 or more employees, provided they are engaged in only a few simple, related activities. On the other hand, a middle-level manager might have all he or she could do to control the activities managed by the supervisors of six different departments.

Are authority and responsibility the same thing?

No. Authority should go hand in hand with responsibility, but the two are no more alike than are the two sides of a coin.

Your responsibilities are those things you are held accountable for—like costs, on-time deliveries, and good housekeeping. Responsibilities are also spoken of as your duties—like checking time cards, investigating accidents, scheduling employees, or keeping production records.

Authority is the power you need to carry out your responsibilities. A supervisor's authority includes the right to make decisions, to take action to control costs and quality, and to exercise necessary discipline over the employees assigned to help carry out these responsibilities.

It's an axiom that you shouldn't be given a responsibility without enough authority to carry it out. A supervisor who is given responsibility for seeing that quality is up to specifications must also be given authority to stop the production line when the quality falls off or to take any steps considered necessary to correct the condition.

Where does your organizational authority come from?

Authority, like responsibility, is usually handed down to supervisors from their immediate bosses. The bosses, in turn, received their authority and responsibilities from their immediate superiors.

And so it goes, on up to the company president, who received assignments from the board of directors.

The biggest chunk of authority and responsibility rests with the company president, who may split this chunk in as few as three pieces (to the vice presidents of production, sales, and financing) or as many as twenty (to vice presidents in charge of twenty different products). As the responsibilities and authorities come down the line to you, the pieces get smaller and smaller, but they also get much more specific.

For example, a plant superintendent may have the responsibility for producing goods in sufficient quantities to meet sales requirements, while the supervisor's responsibility may be to see that ten milling machines are operated at optimum capacity so that 200,000 product units are produced each month. Similarly, the plant superintendent's authority may permit the exercise of broad disciplinary measures, while the supervisor's may be limited to recommending disciplinary action for employees who break rules or whose output is not up to production and quality standards.

Most companies try to make the responsibility and the authority at each level of management fairly consistent. For instance, a supervisor in Department A should have the same general responsibilities as a supervisor in Department Z. Their authority would be generally the same even though the specific duties of each might differ widely.

What other sources can you draw on for your authority?

In addition to your organizational imperative to get things done, you may often need to draw from other, more personal sources. Your employer tries to establish your organizational rights by granting you a title or a rank, by depicting your position on an organization chart, or by some visible demonstration of status such as a desk or an office or some special privilege. Ordinarily you must reinforce this authority, or power, with one of the following:

Your job knowledge or skills
Your personal influence in the organization (whom you know and can get to help you or your team)
Your personal charm (if you have it)
Your ability to see that things get done (performance)
Your persuasive ability (a communications skill)
Your muscle or physical strength (occasionally)

All these sources are important because employees tend to restrict their acknowledgment of organizational rights over them. They expect their supervisors to show a little more real power than

CHAPTER 5: ORGANIZING AN EFFECTIVE DEPARTMENT

that. When employees come to accept your authority as deserved or earned (acceptance theory of authority rather than institutional), you will find that your relationships with people will improve.

Should a distinction be drawn between responsibility, authority, and accountability?

Yes, although it may appear to you to be only a technical one. As your boss, for example, I might be held accountable to higher management for the way in which operating supplies are conserved in my department. But I have the prerogative to delegate this responsibility to you, if I also grant you the authority to take any steps needed to protect these supplies. If you were to misuse these supplies or to lose track of them, I might discipline you for failing to discharge your responsibility in this matter; but I'd still be held accountable to my boss (and would be subject to discipline) for what happened, no matter which one of us was at fault. Similarly, when you delegate a minor responsibility to one of your employees (together with the necessary authority to carry it out), you will still be held accountable to your boss for the way in which this responsibility is carried out by your subordinate. In other words, you can delegate responsibility, but you cannot delegate accountability.

How much leeway does a supervisor have in taking authoritative action?

You can't draw a hard-and-fast rule to follow. Generally speaking, a company may establish three rough classifications of authority for supervisors, within which they may make decisions:

Class 1. Complete Authority. Supervisors can take action without consulting their superiors.
Class 2. Limited Authority. Supervisors can take action they deem fit so long as they tell their superiors about it afterward.
Class 3. No Authority. Supervisors can take no action until they first check with their superiors.

If many decisions fall into class 3, the supervisor will become little more than a messenger. To improve this situation, first learn more about your company's policy and then spend time finding out how your bosses would act. If you can convince them that you would handle matters as they might, your bosses are more likely to transfer class 3 decisions to class 2, and as you prove yourself, from class 2 to class 1.

Note that the existing company policy would still prevail. The big change would be in permitting supervisory discretion, and this would be because you have demonstrated that you are qualified to translate front-office policy into front-line action.

Who can delegate authority and responsibility?

Any members of management, including supervisors, can usually delegate some of their responsibility—and their authority. Remember, the two must go together.

A supervisor, for instance, who has responsibility for seeing that proper records are kept in the department may delegate that responsibility to a records clerk. But the clerk must also be given the authority to collect time sheets from the employees and to interview them if the data seems inaccurate. The supervisor wouldn't, however, delegate to the records clerk the authority to discipline an employee. Likewise, a supervisor can't delegate the accountability for seeing that accurate records are kept.

What is the chain of command?

The term *chain of command* is a military phrase used to imply that orders and information in an organization should originate at the top, then proceed toward the bottom from one higher management level to the next lower without skipping any levels or crossing over to another chain of command. The same procedure would be followed by information and requests going up the line.

Is it a bad practice to go out of channels?

It's best to conform to the practice in your company. Channel is just a word to indicate the normal path that information, orders, or requests should travel when following the chain of command. The channel for customer orders to travel from the sales manager to the production supervisor might be from the sales manager to the production manager, from the production manager to the department superintendent, and from the department superintendent to the supervisor. It would be going out of channels if the sales manager gave the order directly to the supervisor.

The channel used by a supervisor to ask for a raise might be from the superior to the department head, from the department head to the production manager, and from the production manager to the vice president. The supervisor who asked the vice president for a raise without having seen each one of the other managers in progression would be going out of channels.

Since authority and responsibility are delegated through the channels of a chain of command, for the most part it's better to handle your affairs (especially decisions) through them, too. It avoids your making changes without letting your boss know what's going on and prevents others from thinking another manager is bypassing the boss.

On the other hand, there are occasions when chain-of-command channels should be circumvented. In emergencies or when time is essential, it makes sense to get a decision or advice from a higher authority other than your boss if your boss is not readily available.

For purposes of keeping people informed and for exchanging information, channels sometimes get in the way. There's really nothing wrong with your discussing matters with people in other departments or on other levels of the company—so long as you don't betray confidences. If you do cross channels, it's a good practice to tell your boss you are doing so, and why. That way, you won't seem to be doing something behind your boss's back. And that is something you should never do.

How do staff people exert influence?

Staff departments exert influence, rather than real authority, because their responsibility is to advise and guide, not to take action themselves.

Before the days of staff departments and when companies were smaller, a store manager or a company superintendent tried to be informed on all kinds of subjects related to their fields. These subjects included personnel management, merchandising, cost control, quality control, etc. As companies grew larger and processes became more complex, many managers found it was wiser to employ assistants who could devote their full time and attention to becoming authorities in each of these phases of operations. These assistants have become known as staff assistants, and the departments they manage are called *staff departments*.

It's usually a mistake to assume that a staff department tells you how to do something. More often than not the staff department suggests that you do something differently, or advises that your department is off target (on quality, for instance), or provides information for your guidance. This isn't evasion. It's an honest recognition that the line people must retain the authority to run the company, but that to stand up to today's competition, you need the counsel of a specialist in these side areas.

If supervisors are smart, they will make every use they can of the staff department's knowledge. If you were building a house yourself for the first time and someone offered to furnish you free the advice of a first-rate carpenter, a top-notch mason, a heating specialist, and a journeyman painter, you'd jump at the chance. The same holds true in accepting the advice and guidance available from the staff departments and other specialists in your company when you are tackling a management problem.

When should you delegate some of your work?

Delegate when you find you can't personally keep up with everything you think you should do. Just giving minor time-consuming tasks to others will save your time for bigger things. Let one employee double-check the production report, for example, and send another employee to see who wants to work overtime.

Plan to have certain jobs taken over when you're absent from your department in an emergency or during vacation. Restrict the arrangement to routine matters, if you will, and to those requiring a minimum of authority. But do try to get rid of the task of filling out routine requisitions and reports, making calculations and entries, checking supplies, and running errands.

How can you do a better job of delegating?

Start by seeing yourself as a manager. Recognize that no matter how capable you might be, you'll always have more responsibilities than you can carry out yourself.

The trick of delegating is to concentrate on the most important matters yourself. Keep a close eye, for instance, on the trend of production costs; that's a big item. But let someone else check the temperature of the quenching oil in the heat treater. That's less important.

Trouble begins when you can't distinguish between the big and the little matters. You may think you can put off checking the production record; it can wait until the day of reckoning at the end of the month. You may think that unless the quenching oil temperature is just right, the heat treater will spoil a $500 die today. But in the long run you'll lose your sanity if you don't see that the small jobs must get done by someone else.

Be ready, too, to give up certain work that you enjoy. A supervisor must learn to let go of those tasks that rightfully belong to a subordinate. Otherwise, larger and more demanding assignments may not get done. And don't worry too much about getting blamed by your boss for delegating to an employee work the boss has given to you. Generally speaking, supervisors should be interested only in seeing that the job is done in the right way, not in who carries it out. See Figure 5-3 for an idea on how to decide on what jobs to target for delegation.

Should you delegate everything?

Don't go too far. Some things are yours only. When a duty involves technical knowledge that only you possess, it would be wrong to let someone less able take over. And it's wrong to trust confidential information to others.

CHAPTER 5: ORGANIZING AN EFFECTIVE DEPARTMENT

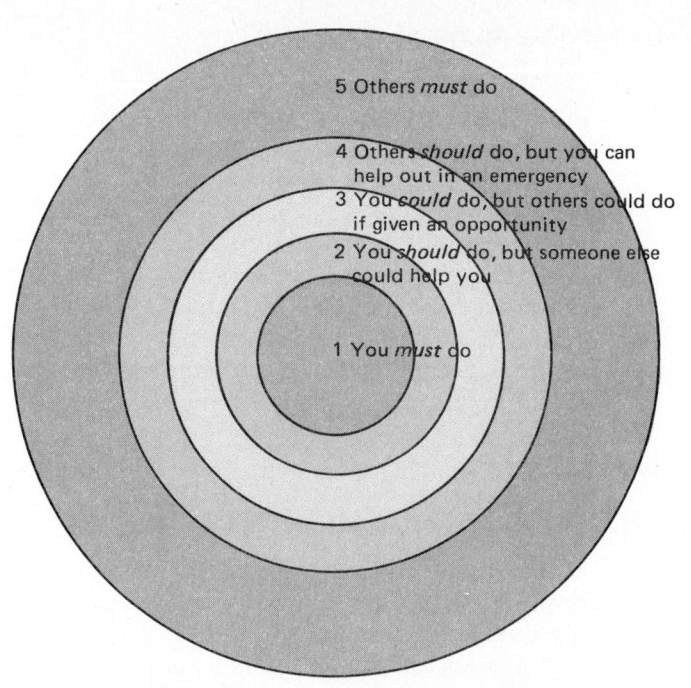

- 5 Others *must* do
- 4 Others *should* do, but you can help out in an emergency
- 3 You *could* do, but others could do if given an opportunity
- 2 You *should* do, but someone else could help you
- 1 You *must* do

Figure 5-3. Supervisor's Task and Delegation Chart.

What should you tell employees about jobs delegated to them?

Give them a clear statement of what they are to do, how far they can go, and how much checking you intend to do. Let employees know the relative importance of the job so that they can judge how much attention it should receive. There's no point in letting an employee think that making a tally will lead to a promotion, if you consider it just a routine task.

Tell workers why you delegated the job to them. If it shows you have confidence in them, they will try that much harder. But if they think you're pushing off all the dirty jobs on them, they may deliberately make mistakes.

Don't mislead employees about their authority; you don't want them trying to crack your whip. But do define the scope of the task and see that others in your department know that this new task isn't something an employee has assumed without authorization. Let the others know that you gave out the assignment and that you expect them to cooperate in carrying it out.

Why should an employee accept a delegated job?

Employees who accept a delegated job outside of their own responsibilities are really taking the job on speculation. They have a right to know the advantages of the added work.

An employee who takes on an extra duty gets a chance to learn. For example, if the employee has never seen how the individual records in the department are tabulated, here's a chance to get a better perception of what's going on.

A delegated job provides more job satisfaction. Employees thrive on varied assignments. This is a chance to build interest by letting an employee do something out of the normal.

Delegation is sometimes a reward for other work well done. If you can truthfully say you wouldn't trust anyone else with a certain delegated task, this will help build an employee's pride and feeling of status.

Are there any organizational don'ts?

Yes, but not very many. Once an organization is set up, pragmatism and practicality ought to prevail. In fact, some odd—and informal—arrangements occasionally work out very well. For example, a highly successful firm operated for years without a visual organization chart. Its president thought the staff would develop the most effective relationships without one; apparently it did. Nevertheless, in the design stages at least, there are a few hazards of organization that ought to be guarded against.

1. Don't let the chain of command get too long. Keep the number of responsibility levels at a minimum; otherwise, some information never trickles all the way to the bottom.
2. Don't ask one person to report to two bosses. Anyone caught this way knows the dilemma: Which boss's work comes first?
3. Don't make fuzzy job assignments. A gray area between two positions invites overlap, conflict, and duplication of effort.
4. Don't put responsibilities with different objectives into the same group. To make the production department responsible for monitoring the quality of its own output with the power of acceptance or rejection, for example, can lead to harmful collusion.
5. Don't be too rigid. Try to retain flexibility for contingent situations—those problems that inevitably crop up and need nonstandard assignments. It has been said that Napoleon would not have lost at Waterloo if he had applied contingency management.

How can supervisors best organize the work in their departments?

Use the same approach that top management does. This can be done in four steps, as illustrated in Figure 5-4.

Step 1 Work to be done	Step 2 Main operations	Step 2 Support services	Step 3 Consolidate work	Step 4 Add managerial controls
Transcribe Print Copy Stock supplies Store finished copies Move materials Keep records	Transcribe Print Copy	Store supplies Store copies Move materials Keep records	Central stores	Stockroom Chief

Organization Chart

Supervisor
├── Records
└── Stockroom Chief
    ├── Supplies
    ├── Storage
    └── Materials handling

Transcribe Print Copy

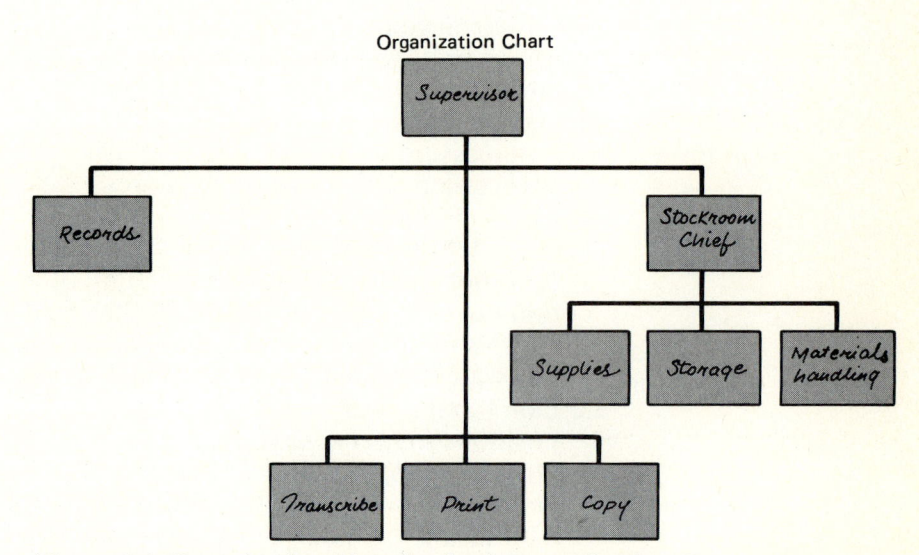

Figure 5-4. Organization Planning for a Reproduction Department.

1. Analyze the work that must be done to accomplish the objectives of the department. In this example of an office records reproduction department, the supervisor knows that the department's work primarily involves transcribing, printing, and copying. The supervisor also realizes that this requires operation of a stockroom for supplies, a storage area for finished copies, and some way of moving materials within the department. Then, too, this supervisor knows that some sort of records of supplies, inventories, costs, orders, and so forth, will have to be maintained.
2. Determine the best pattern of grouping activities for long-term

operation. In this case the supervisor divided the work to be done into main operations and support, or staff, services — a line-staff structure.

3. Consolidate operations or services in such a way as to provide for lowest costs with greatest effectiveness. This supervisor combined supplies, storage, and material handling in one group, leaving recordkeeping as a separate unit.
4. Set up management, or management-oriented, positions to furnish optimum planning, coordination, supervision, and control. In this illustration the supervisor appointed a stockroom chief to head the consolidated stock and supplies handling service, but decided that all other employees would report directly to the supervisor.

Review Questions

1. What is the purpose of an organization chart? Is it possible to do without one?
2. Compare the formal organization with the informal organization.
3. In a manufacturing organization, which departments are likely to be line and which ones staff?
4. In a service organization such as a bank, which departments are likely to be considered line and which staff?
5. Based on what you know of human relations, should managers who have the choice stress authority derived from the institution or stemming from employee acceptance? Why?
6. Why must authority and responsibility be passed together to subordinates?
7. Give examples of companies, departments, or other groups that might likely be structured by using matrix organization. What do these groups have in common?
8. Would it be a good thing to have an especially versatile employee report to the maintenance supervisor as well as to the production supervisor? Why?

A Case in Point The Case of the Backposted Overtime

In the budgeting department of a large utility, the comptroller split his organization into three units. The general accounting section was headed by a manager. Two supervisors reported to him, one for accounts payable and the other for billings. The internal auditing section had the same sort of arrangement: a manager in charge of the department, with the taxes and insurance responsibilities split between two supervisors. The third department, station cost accounting, however, had a department head, George Murphy, but only one supervisor, Tim Coyle. Tim was responsible for timekeeping, job costing, and payroll.

CHAPTER 5: ORGANIZING AN EFFECTIVE DEPARTMENT

Because of unusually heavy power loads in August, the number of repair jobs performed on overtime almost doubled. Accordingly, Tim's staff had a hard time keeping up to date with job costs. Tim's practice was to wait until time charges were verified against job estimates before he authorized their transfer to payroll. This caused a great deal of concern among employees, who felt that payrolls should be kept current with time-worked records.

Early one Monday in late August, George Murphy called Tim into his office and said, "We can't be late again with time charges this week. Will you make certain that we are caught up by Friday?" Tim went back to his desk and thought for a while. Finally, he called the best clerk in the timekeeping section—in fact, the most knowledgeable clerk in the department. "Fred," he said, "I need your help on a touchy problem right away. Beginning tomorrow morning, will you give a hand in the job-cost section? Since I know it so well, I'll take over the timekeeping activity and also make the resolutions of job costs with payroll." Fred agreed.

At the week's end, Tim found that he just didn't have time to fill in for Fred on timekeeping and still handle the resolutions. The result was that overtime on payrolls was still being backposted that Friday. When George Murphy discovered this, he asked Tim what the problem was. Tim's explanation was that he was being asked to do more than he could handle by himself and that he needed extra help if they were ever to catch up.

If you were George Murphy, what would you do? Five alternative approaches are listed below. Rank them in the order in which they appeal to you (1 most attractive, 5 least). You may add another approach in the space provided, if you wish. In any event, be prepared to justify your rankings.

_____**A.** Increase the size of the job-cost staff.

_____**B.** Appoint a new supervisor to be in charge of the job-cost section.

_____**C.** Transfer Fred to the job-cost section and insist that, temporarily at least, Tim delegate responsibility for resolutions to him.

_____**D.** Tell Tim that he must select and train a backstop for himself in each of the sections.

_____**E.** Appoint two new supervisors so that each section has its own supervisor.

If you have another approach, write it here. _____
_____
_____
_____

Action Summary Checklist

	Action Needed Yes / No	Date Completed

1. Your work force's organization focused on departmental responsibilities and objectives. ____ ____   _____
2. Each employee knows what his or her job is and how it relates to others in the department. ____ ____   _____
3. An organization chart constructed for your department. ____ ____   _____
4. Your awareness of, but not conflict with, the informal organization in your department. ____ ____   _____
5. Identification of both line and staff responsibilities in your department and with other company departments. ____ ____   _____
6. Knowledge of where and how your department fits into your company's overall organization structure. ____ ____   _____
7. Identification of your company's and your department's organizational form: functional, divisional or product, geographic, customer, and/or project or task force. ____ ____   _____
8. Estimate of the degree of centralization and decentralization in your company and in your department. Satisfaction with the extent of your own span of control, neither too narrow nor too broad. ____ ____   _____
9. Clear understanding of your own responsibilities and their related authorities according to the classifications on page 79 of the text. ____ ____   _____
10. Full development and utilization of your personal sources of authority. ____ ____   _____
11. Regular use of delegation within your department to relieve yourself of unnecessary work and to develop the skills and confidence of subordinates. ____ ____   _____
12. Willing acceptance of responsibilities delegated from above with an eye toward using them for your own development. ____ ____   _____

Action Summary Checklist (continued)		Action Needed Yes No	Date Completed
	13. Knowledge of the chain of command in your company and general conformance to it.	____ ____	_____
	14. Cooperation with, and use of, company staff departments.	____ ____	_____
	15. Regular review of your department's organization structure to minimize communications problems, avoid having an employee answer to two people, assure clear designation of work duties, and retain flexibility for contingencies.	____ ____	_____

Chapter 6
Exercising Control of People and Processes

Key Concepts

- The control function is inseparably linked to planning. It requires that a supervisor keep continual track of progress toward departmental goals so that corrective action can be taken as soon as possible.

- Good controls are based on reliable, attainable standards of performance. The best standards are based on systematic analysis.

- Budgetary controls place financial restrictions on the actions a supervisor can take in attempting to meet quantity, quality, time, and other interdependent or system-related goals.

- Because control is only one of several functions supervisors must perform, they should take maximum advantage of the exception principle to delegate corrective action to qualified employees.

- Resistance to controls is a natural human reaction. For this reason controls should be fair, be specific and numerical where possible, motivate rather than coerce, be consistently applied, and encourage the greatest degree of self-control possible.

What is the basic purpose of a supervisor's control function?

To keep things in line and to make sure your plans hit their targets. In the restrictive sense, you use controls to make sure that employees are at work on time, that materials aren't wasted or stolen, that employees don't exceed their authority. These controls tend to be the no-noes of an organization, the rules and regulations that set limits of acceptable behavior. In the more constructive sense, controls help to guide you and your department to production goals and quality standards.

What can controls be used for?

For just about anything that needs regulation and guidance. Controls, for example, can be used to regulate:

Employee performance of all kinds, such as attendance, rest periods, productivity, and workmanship.

Machine operation and maintenance, such as its expected daily output, power consumption, and extent of time for out-of-service repairs.

Materials usage, such as the percentage of expected yield and unexpected waste during handling and processing.

Product or service quality, such as the number of rejects that will be accepted or the number of complaints about service that will be tolerated.

Personal authority, such as the extent of independent action employees can take while carrying out the duties outlined in their job descriptions.

Exactly what is a control standard?

A control standard, usually called simply a standard, is a specific performance goal that a product, a service, a machine, an individual, or an organization is expected to meet. It is usually expressed numerically: a weight (14 ounces), a rate (200 units per hour), or a flat target (4 rejects). The numbers may be expressed in any unit—inches, gallons, dollars, or percentages.

Many companies also allow a little leeway from standard, which is called a tolerance. This implies that the performance will be considered to be in control if it falls within specified boundaries. A product, for instance, may be said to meet its 14-ounce standard weight if it weighs no less than 13.75 ounces or no more than 14.25 ounces. The control standard would be stated as 14 ounces, ±0.25 ounces. The tolerance is the ±0.25 ounces.

In what way are plans and controls linked?

Controls are directly related to the goals that have been set during the planning process. In fact, controls are often identical with these goals. Suppose, for example, that as supervisor of a commercial office of a telephone company, you have planned that your department will handle 100 service calls per day during the next month. The 100 calls per day is your goal. It also becomes your control standard. If your department handles 100 calls per day, you have met your target and need exert no corrective controls. If, however, your department handles fewer than 100 calls and begins to fall behind, it is below its control standard. You must take some sort of action to correct this performance.

Take another example. Suppose that you are the supervisor of a machining department in a brass foundry. Your superintendent has advised you that the company has set a goal of only 3 percent rejects of products scheduled to leave your area. In this case you may have to study each separate operation in your department to determine what you can consider its acceptable quality (or workmanship). You must keep in mind that the net effect must be only 3 rejects out of every 100 castings machined.

The lathe operators may be told that they cannot damage any castings at all, since their work is easiest to control. The boring machine operators may be given a standard that allows them to bore center holes no more than 0.1 inch off center. The grinding machine operators may not be given a standard at all in terms of rejects. They may be told that the surface finish of casting they work on must meet the specified dimensions, between ± 0.005 inches. In your estimate, if everything went as wrong as it could for each operator, while still meeting the standards you set, the department will still meet its targeted goal of 3 rejects per 100, regardless of which operation used up all its tolerances.

If the department found that it was rejecting 5 of 100 castings, your job as supervisor would be to find which machine operator had exceeded the limits of control that you had set. Then you would have to decide what caused this to happen. It may be that the machine needs maintenance because it wobbles too much to bore a perfect center. Or the fixture that holds the casting in place while it is being machined may have slipped. Or the tools may need sharpening. Or the employee may need training in how to operate the machine more accurately. Or there is always the possibility that an operator is careless or has willfully damaged a casting. Each of these causes would require a different kind of control action on your part.

Where do the control standards come from? Who sets them?

Many standards are set by the organization itself. They may be set by the accounting department for costs or by the industrial engineering department for wage incentive or time standards. They may be issued by the production-control department for schedule quantities or by the quality-control people for inspection specifications. It is typical for control standards in large organizations to be set by staff specialists. In smaller companies supervisors may set standards themselves. But even in large companies the supervisor may have to take an overall, or department, standard and translate it into standards for each employee or operation.

On what information are control standards based?

Standards are based on one, two, or all three of these sources:

Past Performance. Historical records often provide the basis for controls. If your department has been able to process 150 orders with three clerks in the past, this may be accepted as the standard. The weakness of this historical method is that it presumes that 150 orders represent good performance. Perhaps 200 would be a better target. This might be true if improvements have recently been made in the processing machinery and layouts.

High Hopes. In the absence of any other basis, some supervisors ask for the moon. They set unreasonably high standards for their employees to shoot at. While it is a sound practice to set challenging goals, standards should always be attainable by employees who put forth a reasonable effort. Otherwise, workers will become discouraged, or rebel, and won't try to meet them.

Systematic Analysis. The best standards are set by systematically analyzing what a job entails. This way the standard is based on careful observation and measurement, as with time studies. At the very least, standards should be based on a consideration of all the factors that affect attainment of the standard—such as tooling, equipment, training of the operator, absence of distractions, and clear-cut instructions and specifications.

How accurate are standards and control measurements likely to be?

They won't be perfect. It is the supervisor's responsibility, however, to check regularly to see that measurements are being made as honestly and as accurately as possible.

Unintentional errors creep in from carelessness when original figures are recorded, from mistakes when data is transferred from one record to another in keypunching, or from the halo effect when an observer is impressed by unusually high or low performance.

Deliberate falsification can take place when an operator or a salesperson—whose wages depend on performance—distorts the figures, when an employee covers up for a friend, when someone wants to give the impression of progress by holding up Friday's production count so that it appears in next week's record, or when someone works to lull the supervisor into thinking that everything is going all right.

Inaccuracies aside, it is also very important to check regularly to see that (1) the standards have not changed because of an improvement in machines or methods and (2) the measurements really do help you to make control decisions.

How is the control process carried out?

The control process follows four distinct steps:

1. *Set Performance Standards.* Standards of quantity, quality, and time spell out (*a*) what is expected and (*b*) how much deviation can be tolerated if the person or process fails to come up to the mark. For example, the standard for an airlines ticket counter might be that no customer should have to wait in line more than five minutes. The standard could then be modified to say that if only one out of ten customers had to wait more than five minutes, no corrective action need be taken. The standard would be stated: "waiting time of less than five minutes per customer with a tolerance of one out of ten who might have to wait longer." The guideline is that the more specific the standard, the better, especially when it can be stated with numbers as opposed to vague terms like "good performance" or "minimum waiting time."

2. *Collect Data to Measure Performance.* Accumulation of control data is so routine in most organizations that it is taken for granted. Every time a supervisor or an employee fills out a time card, prepares a production tally, or files a receiving or an inspection report, control data is being collected. Whenever a sales ticket is filled out, a sale rung up in a cash register, or a shipping ticket prepared, control data is being recorded. Of course, all information is not collected in written form. Much information that a good supervisor uses for control is gathered by observation—simply watching how well employees are carrying out their work.

3. *Compare Results with Standards.* From top manager to first-line supervisor, the control system flashes a warning if there is a gap between what was expected (the standard) and what has taken place (the result). If the results are within the tolerance limits, the supervisor's attention can be turned elsewhere. But if the process exceeds the tolerance limits—the gap is too big—then action is called for.

4. *Take Corrective Action.* You must first find the cause of the gap (variance or deviation from standard). Then you must take action to remove or minimize this cause. If travelers are waiting too long in the airline's ticket line, for example, the supervisor may see that there is an unusually high degree of travel because of a holiday. The corrective action is to add another ticket clerk. If, however, the supervisor observes that the clerks are

taking extra-long coffee breaks, this practice will have to be stopped as soon as possible.

To what extent can a supervisor depend on automatic controls?

More and more, operating processes rely on mechanical or automatic control. They try to minimize the human element. We all expect the thermostat to tell the furnace to keep the room warm. In many automobiles we expect a buzzer to tell us whether the seat belt is fastened or whether we are exceeding a preselected speed limit. In some cars we even let a mechanism take over the accelerator so that the speed of the auto is automatically maintained for us. Many processes in business and industry are controlled by the same principles. When a worker feeds a sheet of metal into a press, the machine takes over. When a clerk slips a piece of paper into a copying machine, the machine automatically reproduces the number of copies the clerk has dialed on the control mechanism. The trend toward such automatic controls is very strong.

Human activities, however, still require supervisory control. Supervisors continually have to find ways to make sure that employees meet their job standards. Especially important are standards of (1) attendance, (2) speed and care in feeding or servicing automatically controlled machines, and (3) even greater care needed by employees in joining their efforts with those of people in their own departments and others with whom they interact in their company or client organizations.

What specific kind of controls are most likely to aid or restrict supervisory actions?

These will depend largely on the nature of the organization in which the supervisor works. The following controls, however, are most common:

Quantity Controls. These relate to the demand of almost every organization for some standard of output or production. The quantity of production required is often the basis for all other aspects of control. In other words, a supervisor must first make sure that output quantities measure up. Then the supervisor's attention can turn to controls that specify a certain quality or time, for example.

Quality Controls. If, in meeting the production standard, a department skimps on work quality, there can be trouble. Quantity and quality go hand in hand. The inspection function is intended to make sure that the final product or service lives up to its quality standards (specifications). As a supplement to routine inspections, many companies practice statistical quality control, a way of predicting quality deviations in advance so that a supervisor can take corrective action before a product is spoiled.

Time Controls. Almost every organization must also meet certain deadlines or live within time restraints. A product must be shipped on a certain date. A service must be performed on an agreed-on day. A project must be completed as scheduled. Such time standards point up the fact that it is not enough to get the job done if it isn't finished on time.

Material Controls. These relate to both quality and quantity standards. A company may wish to limit the amount of raw or finished materials it keeps on hand; thus it exercises inventory controls. An apparel firm, for instance, may wish to make sure that the maximum number of skirts is cut from a bolt of cloth so that a minimum amount of cloth is wasted—a material-yield standard.

Cost Controls. The final crunch in exercising controls involves costs. A supervisor may meet the quantity and quality standards, but if, in so doing, the department has been overstaffed or works overtime, it probably won't meet its cost standard.

How do budgets fit into this picture?

Budgetary controls are very similar to cost standards. Typically, the accounting or financial department provides a supervisor with a list of allowable expenses for the month. These will be based on the expectation of a certain output, say, 4,000 units of production. These allowable expenses become the cost standards to be met for the month. At the end of the month the accounting department may issue the supervisor a cost variance report (Figure 6-1). This tells whether the department has met its standards, exceeded them, or fallen below them. Note that in Figure 6-1 the department has exceeded its overall budget by $800. It has, however, met a number of its standards while spending more for material handling, overtime, operating supplies, and maintenance. The supervisor will be expected to do something to bring these cost overruns back into line next month. On the other hand, the department used less than was budgeted for gas, water, steam, and air. If this keeps up, the accounting department may develop a new standard for those expenses and allow the supervisor less money for them in the future.

Some authorities speak of systems control. What is meant by that?

In its simplest terms, systems control means that you can't control one activity or performance factor without affecting the control of another. All activities carried on in a department or a process are interrelated. Quantity, quality, time, materials, and costs cannot

Figure 6-1.

Cost Variance Report

Department Assembly   Dept. no. 707   Month July
No. of units scheduled for production 4,000
No. of units actually produced 4,020
Production variance +20 units

Account Title	Actual	Budget	Variance (+over −under)
Direct labor	$ 8,000	$ 8,000	0
Indirect labor			
Material handling	900	600	+300
Shop clerical	500	500	0
Supervision	1,200	1,200	0
Overtime	100	0	+100
Shift premium	0	0	0
Operating supplies	500	400	+100
Maintenance and repairs	1,900	1,400	+500
Gas, water, steam, air	1,600	1,800	−200
Electrical power	800	800	0
Total controllable budget	$15,500	$14,700	+$800

really be separated if you look at the big picture. They are part of a system.

Take an example. If the sales department wants the production supervisor to push an order in a hurry, the supervisor may have to sacrifice quality (by working too quickly) or costs (by working on overtime). Something in the system has to give. In practice, someone must always decide whether the cost of getting out an order ahead of schedule, for example, can be justified by the benefits involved. One customer may be pleased (a benefit), while several others may be displeased because their orders were bumped back (a cost). Even the customer who is pleased to get an order sooner than expected may be displeased if the quality of the shipment doesn't measure up to expectations.

Supervisors are often at the receiving end of system-control decisions. Just as frequently, they may have to make system-control decisions in their own departments.

Must supervisors spend all their time controlling?

It would appear that way, but by using a simple principle called *management by exception,* supervisors can hold to a minimum the time taken for control activities. Management by exception is a form of delegation in which the supervisor lets things run as they are so long as they fall within prescribed (control) limits of performance. When they get out of line, as in the cost variance report in Figure 6-1, the supervisor steps in and takes corrective action.

Figure 6-2 shows how a supervisor can use the management-by-exception principle as a guideline for delegating much of the control work to subordinates.

For example, take a broiler chef in a fast-food restaurant. The boss says that the chef should expect to broil 180 to 200 hamburgers an hour. This is control zone 1. So long as results fall within the prescribed limits, the chef is completely in charge.

If, however, the requests for hamburgers fall below 180 but are above 150, the chef keeps the grill hot and puts fewer hamburgers into the ready position. If requests build up to 225, the chef moves more hamburgers to the completed stage. This is zone 2. The chef takes this action without first checking with the boss, but tells the boss what has been done.

If business falls from 150 but is more than 100 hamburgers an hour, the chef may ask the boss whether the grill can be turned off for a while. If the requests build up to 250 per hour, the chef may ask if one of the counter clerks can help out. This is zone 3.

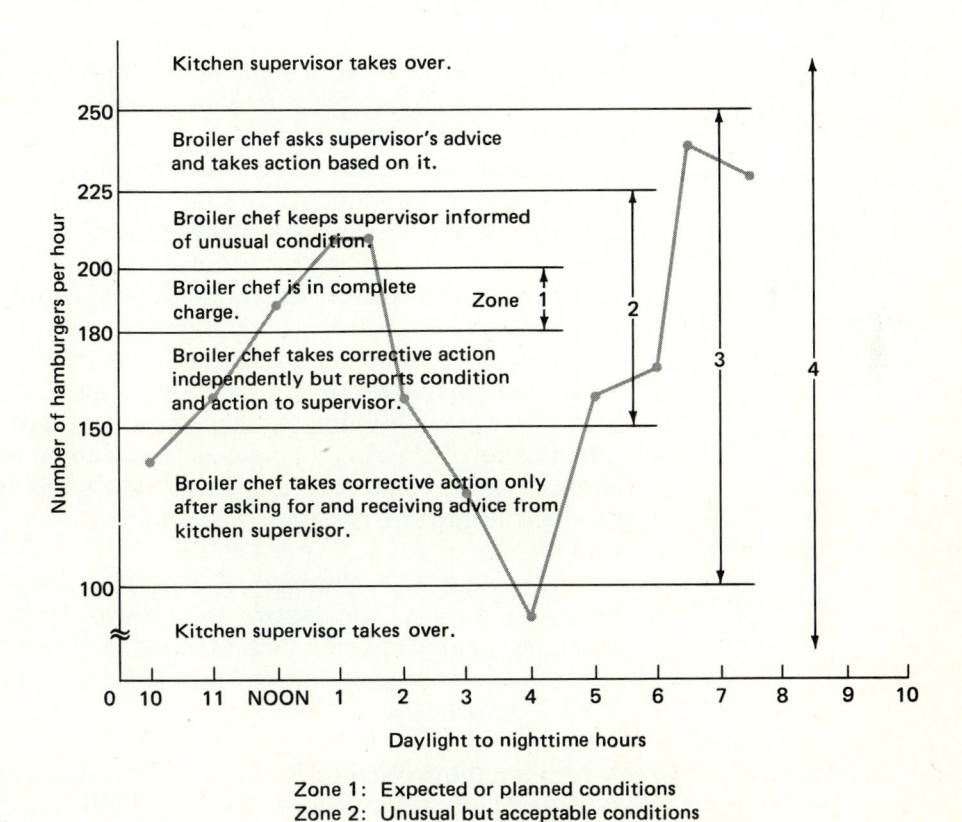

Zone 1: Expected or planned conditions
Zone 2: Unusual but acceptable conditions
Zone 3: Undesirable or highly unusual conditions
Zone 4: Unacceptable conditions

Figure 6-2. Use of Management-by-Exception Chart for Controlling Operation of Hamburger Grill.

CHAPTER 6: EXERCISING CONTROL OF PEOPLE AND PROCESSES

If conditions now move to either extreme—hamburger requests drop below 100 or exceed 250—the chef calls this to the supervisor's attention. This is zone 4. The supervisor may in the first instance (below 100) decide to shut down the grill. In the second instance (above 250) the supervisor may decide to start up an auxiliary grill.

What about the people problem in controls?

Many people do not like to be controlled. They don't like to be told what to do, and they feel boxed in when faced with specific standards. Few persons like to be criticized or corrected. Yet criticism or correction is what control often comes down to. When correction means discipline or termination, controls can seem very harsh indeed. For this reason a supervisor should be realistic about controls. Acknowledge that controls can have a very negative effect on employees, to say nothing to what they may do to the supervisor.

The negative aspects of controls, however, can be minimized. Supervisors should consider any of these more positive approaches:

Emphasize the Value of Controls to Employees. Standards provide employees with feedback that tells them whether they are doing well or not. Standards minimize the need for the supervisor to interfere and often allow the employee to choose the way of doing the job so long as standards are met. The supervisor says, "You do the job, and I will stay out of your hair."

Avoid Arbitrary or Punitive Standards. Employees respond better to standards that can be justified by past records that support the standards. "Our records show that 150 per day is a standard that other operators have consistently met." Standards based on analysis, especially time studies, are even more acceptable. "Let's time this job for an hour or two so that we can be sure the standard is reasonable." Compare this with: "We'll just have to step up our production rate to 175 units each day."

Be Specific; Use Numbers if Possible. Avoid expressions like "improve quality" or "show us better attendance." Instead, use numbers that set specific targets, such as "fewer than two days' absence in the next six months," or "decrease your scrap percentage from 7 out of 100 to 3 out of 100."

Aim for Improvement Rather than Punishment. Capitalize on instances of missed standards to try to help employees learn how to improve their work. "Your output was below standards again last month. Perhaps you and I ought to start all over again to see what it is that is preventing you from meeting them. There may be some place or something that I haven't shown you about this particular operation."

Resort to Punishment as the Last Step. A supervisor must balance rewards with punishment. Most employees respond to positive motivation; many do not. All employees, however, good and poor alike, want to know what the "or else" is about their jobs. The guiding rule is to hold off punishment if you can, but to make it clear to everyone that standards must be met. Specify in advance what the penalty will be for those who don't meet them.

Avoid Threats that You Can't or Won't Back Up. If an employee is to be disciplined for failing to meet a quota or a standard of workmanship, be specific about the nature and timing of the discipline. "If you don't get your production up to 150 per day by the first of April, I will recommend that you be laid off for good." Don't say, "If you don't shape up soon, your head will be in a noose." If you do make the specific threat, it is good to make certain in advance that the company will help you to make it stick.

Be Consistent in Application of Controls. If you have set standards that apply to the work of several employees, it should go without saying that you will be expected to make everyone measure up to them. If you think that exceptions can be made, be prepared to defend that position. In the main, however, standards should be the same for everyone doing the same work. Similarly, rewards or punishment should be the same for all those who meet, or fail to meet, these standards.

What about encouraging self-control?

Self-control is beautiful for those who can exert it. Douglas McGregor insisted that many people need only be given the targets for their work—the standards. After that, he said, they wish to be left alone and to be judged on the basis of their results in meeting or not meeting these targets. Employees will, McGregor said, provide their own control and do not need a supervisor to threaten them or cajole them into meeting standards.

My advice is to give an employee the benefit of the doubt. Give a free hand to those who take charge of themselves. Keep the rein on those who soon show that they need, or expect, the control to come from the supervisor.

When do management goals become control standards?

Very often, as shown when the link between planning and controlling was explained. More specifically, however, many companies convert their organizational goals into control programs by using a system of *Management by Objectives* (MBO). Management by Objectives is a planning and control process that provides managers at each organizational control point a set of goals, or standards, to be attained. The process is usually repeated every 12 months. These MBO goals are similar to the list of supervisory performance goals illustrated in Figure 4-1 in Chapter 4. It is presumed that if all supervisors reach their goals, the organization also will reach its goals. In companies where MBO is practiced to its full extent, the supervisors' goals literally become the standards of performance that must be met. The assumption is that the supervisors are capable of, and will exert, their own controls in striving to meet these objectives. The MBO system also presumes that the supervisors have been given enough freedom of action so that they can meet these goals within the resources provided by staff and budget. In essence, MBO is simply a formalization at managerial levels of the principle of self-control.

Review Questions

1. How are control standards related to the goals established in plans?
2. Of the three chief ways of setting standards, which is the best? Why? What's wrong with the other two?
3. What kind of errors should supervisors look for in control information or in the measurements on which standards are based?
4. What is the ultimate purpose of the control process?
5. Briefly describe five specific controls a supervisor is likely to be concerned with.
6. How are management by exception and control standard tolerances related?
7. Is there anything positive in controls for the people who work in an organization? If so, what?
8. How should a supervisor approach the issue of self-control among employees?

A Case in Point

The Case of the Overheated Copying Machine

Use of the copying machine in the Birdboro Social Security Office had gotten out of hand. Employees were making copies of everything, personal items as well as official documents. Word came down from the regional social security headquarters, addressed to Cora Smith, the office supervisor, "to get this thing under control."

Cora's first effort was to post a notice over the copying machine reminding employees that the machine could be used only for official government business. At the end of the next month, however, the number of copies run off was still as high as ever.

This time, Cora called her employees together and read the riot act to them. "Next person I find using that machine to copy personal work gets suspended on the spot," she threatened. Two days later Cora noticed two employees laughing as they came away from the copying machine. "What's this all about?" she challenged. The employees said nothing, so Cora asked to see what they had been copying. Sheepishly, they held out a dozen or so sheets of paper. They had been copying a slightly off-color limerick that someone in the office had typed up. "Aw, Cora," one said, "we were just having a little fun. After all, what's a few sheets of paper to the government. Why, only last week we ran off dozens of copies of a report that the regional office later canceled."

"That's not the point," said Cora. "In the future, nothing personal goes on that copying machine. You hear me?"

"We hear you," said the employees.

At the end of the month the copy machine's budget for paper usage had again been exceeded. This time Cora decided to take firmer action. She drew up a log sheet and posted it next to the machine. It instructed employees who used the machine to record the date, the time of day, the number of copies run off, their purpose, and the employee's name. Additionally, Cora again called her employees together and described the new system. "Anyone found cheating this system, goes," said Cora.

Two weeks later Cora checked the paper usage and found that the rate of consumption had dropped only a fraction. This month the department office would again exceed its budget.

With that information Cora went to her desk and got the key to the copying machine. She then went to the machine and locked it. Next she posted a sign over the machine that read: "From this time forward anyone who wishes to use the copying machine must fill out a request form and present it to me at my desk. The individual will show me exactly what has been run off when the key is returned."

By the end of the week Cora felt that she had control over use of the copier. On the other hand, Cora was interrupted several times a day to hand out the key and check it back in again.

If you were Cora, what would you do now? Six alternative approaches are listed below. Rank them in the order in which they appeal to you (1 most attractive, 6 least). You may add another approach in the space provided, if you wish. In any event, be prepared to justify your rankings.

_____**A.** Stick to the present system. It is the only way to control this difficult problem.

_____**B.** Explain to the regional offices that it costs more to exert control over copier usage than the extra paper is worth.

_____**C.** Post the monthly paper budget next to the machine.

Ask one employee to check each day's usage and post the cumulative totals daily. Explain that when the budget total is reached, the machine will be inoperative until the beginning of the next month.

_____**D.** Meet with employees to explain the budget and the resultant control problem. Ask them for ideas as to what kind of control procedures might work best. Follow their suggestions.

_____**E.** Call your employees together and tell them that the copy machine problem has gotten ridiculous. You have been too soft so far. You are going to open the machine again, using the log sheet method. But from now on you will act on your threat to suspend anyone using the machine for personal work.

_____**F.** By means of a log sheet, carefully analyze usage for the next month. Based on what you now know, set up a system to allot usage for various legitimate purposes. If greater usage is really needed for official work, ask the regional office to increase your paper budget.

If you have another approach, write it here. _____
_____
_____

Action Summary Checklist		Action Needed Yes No	Date Completed
	1. Departmental standards and controls related to departmental plans and goals.	____ ____	_____
	2. Departmental controls established to cover employee performance, machine operations, materials usage, product or service quality, cost, and job assignment.	____ ____	_____
	3. Control standards clearly written, numerically expressed where possible, and based either on historical records or on systematic analysis.	____ ____	_____
	4. Standards set for employee's personal time to include attendance and tardiness, in-company roaming, rest periods, and quitting time.	____ ____	_____
	5. Standards set for quantity of production or output—for the department as a whole and for individual operations.	____ ____	_____

Action Summary Checklist (continued)

	Action Needed Yes / No	Date Completed
6. Standards set for quality of workmanship, product, and service—for the department's output and for each operation.	____ ____	_____
7. Standards set for materials and supplies usage—yield, waste, storage, and inventory accumulation.	____ ____	_____
8. Standards set for all pertinent time factors, including job times, schedule fulfillment, and project completions.	____ ____	_____
9. Regular check to make sure that control measurements are accurate and relevant to the person or process being controlled.	____ ____	_____
10. Corrective action directed toward causes of variances rather than symptoms.	____ ____	_____
11. Understanding of intent of budgetary controls received and the degree to which you must conform to them.	____ ____	_____
12. Willingness to make the necessary cost-benefit decisions when setting, interpreting, or applying controls.	____ ____	_____
13. Application of the exception principle as often as possible.	____ ____	_____
14. Sensitivity to the people problem in exercising controls; emphasis on motivation rather than punishment.	____ ____	_____
15. Encouragement of employee's self-control whenever feasible.	____ ____	_____

Self-Check for Part 2

Test your comprehension of material in Chapters 4, 5, and 6. Correct answers are in the Appendix.

Multiple Choice Choose the response that best completes each statement below. Write the letter of the response in the space provided.

1. Which of the following should ordinarily be established and stated first?   1. _____
   a. Rules.
   b. Procedures.
   c. Policies.
   d. Goals.
2. In most organizations, supervisors: 2. _____
   a. Are not concerned with plans at all.
   b. Concentrate on short-range plans and goals.
   c. Concentrate on long-range plans and leave day-to-day decisions to workers.
   d. Are mainly responsible for establishing policies.
3. In carrying out company policy, supervisors should: 3. _____
   a. Set their own principles above the company policy.
   b. Try to be sure that the policy fits the specific circumstances.
   c. Take action first, then check policy later.
   d. Always talk it over with their superiors first.
4. Once an organization firms up its policies, it: 4. _____
   a. Can be sure that they won't ever need changing.
   b. Must be prepared to adapt them to new circumstances.
   c. Can leave it all up to the supervisory staff.
   d. Has removed all discretion from the supervisor.
5. If you were a supervisor who had to lay off an employee during a recession because of the employee's low seniority, it would be a good thing to say that you were following company policy but: 5. _____

a. You disagreed with it.
b. It appeared to be fair.
c. It was unfair in this case.
d. The union had dictated it.

True-False Indicate whether each of the following statements is true or false by writing *T* or *F* in the answer column.

6. Plans must be guided by planning premises, which are beliefs about future resources and limitations, strengths and weaknesses. 6. ____
7. Regulations are one of the chief techniques by which management exercises organizational control. 7. ____
8. An obligation on the part of supervisors to see that time records filed by their employees are correct is a liability of the supervisory position. 8. ____
9. Most good organizations establish a chain of command through which authority and responsibility are progressively delegated. 9. ____
10. When a supervisor is able to lead others because of his or her personal characteristics or job skills, the supervisor's authority may be said to be based partly on acceptance. 10. ____
11. When a company has carefully prescribed its managerial relationships with regard to responsibilities and authorities, it is unlikely that significant informal organizational relationships will spring up. 11. ____
12. The final judgment of an organization's structure is whether it efficiently leads to meeting objectives, not whether it is symmetrical or orderly. 12. ____
13. A supervisor should try to delegate as much work as possible to competent subordinates. 13. ____
14. System control often requires that the cost of a course of action be weighed against the benefit expected from the action. 14. ____
15. A goal of control is to reduce variances from established standards. 15. ____
16. Control is the main tool managers have to assure adequate progress is being made toward meeting goals. 16. ____
17. Quantity controls and cost budgets should always be set up in such a way that they do not influence each other. 17. ____
18. Management by exception encourages employees to control their own performance in many situations. 18. ____

19. Properly designed control will function mainly to improve performance rather than to place blame. 19. ____
20. Management by Objectives makes the establishment of control standards unnecessary. 20. ____

Problem Match the specific standards and controls described in the following statements with the general type of control listed below. Place the appropriate control letter on each line.

_____ The industrial engineering department uses a stopwatch to determine how long an operator should take to put together two parts of a radio assembly.

_____ The pattern maker at a guitar factory lays out the work so that 15 guitar heads can be cut out of a 4- by 8-foot sheet of plywood.

_____ The purchasing manager of the state health commission instructs the office manager that a new supply of copying paper should be ordered when there are still two boxes of paper on hand.

_____ A supervisor gives the punch press operator in a container plant a quota of 5,000 caps per day.

_____ The sales manager of a radio station gives each salesperson a travel allowance of $200 for the month.

_____ The chef in a fast-food restaurant is told that the hamburgers must weigh at least one-quarter pound before cooking.

TYPE OF CONTROL

A. Quantity control
B. Quality control
C. Material control
D. Time control
E. Cost control

PART 3
MANAGING PEOPLE AT WORK

By all odds, the task of managing people at work is the most difficult. Supervisors must develop a whole range of skills in the area of interpersonal relationships — with their employees, associates, and superiors.

Chapter 7 helps supervisors to see clearly the individuality and basic needs of each person in order to motivate employees in a variety of ways.

Chapter 8 explains the power of group influence on individuals in the work force and shows supervisors how to direct that power toward productive ends.

Chapter 9 stresses the need for supervisors to accept the inevitability of conflict within their departments while suggesting ways of minimizing this conflict and encouraging cooperation.

Chapter 10 outlines the basic skills and techniques of communication so that supervisors may use them to develop a tightly knit departmental organization.

Chapter 11 provides models that show supervisors how to apply speaking and listening techniques so as to improve the quality of supervisory orders and instructions.

Chapter 7
Individual Motivation

Key Concepts

- There is no one best way to handle interpersonal relationships. They depend on the particular situation (its urgencies and its technical, social, or economic pressures) and who is involved in it. All human relationships are complex, with many influencing elements often hidden deep beneath the surface evidence.

- Individual behavior depends on a vast heritage of genealogical characteristics and is shaped by the forces of home environment, education, and work experience. This individuality causes people to behave the way they do, even though their behavior often appears illogical to others.

- While it may appear that most people work mainly to satisfy their needs for food, shelter, and clothing, it is a fact that today most people expect much more from their work in the way of social relationships, self-esteem, and meaningful work.

- A contented work force and above-normal productivity do not necessarily go hand in hand. Permissiveness and indulgence, for example, induce careless and indifferent work habits. By setting high work standards and motivating employees to attain them, a supervisor must expect occasionally to cause tensions and outspoken disagreements. These exchanges, when resolved without delay, are healthy and tend to hold morale high.

- Good human relations at work rarely occurs accidentally. It is instilled and nurtured by the supervisor in charge. Supervisors can go a long way in establishing good human relations merely by treating their staffs with respect and granting the consideration each person deserves as a unique individual, regardless of his or her relative status within the organization.

Why isn't good human relations just plain horse sense?

Because this is a dangerous oversimplification. Life and business experiences are full of paradoxes and inconsistencies that show that good intentions and straight-line reasoning are not enough.

Consider this example. Joe Smith supervises two men who work side by side on an assembly line in an auto plant. Their job is to attach the garnish (or trim) to the painted body. For some time Ed and Al, the men involved, had been complaining of knicks and cuts received from handling the sharp pieces of metal. Finally Joe decides the best way to cure the problem is to insist that both men wear gloves on the job. On Monday he approaches Ed and Al together. "Boys," says Joe, "the safety department has approved the issuance of work gloves for this job. This should prevent the rash of cuts you've been getting. Here's a pair of gloves for each of you. From now on, I'll expect to see you wearing them all the time."

The next day Joe had to ask Ed on three separate occasions to put his gloves on. Al wore his all the time. At the week's end Al was sold on the value of the gloves. But Ed just stuck his in his pants pocket. "They slow me down so I can't keep up with the line," he told Joe. But to Al, he said, "This work-glove idea is just an excuse to justify speeding up the line. If you give in on this issue, they'll make it even harder the next time."

Why do two men, handled the same way in the same situation, have such differing reactions? After all, weren't Joe's intentions good? Didn't he try to settle Ed's and Al's complaints about the cuts? Wasn't his solution a logical one?

Isn't human relations just applied psychology?

No. Human relations in industry is not psychology, sociology, or anthropology. Most of all, it is not psychiatry. While these four sciences aid in our understanding of what happens to people when they come to work, labels such as these are more misleading than enlightening.

When a job applicant fills out an interview form, the science of psychology is being applied. When a manager asks a supervisor what the employees think about the new rates, the manager is acknowledging the presence of sociological forces. When a company in Michigan shuts down on the first day of the hunting season because it knows from past experience that most of the workers will take off anyway, anthropologists may identify this action as a concession to group cultures. When an office manager listens to a near-hysterical clerk without interrupting, the manager may be borrowing a technique from the psychiatrist.

All the above actions involve the behavior of people at work. It has become common and convenient practice to call this behavior human relations. The operative words are people, behavior, and work.

Where do you find the important action in human relations?

Human relations is something that takes place between people—between an employee and the boss, between one worker and another, between a staff specialist and a line supervisor, between a manager and a superior. It takes place between individuals and between an individual and a group. The human interactions may be between executives and their departments, between managers and their associates, or, inversely, between workers and management in general. It takes place between two or more groups also. It may be between the sales department and the accounting office, between the production department and the maintenance department, or between two factors in the same group.

Why do people act the way they do?

If you mean, "Why don't employees act the way you wish they would?" the answer will take a long time. But if you are really asking, "Why do people act in such unpredictable ways?" the answer is simple: People do as they must. Their actions, which may look irrational to someone who doesn't understand them, are in reality very logical. If you could peer into their backgrounds and into their emotional makeup, you'd be able to predict with startling accuracy how this person will react to criticism or how that person will act when told to change over to the second shift.

The dog who's been scratched by a cat steers clear of all cats. Workers who have learned from one boss that the only time they are treated like human beings is when the work load is going to be increased will go on the defensive when a new boss tries to be friendly. To the new boss the workers' actions look absurd. But to the employees, it's the only logical thing to do.

So it goes—each person is the product of parents, home, education, social life, and work experience. Consequently, by the time supervisors deal with employees, they are dealing with people who have brought all their previous experiences to the job.

Then are all people different?

Each person is a distinct individual. In detail, his or her reactions will be different from anyone else's. To understand human relations, you must know first why people do things before you can predict what they will do. If you know that Bill dislikes his job because it requires concentration, you can make a good guess that Bill will make it hard for you to change the job by increasing its complexity. If Mary works at your company because of the conversation she has with her associates, you can predict that Mary will be hard to get along with if she's assigned to a spot in an isolated area.

The important tool in dealing with people is the recognition that although what they do is likely to differ, the underlying reasons for their doing anything are very similar. These reasons, incidentally, are called motives, or needs.

What determines an individual's personality?

Just about everything. An individual's personality cannot be neatly pigeonholed (as we so often try to do) as "pleasant" or "outgoing" or "friendly" or "ill-tempered" or "unpleasant" or "suspicious" or "defensive." An individual's personality is the sum total of what the person is today: the clothing worn, the food preferred, the conversation enjoyed or avoided, the manners and gestures used, the methods of thought practiced, the way situations are handled. Each person's personality is uniquely different from anyone else's. It is the result of heredity, upbringing, schooling or lack of it, neighborhoods, work and play experiences, parents' influence, religion —all the social forces around us. From all these influences people learn to shape their individuality in a way that enables them to cope with life's encounters, with work, with living together, with age, with success and failure. As a result, personality is the total expression of an individual's unique way of meeting life.

What do employees want from life—and their work?

We all seek satisfaction from life for what a famous psychologist A. H. Maslow, called the "five basic needs." We seek a good part of these satisfactions at our work. Dr. Maslow outlined the basic needs and conceived of them as a sort of hierarchy with the most compelling needs first and the more sophisticated last. Maslow's hierarchy of needs is illustrated in Figure 7-1.

We Want to Be Alive and to Stay Alive. We need to breathe, eat, sleep, reproduce, see, hear, and feel. But in today's world these needs rarely dominate us. True, according to Masters and Johnson, most men and women don't get all the sex they need. But all in all, our first-level needs are satisfied. Only an occasional experience—a couple of days without sleep, a day on a diet without food, a frantic 30 seconds under water—reminds us that these basic needs are still with us.

We Want to Feel Safe. We like to feel that we are safe from accident or pain, from competitors or criminals, from an uncertain future or a changing today. Not one of us ever feels completely safe. Yet most of us feel reasonably safe. After all, we have laws, police, insurance, social security, and union contracts to protect us.

CHAPTER 7: INDIVIDUAL MOTIVATION

```
           Self-actualization
                Need
     To do the work we want to do
          Esteem Need
       To be respected by others
          Social Need
      To be with others we like
          Safety Need
   To feel free from threats or harm
        Physiological Need
      To be alive and to stay alive
```

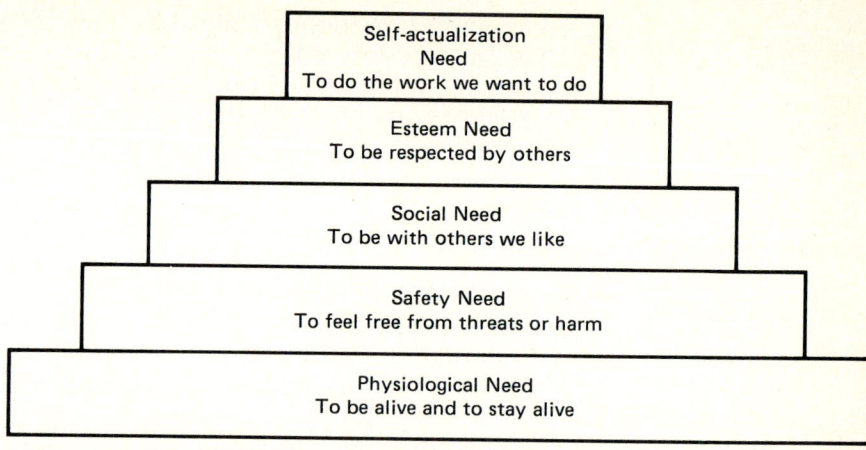

Figure 7-1. Maslow's Hierarchy of Needs.

A. H. Maslow, "A Theory of Human Motivations: The Basic Needs," in H. Leavitt and L. Pondy (eds.), Readings in Managerial Psychology, *University of Chicago Press, Chicago, 1964.*

We Want to Be Social. From the beginning of time we have lived together in tribes and family groups. Today these group ties are stronger than ever. We marry, join clubs, and even pray in groups. Social need varies widely from person to person just as other needs do. Few of us want to be hermits. Although not all people are capable of frank and deep relationships, even with their wives or husbands and close friends, to a greater or lesser degree this social need operates in all of us.

We Need to Feel Worthy and Respected. When we talk about our self-respect or our dignity, this is the need we are expressing. When a person isn't completely adjusted to life, this need may show itself as undue pride in achievements, self-importance, boastfulness—a swelled head.

Because many of our other needs are so easily satisfied in the modern world, this need often becomes one of the most demanding. Look what we go through to maintain the need to think well of ourselves—and have others do likewise. When a wife insists her husband wear a jacket to a party, she's expressing this need. When we buy a new car even though the old one is in good shape, we're giving way to our desire to show ourselves off.

We even modify our personalities to get the esteem of others. No doubt you've put on your company manners when out visiting. It's natural, we say, to act more refined in public than at home—or to cover up our less acceptable traits.

We Need to Do the Work We Like. This is why many people who don't like their jobs turn to hobbies for expression, and why so many other people can get wrapped up in their work. We all know men and women who enjoy the hard burden of laboring work—or machinists who hurry home from work to run their own lathes. This need rarely is the be-all and end-all of our lives, but there are very few of us who aren't influenced by it.

In the 1960s and early 1970s many young people dropped out of society or set out to "do their own thing." This was largely an expression of the desire to fulfill oneself—what Maslow called "self-actualization."

Which of these needs is the most powerful?

The one or ones that have not yet been satisfied. Maslow's greatest insight was that once a need has been satisfied, it will no longer motivate a person to greater effort. If a worker has what is required in the way of job security, for example, offering more of it—such as guaranteeing employment for the next five years—will normally not cause the person to work any harder. The supervisor who wishes to see greater effort generated will have to move to an unsatisfied need, such as the desire to be with other people on the job, if this employee is expected to work harder.

In what way can a job satisfy a person's needs?

It's a fact: Many people are happier at work than at home! Why? Because a satisfying job with a good supervisor goes such a long way toward making life worth living. While all of us may complain about our job (or our boss) from time to time, most of us respond favorably to the stability of the work situation. At home Jane may have a nagging husband, sick children, and a stack of bills to greet her at the end of the month. At work Jane can have an appreciative supervisor, a neat job with a quota she can meet each day, and assurance of a paycheck (and other benefits) at the week's end. No wonder Jane enjoys herself more at work than at home.

Or look at it this way. A rewarding job with a decent company and a straight-shooting boss easily provides the first two basic needs: (1) a livelihood that keeps the wolf away from the door and (2) a sense of safety from the fears of layoff, old age, or accidents. Satisfaction from the other three basic needs—to be social, to be respected, and to do the work we like—is often more a function of a person's supervisor than of the job itself.

A good supervisor can see that a person's job satisfies the social need by demonstrating to the rest of the work group the desirability of taking in a new worker. For instance, "This is Pete Brown, our new punch press operator. We're glad to have him with the company, and I've told him what a great bunch you all are. How about taking him along to the cafeteria at lunch time?"

To satisfy the esteem need, a good supervisor will make sure that workers know their work is appreciated. For example, "Pete, here's your locker. I think you'll agree that this is a pretty clean washroom. We feel that if we hire a good man, we've got to give him good conditions to work in so that he can do the best possible work."

To satisfy the desire to do worthwhile work, a good supervisor gives a lot of thought to putting workers on the job for which they have the most aptitude and training. Like saying, "Since you've worked this type of machine before, Pete, suppose you start on this one. When you've gotten the hang of things around here, we'll see about giving you a chance to learn some of the better-paying jobs."

If people all have the same fundamental needs, how far can a supervisor go in "push-button" human relations?

Not very far at all. There is a great danger in oversimplifying the analysis of human needs, especially at work.

One explanation of human behavior, for example, is that it depends on each employee's expectancy (or estimate) of what his or her actions may or may not bring. In effect, the employee makes three estimates: (1) Can I do what management is asking me to do? (2) If I can do it, will management be satisfied and reward me? (3) Will the reward given me be worth the effort? As you can see, a person's effort will be greatly influenced by the answers to these questions. The supervisor may go through the right motions, according to Maslow, and still find that the employee doesn't turn out as anticipated.

Satisfaction and dissatisfaction are rather vague terms, aren't they?

Yes. One noted behavioral observer, however, has found a way to be specific about them when they apply to work. Frederick Herzberg, in *Work and the Nature of Man* (The World Publishing Company, Cleveland, 1966), set down these interpretations:

Satisfaction for employees comes only from truly motivating factors such as interesting and challenging work, utilization of one's capabilities, opportunity to do something meaningful, recognition for achievement, and responsibility for one's own work.

Dissatisfaction occurs when the following factors are not present on the job: good pay, adequate holidays, long-enough vacations, paid insurance and pensions, good working conditions, and congenial co-workers.

Herzberg bases these definitions on his two-factor theory. He says that every human being has two motivational tracks: (1) a lower-level one, animal in nature and bent only on surviving; and (2) a higher-level one, uniquely human in nature and directed toward adjusting to oneself. Herzberg labels the first set of motivations "hygiene," or "maintenance," factors. We need to satisfy them, he reasons, to keep alive. People try to avoid pain and unpleasantness in life; they do the same on the job. Satisfaction of these needs provides only hygiene for the person. These factors physically maintain, but they do not motivate. If they are not present in the workplace, an employee will be dissatisfied and may look for a job elsewhere that provides these factors. But the employee will not work harder just because they are given. For example, a general pay increase may keep employees from quitting, but it will rarely motivate an employee to work harder.

On the other hand, Herzberg says, certain other factors provide genuine and positive motivation and should be called satisfiers. Without splitting hairs, we can see that generally the company must provide the factors that prevent dissatisfaction. The supervisor tends to provide the factors that satisfy. Few supervisors can establish the basic pay rates for the organization. Almost all supervisors can motivate. For example, the supervisor can provide an employee with a specific, challenging goal: "Not many people can stack more than 200 cartons an hour. If you can stack 200 an hour today, you'll be a great asset to this department."

Similarly, a supervisor can show that an employee's work is appreciated by saying: "The boss asked me today who typed these especially neat reports. I was pleased to be able to say it was you."

The supervisor can also help to make work more interesting: "Why don't we take 15 minutes today to see whether together we can find a way to break the monotony in your job?"

And the supervisor can always extend responsibility by saying to an employee: "Beginning today, will you make the decision as to whether off-grade products should be reworked or thrown away? If you make an occasional mistake, don't worry about it. Your judgment is as good as mine, and I've learned that we can't be 100 percent perfect in these decisions."

Is the object of good human relations to have one big happy family?

Have you ever known a family in which there wasn't some discontent? Where one child didn't feel that another one was favored by a parent? Or where there wasn't an occasional spat between husband and wife? Or where there wasn't a disreputable relative hidden somewhere? I can't believe you haven't. It's the same way in business. As a responsible supervisor, you strive for harmonious relationships with your employees and with the others with whom you associate. But it would be foolish to expect that everything is going to be smooth all the time—or even most of the time. It's only natural for people to have differences of opinions and arguments.

What you should aim for in your department is to have the arguments settled in a peaceful and reasonable manner. Keep emotions and epithets out of it. Sure, you can expect occasional name-calling and loud voices and red necks. But the general level of human relations should be friendly. An attitude of: "Okay, let's pull this issue apart. Tell me exactly what's eating you about this assignment. When I've seen your point, I won't promise I'll agree with you. But I'll be a lot better able to give you a straight answer then." After your decision, say to the employee: "Don't apologize for making an issue about it. That's your prerogative. And I'm glad you exercised it to get this matter cleared up. But how about in the future coming to me first before you get so hot and bothered about it?"

What happens when workers don't get satisfaction from their jobs?

Morale will be down, attitudes not "right." Most important to you, unsatisfied workers don't produce as much or as well as those who find their work rewarding.

Isn't job satisfaction primarily the company's responsibility—not the supervisor's?

The company's stake in good human relationships is just as big as the supervisor's. When a company helps the supervisor to establish the right climate for good human relations, the supervisor's job with people is much easier. But your relationship with your employees is a very personal one. No amount of policies and procedures, fancy cafeterias, generous fringe benefits, or sparkling rest rooms can take the place of a supervisor who is interested in people and treats them wisely and well. From your point of view, responsibility for employees' job satisfaction is one you share jointly with the company.

Does good human relations really pay off?

Early in your career as a supervisor you'll find this recurrent criticism of the practice of human relations in industry: "It makes good talk, but it doesn't pay the bills; whenever the squeeze is on to cut costs, all the human relations frills will go out the window." That's the trouble with human relations. It's been hard for many companies to prove that its practice saves money. Whenever you come across supervisors who don't believe in good human relations (or who mistake softness for the real thing), they will be able to quote you lots of examples of well-meaning supervisors who got trampled on by employees they'd tried to do right by.

On the other hand, the casebooks are full of proof that supervisors who are intelligent in their dealings with people are able to show more production, lower costs, and greater quality. Good human relations doesn't mean being foolishly soft or weak or negligent of people's intent. Neither does it mean treating people as if they weren't people—which was the mistake of most supervisors for the 20 or 30 years preceding the Great Depression. Good human relations is an art and a science; it's firm yet flexible, and it's the most difficult ambition in the world to achieve. Be assured that the results are rewarding—in dollars and cents as well as in personal satisfaction for you and the people you supervise.

Review Questions

1. Provide an example from your own experience to show how two or three people reacted differently to almost the same set of circumstances. Give an explanation of the reasons for these differences.
2. Think of a possible confrontation between an employee and a supervisor. Show how their viewpoints and objectives might vary.
3. Do you think that the order of priorities for Maslow's five basic needs changes as a person matures? Why?
4. Comment on the relationship between an individual's need for esteem and need to do meaningful work.
5. When worker motivation in a department is still low despite good pay, fringe benefits, and excellent working conditions, what can a supervisor do to increase motivation?
6. How would you draw the line between (**a**) a supervisor who is well liked and whose department is productive and (**b**) a supervisor who is well liked but whose department is not particularly effective?
7. Contrast a supervisor who tries to manipulate employees and one who tries to motivate them.

A Case in Point: The Case of the Conflicting Coffee Breaks

Two employees, Janet and Martha, work side by side as bank tellers. For several months they have relieved one another for their coffee breaks. Janet takes the first break from 9:45 to 10 a.m.; Martha, the second one from 10 to 10:15 a.m. Beginning this month, however, a new supermarket opened in the shopping center, and there is a large influx of housewives who come in to cash checks right after 10 a.m. Accordingly, Jack Smith, their boss, asked Martha to postpone her coffee break until after 10:30 a.m., but told Janet she could continue on the same break as before. Martha thought this request over; when she came in the next day, she told Mr. Smith that the new arrangement was unfair. If anyone should postpone her break, it should be Janet because she has had the early one for a long time. When Mr. Smith asked Janet her opinion, Janet said that she had been handling the peak load alone from 10 to 10:15 a.m. for a long while. Now she ought to get the choice because she is still going to be on duty during the extended peak period.

If you were Jack Smith, what would you do? Five alternative approaches are listed below. Rank them in the order in which they appeal to you (1 most attractive, 5 least). You may add another approach in the space provided, if you wish. In any event, be prepared to justify your rankings.

_____ **A.** Tell Martha that she is selfish for not going along with a simple adjustment and insist that your request be followed.

_____ **B.** Agree to Martha's suggestion instead, and tell Janet you expect her to cooperate.

_____ **C.** Point out that the morning hours are busy for only a very short time, so that this shouldn't be a factor.

_____ **D.** Ask Martha and Janet to resolve this problem between themselves, so long as there is double coverage from 10 to 10:30.

_____ **E.** Set up a rotating schedule.

If you have another approach, write it here. _____
_____
_____

Action Summary Checklist		Action Needed Yes No	Date Completed
	1. Human problems approached from an informed point of view rather than assuming that common sense is all that is needed.	___ ___	_____
	2. Alert to human interactions as well as to production problems.	___ ___	_____
	3. Identification of differences in motivation, goals, and performance among your employees.	___ ___	_____
	4. Assessment of each employee as to which levels of Maslow's hierarchy of needs are most important.	___ ___	_____
	5. In trying to motivate employees, searching always for the unsatisfied need.	___ ___	_____

Action Summary Checklist (continued)

	Action Needed		Date Completed
	Yes	No	

6. Provision of "satisfiers" at work for those employees who respond to positive motivation. ____ ____ _____
7. Open praise for employees who do a good job. ____ ____ _____
8. Opportunity for employees to apply their own self-discipline. ____ ____ _____
9. Challenging assignments for employees who want to achieve. ____ ____ _____
10. Wariness of your own desire to excel to the extent you become so task-oriented that you minimize human relationships. ____ ____ _____
11. Friendship to those employees who value social relationships highly. ____ ____ _____
12. Respect for those individuals to whom physiological needs are still their strongest source of motivation. ____ ____ _____
13. Maintenance of a general atmosphere of courtesy and comradeship in your department, despite occasional flare-ups. ____ ____ _____
14. Feedback to higher management of the absence of "hygiene" factors, which may dissatisfy employees. ____ ____ _____
15. Restraint in jumping to conclusions about personalities; an attitude of "live and let live" with respect to personal preferences. ____ ____ _____

Chapter 8
Work Group Behavior

Key Concepts

- Because supervision is involved with organized human effort, group relations are present in every situation; the characteristics of a particular group's behavior must be weighed just as carefully as the behavioral characteristics of an individual. Work groups may be either formal, established consciously by management, or informal, spontaneously created by members because of mutual interests and enthusiasms.

- With groups especially, the principle of participation presents an effective approach. By recognizing the force a group exerts in attaining (or in blocking) goals, a supervisor who invites participation encourages the group to direct its influence in a productive manner.

- Employees can be loyal both to the group and to the supervisor. Little is to be gained by forcing an individual to choose between the two, since both provide certain satisfactions.

- Because groups exert such tremendous influences in the work situation, supervisors must tune their senses to the feelings of groups as well as of individuals. Before supervisors can successfully cope with, or redirect, nonproductive behavior, they must know how people in the work force feel about themselves, their work group, the work itself, and their supervisors.

- Supervisors must respect both the power and the legitimate interests of work groups without abandoning the responsibility of management to the group or relinquishing essential authority. Adequate care will usually allow organization goals to be met without ignoring the rights and expectations of either individuals or groups.

What is meant by group dynamics?

This term is applied to the forces brought to bear by individuals, singly or collectively, in a group activity. The choice of the word *dynamics* is especially important. It implies change. For example, you set out to explain to Paul why he should operate a slightly more complex machine without receiving an increase in his pay rate. He enters the situation with the conviction that you are trying to take advantage of him. You begin with the view that he's got to accept your word. After five minutes of talking, you see that Paul isn't going to take this decision lying down; furthermore, you believe he has a legitimate argument you hadn't anticipated. Paul, on the other hand, thinks you aren't going to go to bat in his behalf, and although he's still apparently listening, he's made up his mind to see his shop steward as soon as he can. Since the conversation began, your attitude has changed and so has Paul's. That's dynamic.

Any two people can make up a group. Their interaction is *group dynamics*. As more and more people get into the group, the situation gets more dynamic. As time elapses, the situation gets even more dynamic. As new factors enter the situation (like a change in workplace lighting, an announcement of a pay increase at the company next door), the situation gets still more dynamic.

More than one person — plus change — adds up to group dynamics.

What does this have to do with the supervisor?

Just about everything. You must first recognize that all situations are dynamic. Then you've got to develop a way of following the direction of, and coping with, the evolving situation. All too often in group dynamics the supervisor is a couple of laps behind the field. He or she is trying to solve the situation as it was five minutes ago — or five days ago — not as it is right now.

Which groups take priority: the formal or the informal ones?

Formal groups do, such as your own department or assigned work teams within your department. They have been set up routinely to carry out the work in the best fashion. But informal groups require your attention and consideration, too. A supervisor must be realistic about the formation of informal groups within his or her department.

Informal groups are inevitable. They'll form at the water fountain and in the locker room. They will be made up of car poolers and those with common interests in sports or politics. You will find them everywhere. There is no way to blot them out.

Informal groups can be very powerful and exert a strong influ-

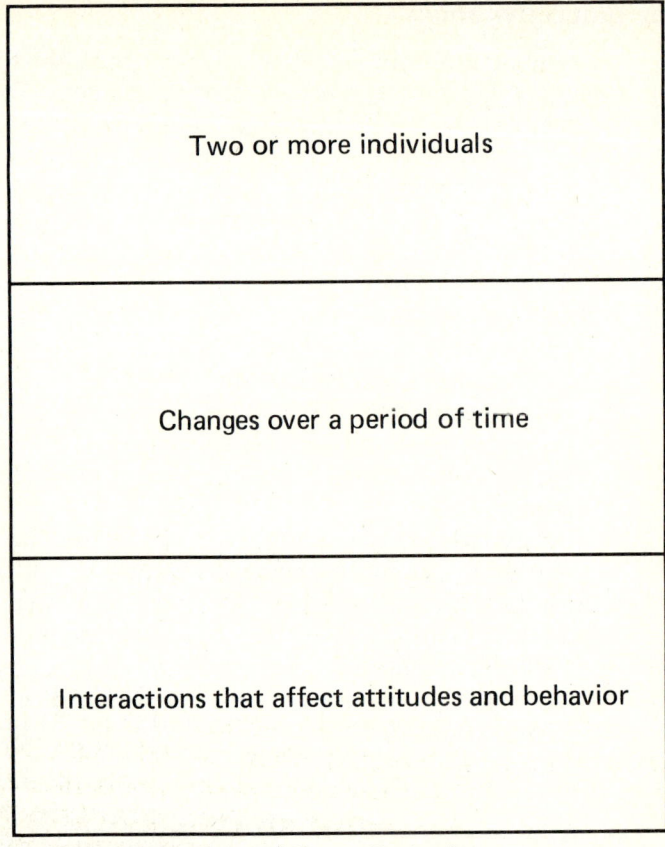

```
┌─────────────────────────────────────┐
│                                     │
│       Two or more individuals       │
│                                     │
├─────────────────────────────────────┤
│                                     │
│                                     │
│       Changes over a period of time │
│                                     │
│                                     │
├─────────────────────────────────────┤
│                                     │
│                                     │
│  Interactions that affect attitudes and behavior │
│                                     │
│                                     │
└─────────────────────────────────────┘
```

Figure 8-1. Ingredients of Group Dynamics.

ence on your employees. They command loyalty and often demand conformity. Most important, groups like this can work on your behalf or they can work against you.

To whom does the individual employee owe loyalty: the group or the supervisor?

There is no reason why an employee cannot be loyal to both. An employee warms up to various informal groups for friendship and companionship. A rank-and-file worker is more likely to identify with a buddy than with the boss. In a time of layoffs or other threats, an employee may reasonably look to the group for protection.

On the other hand, an employee looks to the good supervisor for knowledge about the job, personal training and development, direction and instruction, encouragement, respect, and understanding. The wise supervisor doesn't force an employee to choose between the group and the boss.

Which goals come first: the individual's, the group's, or the organization's?

If anything is to be accomplished, groups as well as individuals must place their goals second to those of the organization. The trick to good supervision, however, is to find a way to keep the goals of all three in harmony. Mary, for example, wants to get the job done as soon as she can so that she can take a break. The group wants to stretch it out so that there will be overtime. The supervisor, who must represent the organization, wants to get the job done on schedule so that a shipment can be made on time and at a specified labor cost. Mary and the supervisor are pulling in the same direction. The group is not. The supervisor has to find a way to persuade or insist that the group go along with the company goals; for example, "We'll all lose this order if we don't get it out by 4 p.m." or "Our deadline is 4 p.m. We've been able to make it dozens of times in the past, and regardless, there will be no overtime approved for this shipment."

What are work groups likely to do best?

Solve work problems. Groups, formal or informal, seem to have an uncanny knack for unsnarling complex work situations. In a few minutes they can straighten out crossover procedures between employees. They often know causes of difficulty hidden from the supervisor. Typically, they are acutely aware of personality conflicts between their members. Thus, a group's ability to put together jointly held know-how in a constructive manner is one that experienced supervisors like to tap. The technique of securing group aid this way, in solving departmental problems, is called participation.

In what ways are groups most likely to cause problems?

By ganging up to present mass resistance (spoken or silent) and by pressuring individual members to conform to the group's standards. Strong work groups stick together. They will protect one of their loyal members, and they will force a nonconformist to go along with the majority. The pressure can be so strong that even an eager beaver or a loner can be made to fall in line or to quit. Groups are powerful. Their support is to be cherished, and their enmity can be awesome. For these reasons prudent supervisors seek the group's help in establishing attainable work goals.

How can a supervisor set goals with the work group without sacrificing authority?

Unless the group of people you supervise believe that what you want them to do is to their advantage as well as to yours, you'll have little success as a supervisor. The solution lies in permitting the group to set their goals along with you and in showing them that these goals are attained through group action—teamwork.

It may be only natural for you to think that permitting the group to get into decision making will be hazardous to your authority. It needn't be. First, make it clear that you'll always retain a veto power over a group decision (but don't exercise it unless absolutely necessary). Second, establish ground rules beforehand for their participation and make these limitations clear. Finally, provide enough information for the group so that they can see situations as you do. When people don't have enough facts, they rebel against authority.

In dealing with work groups, try to make your role that of coach. Help employees to see why cost cutting, for instance, is desirable and necessary to ward off layoffs. Encourage them to discuss ways to cut costs. Welcome their suggestions. Try to find ways of putting even relatively insignificant ideas to work, and report the team's achievements frequently. Emphasize that good records are the result of the team's united effort, not your own bright ideas.

Of course certain decisions, such as those concerning work standards or quality specifications, may be beyond the group's control or even yours. Consequently, you should make it clear at the start what work conditions are off limits for group participation.

Why is group participation so effective?

You'll hear a lot about the wonders of participation, and most of what you'll hear is true. In today's employer-employee relations, few techniques have been so successful in developing harmony and the attainment of common goals as has the development of participation by supervision.

Participation is an amazingly simple way to inspire people; its simplicity lies in the definition of the word. To participate is "to share in common with others."

Sharing, then, is the secret. You must share knowledge and information with others in order to gain their cooperation. You must share your own experience so that employees will benefit from it. You must share the decision-making process itself so that employees can do some things the way they'd like to, and you must share credit for achievement.

Once you've learned how to share, participation is self-perpetuating. Supervision becomes easier when employees begin to share responsibility with you. No longer do you alone have to watch for every possibility. An employee will report an overheated motor, raw material with flaws, or an impending bottleneck. Employees won't wait for you to tell them what to do in an emergency. You'll find them using their own initiative to keep up production. So sharing pays off as employees share your burdens and their production records with you.

How often can group participation be expected to work in your behalf?

Only as often as the group's discussion of a situation leads them logically or emotionally, or both, to the conclusion that what you wish is good for them. Keep in mind that merely permitting participation will not manipulate the group to your point of view. The larger the group, the more forces are at work in it with which your ideas must cope.

If the majority can be expected to agree with your inclinations when given the same view of the facts you have, then the majority may sway group attitudes in your direction. But even this won't always be the case. If, for example, Mary is cantankerous, but because of seniority or outspokenness has the respect or fear of the rest of the people in the steno pool, the group may never buy an idea of yours that discredits her. Conversely, the group may (for reasons that are hard to determine) rebel against Mary and accept your new idea.

There are two rules of thumb to guide you: (1) Without group support your chance of achievement is slim. (2) Your best chance for winning group support is by letting the forces within the group itself struggle toward a decision with minimum interference from you. This isn't to say you must stand helplessly by while the group strikes off in the wrong direction. You can supply sound direction by providing facts that might be overlooked and by asking the group to weigh the pros and cons of various alternatives.

How can you tell how a group feels about you?

Surprisingly, one way is to let the group know how you feel about them. In other words, if you're puzzled or angered by the group's behavior, tell them so in clear terms. Then give them a chance to present their excuses or to strike back at you. If you can take a stiff rebuttal or candid criticism, you're likely to discover how the group really feels about your managerial techniques.

Here's an example. Supervisor Jane is being pressed for better quality control in her department, but month-end reports show that her department is losing ground. Now it does her no good to hold private ideas about who's sabotaging her or to complain about the matter to the other supervisors. It would be far better for Jane to lay her thoughts on the line. She can call her work group together and say, "I won't make a secret of how I feel. I've asked for your help in licking this quality problem, and all I get is the feeling that you're trying to make a monkey out of me. I don't like it. In fact, I'm downright angry about it. As far as I can see, the fault is yours, not mine. Now, can you tell me where I'm wrong?" This brings her feeling out into the open. In reply she may — if she can bite her tongue for five minutes — get a response from someone in the group that will show where the trouble lies. Or she may get no verbal response at all. Instead, she may find a subtle shift in the ways in which the group performs and even an improvement in the quality of workmanship.

Why worry about how people feel about you? Supervising isn't a popularity contest. In the long run, you call the signals, don't you?

A supervisor's first responsibility is to be effective. This doesn't necessarily mean that supervisors have to be popular to be effective, but we acquire many ingrained habits that stand in the way of achievement. Many supervisors are naggers without realizing it. Many supervisors have the best intentions when they offer advice, but don't realize that their subordinates think this demonstrates a lack of confidence in them. Other supervisors dominate conversations with their employees without recognizing this breeds a resentment that deafens the employees' ears to instructions. If we could find out how others, especially groups, react to our manner, we might be able to eliminate or minimize those affronts and irritations we don't intend.

How changeable are group attitudes?

They can be very changeable. Take a group's attitude, for example, on a proposed change in its work procedure. Initially, all members may resist it. Then one or two try it out and find that it is not so bad as they thought. They persuade a few of their friends to try it out. Soon, like passengers who rush from one side of a boat to another, they can dramatically change the weight of the group's position. Even the reluctant members are swept along with the crowd. Obviously, this effect can be helpful or troublesome. It is a force to be dealt with. (See Fig. 8-1.)

Why are some groups influential, others weak?

One union will call a strike only to see it fizzle out in a week or two. Another union, with a much less clear-cut issue at stake, may go out on strike and stay on strike for months. The first group of strikers is a weak group, the latter a strong one.

Strong groups, contrary to what you might suspect, are ones in which there are lots of conflict and frequent arguments. But where arguments are welcomed, agreements are stronger, too, and the pressure to conform is great.

Weak groups are those in which the objectives are not very important to most members or in which a few strong leaders make all the decisions. The objectives in strong groups and weak groups are represented in Figure 8-2.

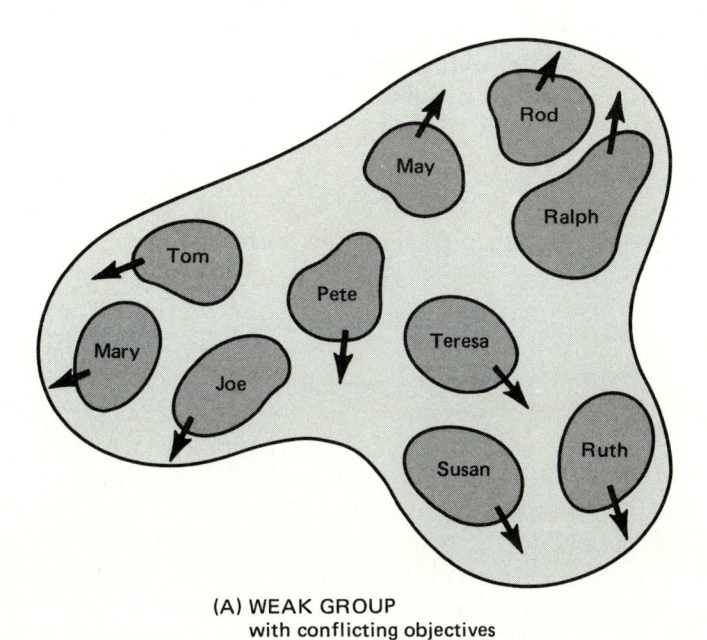

(A) WEAK GROUP
with conflicting objectives

(B) STRONG, COHESIVE GROUP
with unified objectives

Figure 8-2. Weak and Strong Groups.

CHAPTER 8: WORK GROUP BEHAVIOR

In the work groups you supervise, try to find out what the workers want as a group. Then help them to set these goals themselves. Try to show that your interest is in seeing that group goals are achieved and that you aren't the roadblock to job security, better pay, more rewarding work. The work groups you supervise will then be strong groups. Properly inspired, the groups will have goals very similar to yours.

It's when supervisors set themselves against work groups that the group becomes either strongly against the supervisor and the company, or weak and easily seized by a strong leader who may be against the supervisor or the objectives that best satisfy both company and worker.

Why are some groups made up of troublemakers rather than good workers?

At least one significant study has been made to show that the nature of some work itself somehow attracts, or develops, troublemakers. But it's hard to conclude that's the case most of the time. It's better if you can take the broad view that the group you supervise is also one of the groups of which you, too, are a member. While your company and your boss may have given you a certain amount of authority, that doesn't guarantee that you'll be the leader, or the only leader, in that group. If you're in tune with the group, however, there's a good chance you can find a way to make your kind of leadership and authority harmonize with the group's outlook. If so, even the existing troublemakers in the group won't be able to develop or to encourage the group to challenge you, your objectives, and your way of doing things. It's when the other leadership in the group supersedes yours that the good workers become troublemakers in your eyes.

Which comes first, the individual or the group?

It's almost impossible to say. We do know that the group is not just the sum of the individuals in it. Individually each of your employees may be loyal and honest, but in a group each person may be more loyal to the group's interest than to you. As a result, the individual may cheat a little on output or quality, if that's the standard the group respects.

It seems unavoidable that you must place your bets on the group's being collectively stronger than any of its individuals. Few individuals can stand up to group pressures for long. The person who does so may keep on working in your department, but is no longer a member of that group. Such employees become oddballs, difficult for you to deal with fairly and intelligently because you're never sure what standards of performance to impose on them—

theirs or the department's. For that reason don't press individuals to support you rather than the work group. Accept the fact that they will be loyal to you when this loyalty doesn't put them at odds with their peers.

By and large the supervisor's charge is to treat each person as individually as possible without challenging the prerogatives of the group the individual works in. The work group is an organization for which you are expected to provide direction and inspiration, not moral judgments.

Review Questions

1. Describe a situation from your own experience in which you were part of both a formal group and an informal group within the same organization.
2. Should a supervisor force an employee to choose between loyalty to the group and loyalty to the supervisor? Why or why not?
3. Why would an experienced supervisor encourage group participation in solving a work problem?
4. Which kind of supervision would you prefer if you had your choice: one in which the supervisor carefully and fairly laid out the work but was very firm about your following instructions, or one in which the supervisor carefully and fairly spelled out what results were expected but left it up to you to figure out how to accomplish them? Why?
5. What kind of problems can work groups cause that a supervisor should be especially conscious of?
6. Think of a group in your own experience that has changed some of its attitudes or beliefs over a period of time. What caused the change? Was it rapid or gradual? How did it take place?
7. What are some forces likely to create a strong group? A weak group?
8. As a supervisor, what would be your overall goals in establishing relations with your work group?

A Case in Point: The Case of the Sixteen Drafters

Tony C. supervises 16 drafters. Most of their work involves routine detailing of prints and drawings prepared by design engineers in another department. Occasionally some of the work, however, is more difficult and calls for the drafter to apply design-level thinking before the drawing is to be detailed. Tony C. has found out that George Smith is particularly good at this work. George had studied engineering at one time, and during the war he had actually worked as a designer in an aircraft plant. George made no complaint about these assignments, but one morning this week Tony C. was confronted in his office by three of his older drafters. "We're beginning to get annoyed at the way you give all the choice design work to George," said the spokesman.

"Choice work!" replied Tony C. "That's difficult, demanding work. If I gave it to half of the people in this department, there would be nothing but hassles. Besides, George isn't complaining."

"That's not the point," said the spokesman. "We think that such work should be spread around so that everybody who wants it gets a crack at it."

Tony C. replied that he wouldn't trust it with just any employee, and that the drafters could go back to their drawing boards.

The following day when Tony C. asked George to fill in a design element on one of the prints, George said, "You've been taking advantage of me by asking me to do all the hard work. If I'm so good, why don't you see that I get promoted to the design department? Let someone else do this kind of work from now on."

If you were Tony C., what would you do? Five alternative approaches are listed below. Rank them in the order in which they appeal to you (1 most attractive, 5 least). You may add another approach in the space provided, if you wish. In any event, be prepared to justify your rankings.

_____**A.** Have George's job upgraded so that he gets a higher rate than the others in the department.

_____**B.** Assign the work to others in the department, but only to those you know can do the job well.

_____**C.** Insist that George do any work he's assigned.

_____**D.** Rotate the assignment until everyone has had an opportunity to try it. Then, in the future make such assignments only to those who do it well and who want to do that kind of work.

_____**E.** Call the group together for a short meeting. Tell them you're interested in their opinions about how this work should be assigned.

If you have another approach, write it here. _____
_____
_____
_____
_____
_____
_____

Action Summary Checklist		Action Needed Yes No	Date Completed

1. Alert to the dynamics of group relationships in your department. ____ ____ ____
2. Awareness of, but not prying into, informal groups in your department. ____ ____ ____
3. Willingness to share employees' loyalties with their work group, formal and informal. ____ ____ ____
4. Integration of individual and group goals with company goals. ____ ____ ____
5. Opportunity for employees collectively to help solve production and other work-related problems. ____ ____ ____
6. Sharing of relevant job information and know-how with employees, individually or in groups. ____ ____ ____
7. Action as a facilitator when work groups struggle to resolve intragroup squabbles. ____ ____ ____
8. Recognition that many individuals will look to you for protection from unreasonable group pressures so as to assure personal freedom of action. ____ ____ ____
9. Observant of changes in group behavior that may signal a radical shift in group attitudes, favorable or unfavorable, toward their work, the company, or you. ____ ____ ____
10. Ability to describe personality characteristics of your departmental work group and informal groups within it. ____ ____ ____
11. Assessment of your departmental work group as weak or strong. ____ ____ ____
12. Development of a strong and cohesive departmental work group that is in general agreement with company objectives for it. ____ ____ ____
13. Assurance that your work group, while moving toward its departmental objectives, also works in harmony with other company departments toward the greater objectives of the entire program. ____ ____ ____

CHAPTER 8: WORK GROUP BEHAVIOR

Action Summary Checklist (continued)

	Action Needed		Date Completed
	Yes	No	
14. Firm stand on goals, policies, procedures, and rules that are judged to be inflexible if work is to be coordinated in a safe and productive way.	____	____	_____
15. Reliance on performance as the best indicator of individual and group morale.	____	____	_____

Chapter 9
Conflict and Cooperation

Key Concepts

- Conflicts are natural in any organization. The supervisor's responsibilities are to try to understand the causes of conflicts and resolve them in a way that will contribute to meeting the objectives of the work group. Establishing open communications among the people really involved, in an atmosphere of respect and flexibility, is the key to accomplishing this.

- Being sensitive to others is a technique for building mutual understanding, not for shucking off supervisory responsibility to individuals in the group. The supervisor still maintains discipline and makes decisions as needed. The supervisor's obligation is to understand how others feel and to build a communications bridge to them, not to abandon responsibility.

- Attitudes, and the degree to which they influence behavior of both individuals and groups, are highly individualistic. Furthermore, attitudes are the result of long-term conditioning; consequently, they cannot simply be ordered into existence by management.

- Contrary to what might be supposed, employee attitudes toward their supervisors are generally positive, especially toward supervisors who set firm but reasonable performance standards. It is especially likely that when supervisors' attitudes are positive, their subordinates' attitudes will likewise be positive.

- Sympathetic understanding of the reasons for an employee's point of view, especially when the understanding is indicated to the employee by attentive listening, is one of the most effective ways for a supervisor to induce cooperative, productive attitudes. Transactional analysis can help avoid certain blocks to the needed communication.

Is the presence of bickering and disputes a sign of poor supervision?

Not necessarily. It is human to quarrel and complain. When many people must work together, conflict is inevitable. Accordingly, a small amount of conflict can be a good thing. When there is no end of quarreling and confrontation, supervisors should begin to worry about how good a job they are doing.

What are the main sources of conflict in an organization?

They are many. People with different ideas about what should be done and how to do it are a common source. Departments that are sometimes at cross-purposes—like production and maintenance, production control and sales, sales and credit, accounting and retailing, purchasing and engineering—cause intergroup difficulties. But most of the causes of conflict in a department are closely related to the work itself: how it is laid out and the way in which the supervisor manages the employees. In particular, a supervisor should be on guard against these situations:

1. A one-way pattern of communications: The supervisor makes most of the decisions and hands down orders and instructions all the time.
2. Unpredictability: The supervisor insists that something be done this way today and that way tomorrow.
3. Change: in methods, materials, or specifications; in organization relationships; in company policy. Employees work best when there is a certain degree of stability in the department.

What's a good way to handle conflict in your department?

First, be alert to its presence. Next, seek its causes. Then meet it head-on. A basic approach involves four steps:

1. Decide what you wish to be accomplished. Do you want peace and quiet at any price? Or do you want better workmanship? Greater productivity? A project finished on time? Fewer mistakes in transcribing? An end to delays caused by quarrels between the maintenance person and your production operator? Nothing will be resolved unless you first make up your mind what the desired outcome should be.

2. Call together the people who can best settle the issue. If the conflict is strictly between you and one employee, limit the confrontation to the two of you. If others are involved, invite them into the discussion. If a disinterested party, such as the quality-control department, can shed light on the subject, ask for its participation. If a referee or someone who can speak authoritatively about the company's viewpoint is needed, then get your boss into the act.
3. Be ready to bargain, not hand out edicts. Conflicts are truly settled by negotiation. A short answer tends only to put off the problem, and it will recur. If you keep your eye on the objective you have set, there are usually many ways to attain it. Remember that each individual has an objective, too. If the maintenance department, for example, can provide the necessary repairs while still keeping their costs in line — and dependable repairs are your objective — then try to let them do it their way.
4. Don't be distracted by the red herring of personalities. While many people do rub one another the wrong way, most conflicts have a much more tangible basis. That's the value of keeping the eyes of all concerned on the main objective. It tends to push personality conflicts into the background. Finally, try not to get emotionally involved yourself. Above all, don't choose sides.

How can you avoid prolonging a touchy situation?

As we said earlier, the best thing is to face up to conflict as soon as you are sure it has substance. In other words, don't heat up a minor dispute by jumping the gun. But do try to resolve it clearly once you've seen more than smoke. Because conflict is unpleasant to most of us and because it is not easy to settle, you should guard against certain practices that tend to prolong it. For example, you should check to see that you are not making any of the following mistakes:

Avoiding conversations or contact with those who are involved. You're angry at Sue, for example, and you're not going to speak to her. Or you purposely cut out the bowling night with the purchasing supervisor who is undercutting you.

Emphasizing orders and instructions while cutting off an employee's opportunities to talk up to you, or relying on a flurry of written memos and bulletin board notices. This encourages employees to carp among themselves and to inflate the issues so that they become harder to resolve.

Switching from compliments to complaints. You feel you were nice to Sam, for example, and he didn't cooperate. Okay, now you'll show him what it's like by throwing a few zingers to him.

Allowing the injured parties to gang up. One unhappy person can "infect" several others. If it is your department against the sales-order department, for example, continued silent combat will build up their solidarity; and when you finally try to settle the issue, it will be stickier than ever.

People speak of the value of gaining sensitivity. Why?

In your dealings with other people, especially those who are members of your work force, many authorities believe that you can establish better long-term relations with them if you are sensitive to the way they feel, both about you and about your behavior toward them. The rationale goes something like this: If you're in tune with employees' feelings, your timing of instructions, changes, requests, and criticisms — and your way of going about all this — will be more effective.

The sensitivity point of view assumes that few of us really know how we affect other people. It also assumes that if we had a chance to see ourselves as others see us, we'd change our ways and adopt a more acceptable manner. Unfortunately, these sensitivity authorities generally assume that under normal conditions others disguise their true feelings so well that the chances of our finding out about ourselves are very slim. Accordingly, the prescribed way to acquire this learning is to take part in a sensitivity-training laboratory — often called laboratory, or controlled, training.

What is the significance of a hidden agenda?

One point of view of the sensitivity-training people is that so many ordinary business meetings (where, for instance, supervisors sit down to resolve production or cost problems) get nowhere because each member nurses a hidden agenda. This hidden agenda prevents the group from making real progress in solving their mutual problems, as can be seen in Figure 9-1. For example, Teresa, the production-control supervisor, may feel the meeting has been called to make her the scapegoat of a delayed shipment. Consequently, she comes to the meeting with the intention of placing the blame on the purchasing agent for not having stocked the right quantity of subassemblies. This is Teresa's hidden agenda. Until the group gets Teresa to put this agenda on the table, the group meeting will accomplish very little. Proponents of sensitivity argue that it would be far better for the purposes of the meeting if Teresa were to say what is on her mind — that she thinks she is going to be made the goat, that others are to blame. In that way, other participants would know how Teresa feels and could clear the air of recriminations before settling down to solutions that usually require teamwork.

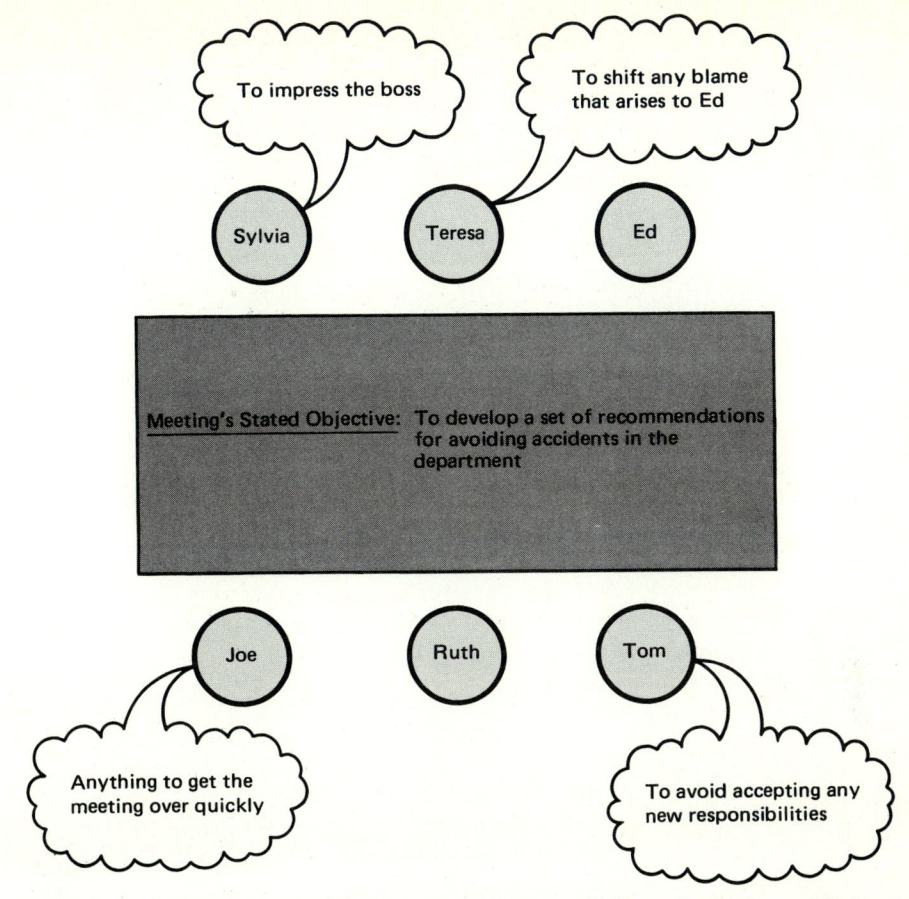

Figure 9-1. Examples of Hidden Agendas at a Safety Committee Meeting.

Must you be superhuman to get along with everybody?

You would be if you did. That's why psychologists stress the value of accepting yourself pretty much as you are—not smugly, of course, but recognizing that you have many faults that keep you from doing a perfect job and sometimes make you difficult to live with.

If you expect perfection from yourself, for example, chances are that you will become almost impossible for others to get along with because you tend to expect perfection from them, too. Worse still, you expect perfection from them in a lot of matters they couldn't care less about. On the other hand, it's just as dangerous to shield yourself from your own personality deficiencies and to make excuses for them. Admitting your weaknesses is far better. Try to make concessions where they cause others trouble, but don't blame others for your shortcomings.

Whether you strive for perfection or cover up your weaknesses, it often adds up to misery for others. Sensitivity experts believe that (1) just knowing more about yourself may make you more acceptable to others and (2) permitting others to comment to you about your shortcomings can work magic for you. People will then accept you for what you are and will make allowances for you, and they will also more readily accept, and act upon, your criticism of them.

Does sensitivity imply that a responsive manager doesn't demote, discipline, or fire anybody?

Not at all. If the demands of a particular job are such that a subordinate cannot perform it properly, the supervisor must take action. Sensitivity does not interfere with this action. Its purpose is to help people who are working to do a better, more effective job. Sensitivity flourishes in an atmosphere of success, not failure, and vice versa.

How can you invite candid, open discussion with others without recriminations?

First, be candid. That takes courage on your part, Later, the recriminations won't be so bad and may disappear altogether. The trick in getting others to level with you is to try to separate feelings from facts.

For example, an employee has an irritating way of making remarks to other employees while you're explaining the lineup for the day's work. Get this employee aside and say something like this: "I have no idea what it is you're saying when I'm talking, but it irritates me beyond reason. It makes me want to give you the heaviest kind of work I can find. It's crazy for two grown persons to get a hang-up like this. Maybe my impression of your attitude is all wrong. Is it?" Given this chance, the employee may say, "You bug me, too, the way you lecture us each morning as if we were kids. What's more, you always seem to find a way to make me look like a fool." At that point the person is beginning to bring the hidden agenda into view because you've been willing to expose yours. Surprisingly, once feelings have been discussed—not necessarily resolved—the chances are infinitely better that the two of you will be able to agree better on factual matters.

What is an attitude?

An attitude is a person's point of view. It's a way of looking at something. Even more important, an attitude is a person's readiness to react in a predetermined way.

Baseball batters ready to swing at a pitch, for instance, set their feet, position their bats, keep their eyes on the pitcher. They have learned from experience that this attitude gives the best chance of getting a hit. In the same way you and your employees learn from your experience to assume a readiness to react when faced with a situation. Employee attitudes toward lateness determine how conscientiously they try to get to work on time. Your attitude toward lateness will determine how much emphasis you place on tardiness as a measure of employee performance.

When are attitudes positive?

Attitudes that reflect optimism and enthusiasm—what professional athletes call desire—are positive. People who are positive in their thinking look for the good things in other people and in their own work. They seek to change and improve those conditions they don't like, rather than merely to complain about them. People who have negative attitudes tend to see only the bad side. They dwell on their own misfortunes and those of others. Unfortunately, negative attitudes, like positive ones, are contagious. An employee who begins a working career cheerfully may have that positive outlook eroded by the constant fault-finding of sour-dispositioned associates or supervisors.

What causes poor attitudes?

When an employee faces a situation the way you'd like—such as accepting your corrections with good grace—you're likely to say that the worker has a good attitude. But if the same worker irks you by habitually failing to keep the area neat, you may find yourself saying that the employee's attitude is poor. How do you explain this contradiction? How can the same person's attitude be good one time and bad the next?

It could be that the employee's attitudes are fine from the employer's point of view. In the first instance you seem considerate and helpful when it comes to showing how to do a job. Your favorable action has developed in the worker a good attitude toward criticism. In the second instance this same worker may have learned that you are soft about discipline for sloppy housekeeping. The worker's observation is that you complain a lot about poor housekeeping, but your bark is worse than your bite. So this worker's attitude toward housekeeping is the one you've taught, even though its's bad.

Is the supervisor always responsible for a worker's attitudes?

No. An employee, just like yourself, has many teachers. Parents, childhood pals, schoolteachers, the person at the next desk, union representatives have all been teaching the employee how to react to things for a long time. These other people may have shown

CHAPTER 9: CONFLICT AND COOPERATION

hundreds of times that it's possible to get away with anything just by giving lip service to what the boss says. If the employee keeps on doing what he or she pleases, you'll have to try hard to build up new, different experiences with this worker. You'll have to show that the old attitude won't be acceptable in relationships with you.

What can you do to understand more about employee attitudes?

To understand a worker's attitude better, you must take an interest in that person, not just as a productive cog in the business machine, but as someone who has dreams and ambitions and troubles just as everyone else has. Your interest should not be superficial, or it will be recognized as such and the person will be harder than ever to reach. In fact, you have to work hard on your own attitudes toward others to get yourself to see each person as a whole.

To begin taking this interest in employees, first form a habit of inquiring into nonwork activities. Begin with less personal things like bowling scores, do-it-yourself projects, or any hobby they are likely to speak freely about. If you continue to show you're interested in their pastimes and their success or failure in them, you'll build their confidence in you. If they have other personal matters they would like to tell you about—family affairs, financial troubles—let them bring up the problems so that you won't be guilty of prying.

Little by little, just listening and showing this sincere interest will reveal the reasons for employee attitudes. You needn't attempt to advise or be overly sympathetic. It isn't necessary. In fact, it can be downright dangerous. For most people your willing ear is enough.

It is usually a mistake to use the direct approach and to ask why an employee's attitude is the way it is. More often than not, the person doesn't know. It's better to take the roundabout road to discover the true attitude and the reasons behind it.

What can you do to change attitudes?

Quite a lot. Understanding attitudes often points the way to changing them. Employees learn the attitudes they have; you can teach them new ones. Don't try this by preaching. Do it by setting favorable examples and by providing employees with favorable experiences.

Suppose Mark is a troublemaker in your department. He complains about his own assignment, continually charges discrimination, and stirs up the other employees to make grievances. In your eyes, his actions show his attitude to be bad.

You want Mark to change his attitude, but why is Mark a troublemaker? That's hard to say, and it takes experience and understanding to find out. But think for a moment about what Mark's experience shows him about his troublemaking attitude: It provides him with plenty of attention; it makes him a hero; it wins grudging admiration from his associates.

Suppose that you could find a way to provide Mark with experiences where his troublemaking didn't get him attention or admiration, and you could find other, more favorable ways to provide experiences that give him the attention and admiration he desires.

For instance, you might find good reason to compliment Mark openly and frequently about his work. You might ask his opinion about new methods that are under consideration. You might enlist his aid in telling other employees about job changes. All these actions on your part are healthy, and they provide Mark with the type of job satisfaction he looks for. Suppose that each time Mark made trouble, you handled his actions discreetly and impersonally and that you avoided any show of emotion or upset. The chances are that the combined effect would be to change his attitude for the better.

You should be cautioned, of course, that attitudes and behaviors aren't often easy to pin down to actual cause and effect; but if you approach each human relations problem without a preconceived notion and with real humility and warmth, attitudes can be changed. The point in Mark's case is that you want to help him, not outsmart him.

Can you always change someone's attitude?

Theoretically the answer is yes, but in practice, no. Some people are just too fixed in their ways to yield very much. Sometimes you, as a supervisor, can do little to change the organizational situations that create unfavorable attitudes. Some combinations of circumstances may be too complex to do much about without professional help from the personnel office or from a psychologist or a psychiatrist.

You also should be aware that a fairly large number of workers are emotionally unstable. The cause of their poor attitudes is a mental illness that is far beyond the lay person's power to treat and is difficult to identify. If you suspect such a condition in one of your employees, don't play parlor psychiatrist. Speak to the company medical staff or to the personnel office, and then follow their advice.

What is an attitude survey?

An attitude survey is a systematic way of finding out how employees feel about their company, their pay, their supervisors, their working conditions, their jobs, and so forth.

The most common type of attitude survey is based on a multiple-choice questionnaire, with which a company can take a kind of vote among its employees to find out their attitudes. Questions are phrased something like this:

Check the one answer that most nearly describes how you feel: *There's too much pressure on my job.* Do you agree, are you undecided, do you disagree?

Another typical question:

My boss really tries to get my ideas about things. Do you agree, are you undecided, do you disagree?

As many as 100 questions may be asked, with room left for written comments. To make the survey more meaningful, it is kept confidential. No employee signs his or her name, and the tabulation is done by a university or a consulting firm so that company officials never see even the handwriting of those surveyed. See Figure 9-1.

Questionnaire answers are tabulated and analyzed. Most companies report survey findings either generally or in specific terms to their employees. It's especially important that once management finds out what employee attitudes are, it takes immediate action to improve conditions where these attitudes are unfavorable. For instance, a survey may show that most employees don't feel free to discuss job matters with their supervisors. Most people who have studied the relationship of attitudes to effort believe that such a condition is unhealthy and prevents a supervisor from getting the necessary cooperation. Consequently, the company and the supervisor should take steps to improve the condition. For you it may mean changing your own attitude and conduct to show that you will set aside time to listen to employee questions, complaints, or suggestions, and that you will listen with interest and welcome the ideas that are presented.

Why don't some people cooperate?

For a very natural reason: They see no personal advantage in doing so. Is this a terrible attitude? Not at all.

Not one of us does anything for nothing. We do some things for money, others for lots of other reasons. Joe works well because he likes the feeling of being with a group of people. Sam works hard because he gets a sense of accomplishment from what he is doing. Mary puts in top effort because her job makes her feel important.

Few persons work for money alone. Because we all expect different satisfactions in different proportions from our work, don't be annoyed when a worker's attitude seems to say, "What's in it for me?" That's your signal to get busy and find some way of providing satisfaction for that employee on the job.

Why isn't high pay the key to cooperation?

Good pay rates are important, but many companies that have sought the high-wage route to workers' affections have been sadly disappointed. Although pay means much to most employees, experience shows that it isn't enough.

One big trouble with pay as an incentive is that employees don't enjoy it while they work. It is after work that the salary brings tangible rewards and good feelings. Consider vacations and pensions. Employees can take advantage of neither while actually on the job. As Herzberg pointed out, your solution to winning employee cooperation is to appeal to employees' needs for respect, for challenge, and for interesting work. Each employee has a different set of these needs; the supervisor's skill lies in trying to adjust the employee's work and working relationships to satisfy the needs as much as is reasonable. The belief is that employees will cooperate to get this kind of treatment.

What's the best formula for winning cooperation?

The best formula is not to seek one. Despite the simplicity of the reasons people work, there is no easy road to securing cooperation. Don't be misled into believing there are gimmicks or pat things to say. There are no standard ways to react that, once memorized, will have employees eating out of your hand. If you attempt to outsmart employees, they will spot your lack of sincerity, and resistance will go up in proportion.

The best way to achieve cooperation is to change your own way of looking at people until you see in them some of the good and bad qualities you see in yourself. Make a point of being sensitive to people. Pause again and again to imagine how employees think about what you tell them or what you ask them to do. Stop talking, too, and listen to what they say about themselves, about the other workers, and about you. For not until you begin to know people will you be able to put into practice some of the simple ideas expressed here for getting along with them.

How can you remove resistance?

There are many methods. Don't use the same one in every situation. Learn them all so you have a choice when resistance shows up.

Try a Success Example. Casey doesn't want to work nights? Tell Casey about Jonesy, who thought he wouldn't like working nights, but who, after trying it for a month, won't work any other shift.

Try Making a Guarantee. Anne is sure the new method won't work? Tell Anne that if she tries it for a week and doesn't find it better than the old way, you'll promise she can switch back again.

Try a Demonstration. The operator thinks the rate on the new job is too tough? Say, "Here, let me show you how easy the machine is to operate. It looks a lot harder than it actually is."

Try Asking Questions. Marie says she can't make bonus. Ask her what she finds hardest about the job, whether she feels it has been properly explained.

Try Just Plain Listening. Sandy won't work overtime today or any other day? Let him rave. Hear all his arguments in a friendly manner. When he's had his complete say, then try persuasion and reasoning.

How do you go about getting cooperation from your associates?

The secret of getting along well with other supervisors is much the same as winning cooperation from your employees: Find out what they want most from their work, then satisfy these desires. Except that with your associates, it's not so much a problem of providing satisfaction as it is of not blocking their goals and ambitions.

Face up to the fact that, to a degree, you and your associates are competing—for raises, promotions, praise, popularity, and a host of other things. If you compete too hard, or compete unfairly, you won't win much cooperation from the other supervisors. Your chances of getting ahead often depend on your ability to run your department in smooth harmony with those departments that interlock with yours.

Winning friends among the other supervisors means intelligent sacrifice. Occasionally you'll have to put aside your wish to make your department look good just so that you don't put the supervisor of the next department behind the eight ball. Willingness to lend a hand when another supervisor falls behind and avoiding hairsplitting when allocating interdepartmental charges and responsibilities will help.

Above all, let other supervisors run their own shows. Don't try to give orders in their departments or encourage disputes between your workers and theirs.

Just as when an individual employee doesn't play ball with the others, if you don't conform to a reasonable degree, you'll have the supervisory group down on you and cooperation will be long in coming. To turn this group solidarity to your advantage, aim at giving the supervisory organization the advantage of your own positive leadership. Help other supervisors set worthwhile goals, and the chances of your all working together will be improved.

How can you get along best with staff people?

Generally speaking, staff people in your organization are almost entirely dependent on you and other supervisors for cooperation. In this case cooperation will breed cooperation. If you cooperate with staff people, their jobs are made infinitely easier. Their superiors judge them by their success in getting your assistance and on the degree to which you accept and act on their advice. So if you cooperate with staff people, you're actually helping them to get more satisfaction from their work; and you can be pretty sure that they'll go a long way toward helping you make a good showing on *your* job.

Wouldn't you like to have a data processing specialist report to your boss: "It's a pleasure to work with a supervisor like Jill. She never seems to hide things or get her back up when I offer suggestions. She's quick to see how what we're doing will improve operations in the long run. Not that Jill buys everything I say. She doesn't. She has her ideas, too. But together, I think Jill and I are really accomplishing things out there."

How can "I'm okay, you're okay" help to resolve personality conflicts?

This kind of analysis, often called transactional analysis (TA), helps to provide insights because it simplifies some of the apparently complex interactions that take place between people. It maintains that four possible relationships are held by the employee and the supervisor:

1. I'm not okay. You're not okay. This negative view implies an employee's dissatisfaction with his or her own behavior, but also, in effect, says that the supervisor's actions are just as bad. It is somewhat like a rebellious child quarreling with a parent. At work it might arise when an employee accused of pilfering materials says that the boss does the same thing.
2. I'm not okay. You're okay. This is often the mark of a person who has lost self-respect or of a person who places all the responsibility on the boss's shoulders. This person often feels unable to do the job without continual assistance from the supervisor. Supervisors should strive to get out from under this kind of dependence.
3. I'm okay. You're not okay. This is the parental kind of role supervisors often assume. Essentially it treats the employee like a child. Such an attitude invites rebellion or loss of any hope the individual may have that the job can be done to your satisfaction.
4. I'm okay. You're okay. This is the mature, or adult, way to handle conflicts. It assumes that each individual respects the

other. Starting from a point of mutual respect, each person tries to understand, not necessarily agree with, the other's point of view. The supervisor says to the employee, "I understand why you may think I'm taking advantage of your good nature, but listen to me long enough so that you understand my point of view. Once we're sure we understand one another, maybe we can come to some sort of agreement that gives you some satisfaction while making sure that the job gets done."

When transactional analysis is used, any of the first three approaches tends to keep the conflict going, even to heat it up. The fourth approach, sometimes called stroking, can be very effective if carried on honestly. It helps to provide a solid basis for cooperation and compromise.

What is the best way to avoid misunderstanding and to gain willing cooperation?

The starting place is respect for others' points of view, no matter how much they vary from your own. For the manager this implies an appreciation of subordinates for what they really are. It's wishful thinking—and downright harmful—to measure someone against a mythical ideal such as the perfect person for the job.

Many managers never learn that their subordinates are constantly evaluating the manager's actions and varying their efforts accordingly. It's certainly the rare subordinate who will risk telling the boss when he or she is making mistakes, particularly if the boss isn't one who takes criticism willingly. Thus, many supervisors never get any critical feedback about themselves. Fortunately, if you can take the first step, you'll find yourself a new and better kind of supervisor. You'll gain a new awareness that there are more consequences to any action involving people than those on the surface. The consequences often interfere with productivity, because people who are working on their own frustrations have less energy to devote to the job.

Of course, it isn't always possible to solve the human problems that can result from a necessary and unpleasant management action; but sensitive supervisors enjoy two distinct advantages over their less sensitive counterparts:

1. An awareness of others' needs aids in avoiding unnecessary human problems that ordinarily seem to be cropping up each day.
2. A pattern of awareness of others' needs in itself tends to blunt the edge of problems and conflicts that cannot be avoided, because subordinates and associates know that the supervisor has tried.

It is smart to show you appreciate employee cooperation, or should you act as if it's something coming to you?

You can overdo your show of appreciation. But neither should employees think you take their efforts for granted. It would be ridiculous, for example, to stand by the time clock congratulating each employee for coming in on time. But it makes sense to look over the attendance record every six months and take a minute to say to each person with a perfect record: "I just reviewed the department's attendance records for the last six months, and I see that you went through those six months without missing a day or being late once. We appreciate that around here. It helps make the department an easier place to work in. Hope you can keep it up."

Yes, it's better to err on the generous side than to get the reputation of being a supervisor who takes a pound of flesh each day but never so much as says thank-you.

Review Questions

1. Why do conflicts arise in an organization?
2. Give an example from your own experience of a conflict that was prolonged rather than resolved because it was mishandled.
3. How could sensitivity training be any better than on-the-job experience in improving interpersonal skills?
4. Give an example of a hidden agenda in some sort of group meeting or discussion.
5. Would it be wise for a supervisor to insist that an employee change his or her attitude? Why or why not?
6. In what ways might an employee give evidence of a poor attitude toward work?
7. Describe some steps that a supervisor might take to change employee attitudes.
8. Can transactional analysis (TA) be of any practical value in handling conflicts?

A Case in Point: The Case of the Unhappy Mixer Operator

In the blending department of a rubber factory, morale was surprisingly high. Employees worked hard in the presence of oppressive heat and unpleasant fumes. Without warning, however, the performance of Pete, a 30-year-old operator of a Banbury mixer, began to deteriorate. The number of batches he mixed per shift fell from 15 to 11, and on two occasions he scorched a batch. When his supervisor talked to Pete to try to find the reason for this slump, Pete said, "Everything is all right. I'm just a little untracked. Leave me alone and I'll get straightened out soon." Despite this assurance, however, Pete's poor work continued. Puzzled, the supervisor checked with the personnel department for advice. An examination of Pete's personnel record showed that twice in the past he had bid for a job elsewhere in the company where working conditions were better. Three weeks ago he had again bid for a job—this time in the company's toolroom. He had been advised that he did not have the necessary educational qualifications for advancement into a skilled trade.

If you were Pete's supervisor, what would you do? Five alternative approaches are listed below. Rank them in the order in which they appeal to you (1 most attractive, 5 least). You may add another approach in the space provided, if you wish. In any event, be prepared to justify your rankings.

_____ **A.** Tell Pete that now that he knows his future is limited, he ought to buckle down and get back on the ball.

_____ **B.** Try to find out what Pete's aspirations are and then work to help him attain them.

_____ **C.** Seek to get Pete transferred somewhere else.

_____ **D.** Interview Pete for his thoughts about how his job in the blending department might be made pleasanter.

_____ **E.** Talk with Pete and tell him you can understand his disappointment, but that there still is an important job for him to do in the blending department.

If you have another approach, write it here. _____
_____
_____
_____

Action Summary Checklist		Action Needed Yes No	Date Completed
	1. Main sources of conflict minimized: one-way, downward communications; inconsistent directives and decisions; continual change in methods, relationships, and policies.	____ ____	_____
	2. Prompt management of departmental conflicts as they surface.	____ ____	_____
	3. Bargaining or compromising approach toward conflicts involving you.	____ ____	_____
	4. Focus on issues and objectives rather than personalities.	____ ____	_____
	5. Emphasis on two-way communications and continued personal contacts even when angry.	____ ____	_____

Action Summary Checklist (continued)

	Action Needed Yes No	Date Completed

6. Sensitivity to the interest of others, associates as well as employees. ___ ___ _____
7. Recognition that demands for perfection are unattainable in most instances and threatening to most people.
8. Willingness to invite candid comments from employees about touchy departmental situations and to listen to them without recriminations. ___ ___ _____
9. Recognition that what is important is employee performance, not their attitudes, although poor attitudes may lead to poor performance. ___ ___ _____
10. Maintenance of your own state of high morale, seeking advice and guidance when it is low. ___ ___ _____
11. Encouraging employee cooperation by seeking to satisfy their needs for respect, challenge, and interesting or meaningful work. ___ ___ _____
12. Getting along with your associates by keeping your eyes on the common objectives of company productivity, quality, and cost control. ___ ___ _____
13. Cooperating with, rather than resisting, the advice and suggestions from staff personnel. ___ ___ _____
14. Seeking to maintain an attitude of I'm okay, you're okay, when dealing with stress situations involving employees or associates. ___ ___ _____
15. Praise for those employees who do cooperate in helping to meet departmental objectives. ___ ___ _____

Chapter 10
Activating the Work Force by Communications

Key Concepts

- Effectiveness of employee communications depends on the extent to which supervision and management strive to maintain an open, honest, and comprehensive network. The resultant effectiveness of the communications effort will become a major factor in strengthening or weakening organizational unity and morale.

- Supervisors who are successful in discharging their total responsibility are those who place themselves at the focal point of the communications network in their organization.

- Information can be exchanged only when reception as well as sending takes place and "noise" is held to a minimum. Observation, listening, and reading are as essential to supervision as demonstration, talking, and writing.

- While information exchange is greatly influenced by nonverbal factors such as anxieties and apprehensions, attitudes and emotions, personality, and tone of voice, a great deal of business information must inevitably take its shape through the tyranny of words.

- Communications techniques are most effective (1) when used in combination, one with another rather than singly; and (2) when appropriately tuned to the situation and individuals involved.

What is the significance of communications when the term is used in connection with supervision?

The term *communications* is defined as the process in human relations of passing information and understanding from one person to another. As a supervisory responsibility, it is frequently called employee communications, although the communicating process is equally important between supervisor and supervisor and between supervisor and boss.

The term communications was, of course, originally applied to mechanical means for transmitting and receiving information, such as newspapers, bulletin board announcements, radio, telephone, and television. Employee communications have many of the qualities and limitations of mechanical means, but they are infinitely more subtle and complex. Try to treat communications carefully.

How does communications activate the organization?

By providing the linking pin between plans and action. You may have put together the best set of plans ever and staffed your department with the best people available, but until something begins to happen, you will have accomplished nothing. Communications with your employees is what puts the whole plan into motion.

When do human communications get off the track?

When we try to get our ideas across to others, human communication (like radio or television transmission) systems suffer from poor reception and interference or from being tuned in on the wrong channel. Poor reception often occurs when a supervisor gives an order that an employee hasn't been conditioned to expect. Interference takes place when a supervisor gives conflicting instructions. An employee may be tuned in on the wrong channel if a supervisor talks about improving work quality when the employee wants to find out about taking the day off. Only through skillful communications can these human transmission failures be avoided. Some experts on communications refer to these distractions as "noise."

Is any one method of communications better than another?

Each situation has its own best method or combination of methods. To show some employees how much you appreciate their cooperation, all you may need to do is give them an occasional pat on the shoulder. But others may need frequent vocal assurance. Still others will believe only what you put down on paper. The most successful communicating is done by supervisors who know many ways of getting their ideas, instructions, and attitudes across.

What are the two basic ways to approach employee communications in your department?

By using either a wheel or a web system (or network). In a wheel system (also called a satellite system), communications tend to be restricted. The supervisor stands at the center, or hub, as shown in

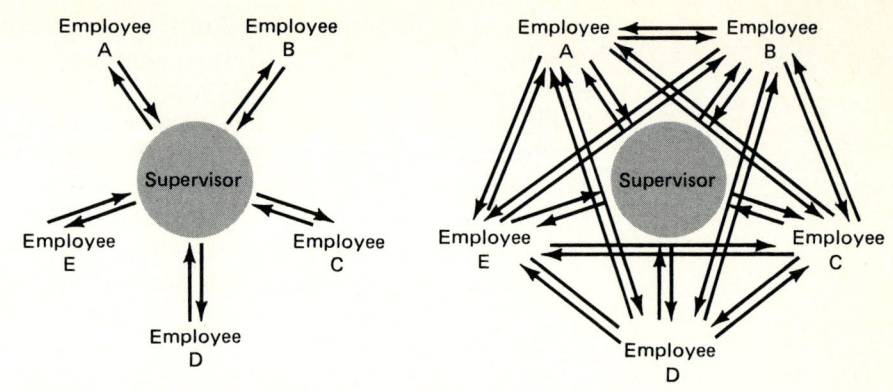

Figure 10-1. Examples of Restricted and Open Communication Systems.

Figure 10-1. Information is passed out to and received from employees via the spokes. Employees are not encouraged to exchange ideas with each other. In a web network, communications tend to be more open. The supervisor still stands at the center of the system, but employees are encouraged to exchange information freely in any channel they can find open.

In the wheel network the supervisor controls the flow of information. This helps to avoid inconsistencies in interpreting what was said. The wheel approach, which seems best with simple, repetitive tasks, protects privacy and allows the supervisor to be very personal in talks with employees. It tends to be slow and ponderous, however, when you are dealing with new or complex problems.

In the web network the supervisor acts more as a facilitator and verifier than a communicator. The system distributes ideas quickly and helps to get agreement for them and their application on a broad front. Drawbacks are that rumors often get out of control and progress toward goals and changes in methods may not be fed back to the supervisor until too late. But the advantages tend to outweigh the disadvantages. Furthermore, an attitude toward open communications invites employee participation in solving problems and helps to build a strong team spirit.

Experts advise, however, that if you have established a communications system that works, don't change it. Employees who have found the way through company channels don't particularly like to have the channels upset.

Should a supervisor use the company grapevine as a means of communication?

Listen to it. It's one way of getting an inkling of what's going on. But don't depend on it for receiving accurate information, and never use it to disseminate information.

The grapevine gets its most active use in the absence of good communications. If you don't tell employees about changes that will affect them, they'll make their own speculations—via the grapevine. As a result, the grapevine carries rumors and outright lies more often than it does the truth. Surveys show that while employees may receive a lot of their information from the rumor mill, they would much rather get it straight from a responsible party—the boss. In fact, you build good will by blocking rumors that come to your attention. So show employees you welcome the chance to tell them the truth about company matters that concern them.

Some authorities, however, believe that if you talk to enough employees and prove yourself to be a reliable source of company information, the grapevine will work for you. This is probably true, but leaking information to the work group deliberately through the grapevine isn't the same thing and will tend to isolate you from them in the long run.

Some people talk about three-dimensional communications. What are they referring to?

Communications should not be a one-way street. For a complex, modern organization to function smoothly, communications must move three ways. Not only must you furnish information downward to employees, but employees must communicate their ideas and feeling upward to you. Because staff and interdepartmental cooperation is so important, there must be horizontal, or sideways, flow of information, too. This up, down, and across process, illustrated in Figure 10-2, is called three-dimensional communications.

Supervisors can't have the answer to everything that is happening in the company, can they?

No. But it is your responsibility to keep informed on matters of importance. If you don't know what's going on, you can't tell others. This applies to many areas that are of real concern to employees like social security, pension plans, the way an incentive is applied, or a leave of absence policy. When an employee asks you something you don't know about, you'll lose face if every time you have to say that you'll find out from someone else. Soon employees will figure you're not in on the know and will go to someone else—like their shop steward—for information.

When you are caught unprepared, however, don't bluff. Don't say something like, "How should I know? Nobody tells me anything." Instead, strive to be in a position of confidence with higher management so that you can say, "I don't know the answer to that

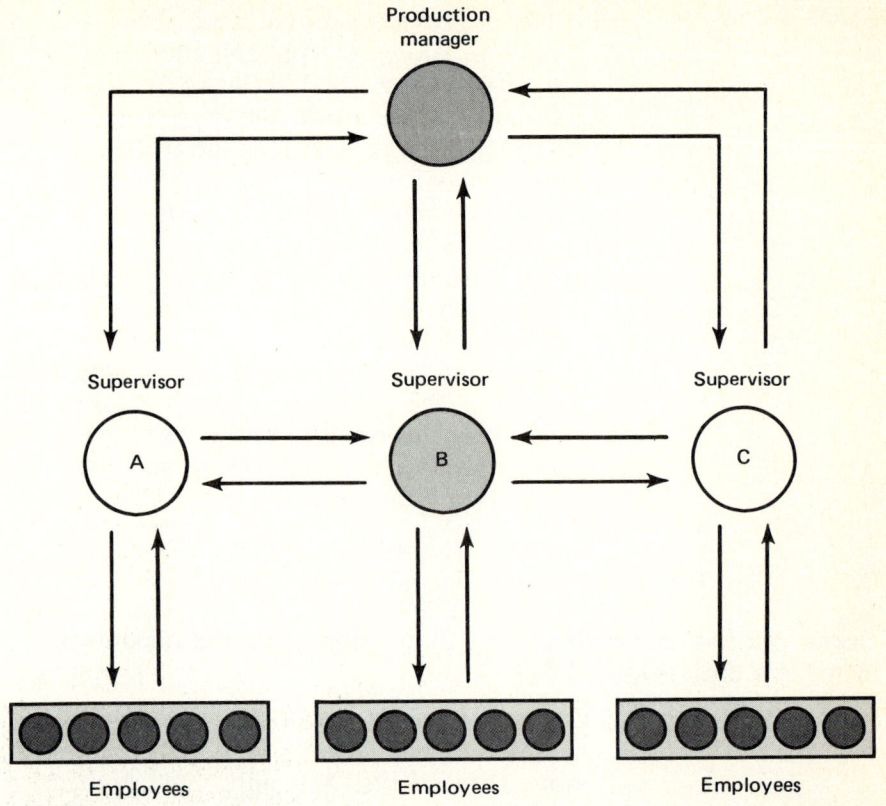

Figure 10-2. Three-Way Communications: Downward, Upward, and Horizontal.

one, but I'll certainly try to find out and let you know as soon as I can."

Do employees believe what you tell them?

Not all the time, any more than you believe everything you hear. But if you shoot as straight as you can in all your conversations with them, they'll look to you as a reliable source of information. It is just as important that employees have confidence in the purpose of your communications. They should never wonder, "Why did the supervisor say that?"

If the reason you complimented an employee yesterday was so that you could stick that person with a hard job today, there will be suspicion the next time you offer praise. If you would build confidence, avoid trickery, and don't blind yourself to the inferences an employee may draw from what you say. Better to be brutally frank about your purpose: "I'm having this heart-to-heart talk with you now because we're going to crack down on low producers," than to pussyfoot about your intentions: "I want to get your ideas as to what you can do to improve your output."

Is there danger in saying too much to employees?

Yes, although this isn't the most common hazard. Supervisors who run off at the mouth continually, who are indiscreet, or who violate confidences do overcommunicate or communicate in the wrong way. It's much better to speak only of what you are certain than to get a reputation for being a blabbermouth.

Some supervisors, too, in their eagerness to keep employees fully informed, try too hard. They find themselves spending too much time communicating information that employees don't need or want.

How can you decide what to talk to employees about?

Talk about those things employees want to know — those concerns that directly affect them or their work. Talk about work methods, company rules, pay practices, the values in employee benefits, opportunities for advancement, your appraisal of how well the employee is doing the job.

Talk also about department and company matters that are news — while they are news. Your influence as a communicator will be watered down if what workers hear from you is only a stale confirmation of something they have learned from another worker or from their union representative. Your employees should depend on you for reliable information.

Are there things you shouldn't talk about?

Yes. Politics and religion are dangerous subjects, as are other intensely personal matters like men versus women and dove versus hawk issues. Steer clear of them — even if an employee brings up the subject.

On the subject of business economics, which should be discussed with employees if they are to get a good perspective on their work environment, be careful to let employees form their own judgments and express their own opinions.

How much communication should you have upward with your boss?

Just as your success as a leader depends on how freely employees will talk to you and tell you what's bothering them, your superior, too, needs similar information from you. Make a point of keeping your boss informed on:

Matters for Which the Boss Is Held Accountable by His or Her Superior. This would include performance standards such as deliveries, output, quality. If you see that you're not going to be able to meet a schedule commitment, don't yield to the temptation of trying to conceal it. Instead, build confidence with your boss by saying, "I want to warn you that job number 1257 won't be finished on time. We ran into off-grade material and had to rework some of the units. I can guarantee that delivery will be made by next Tuesday, however."

Matters That May Cause Controversy. If you've had to take action that may be criticized by another department, your superior should know about it to be able to talk intelligently about it if interdepartment disagreements are brought up. Suppose the quality-control section has advised you to shut down a line because production is off-standard, but you've thought that you must keep it running in order to make a delivery date. Better get to your superior fast — with the facts.

Attitudes and Morale. Middle and top managers are continually frustrated because of their isolation from the work group. They need your advice and consultation as to how people in the company feel, generally or about a specific issue. Make a point of speaking to your boss on this subject regularly. Tell about good reactions as well as bad, but never play the role of stool pigeon or go to the boss with information gained in confidence.

Which kinds of communications are likely to speak louder than words?

Talking and writing are the communications media most frequently used, of course, but regardless of what you say, employees will be most affected by what you communicate to them by your actions. What you do — how you treat them — is the proof of your real intentions. When you go to bat for an employee who is in trouble, that's concrete communication of how well you value that person's contributions to your production team.

Even on simple matters, such as training an employee to do a new job, the act of showing how to do it (demonstration) is eloquent even when no words are spoken.

The best kinds of communications are generally those that combine the spoken or written words with action. Show-and-tell is a good formula for you to remember.

What is body language?

The way your body or facial expressions tip off to others what is really on your mind. These nonverbal signals are revealed by a frown, a nervous touching of your nose, the way you shrug your shoulders, or a gesture with your hands. Don't concern yourself with changing or controlling your body language, but do recognize that many employees will read it to tell how sincere you are.

How can you avoid having an employee take offense at what you say?

Each of us has a great big ego, and some of us are more sensitive than others. The tone of your voice, your choice of words, or your tactlessness may make an employee feel menaced or hurt. Whenever you put something in such a way that an individual may infer a threat to pay or status, personal feelings will get in the way of rational thinking.

Take this example of a statement to an employee: "You remember I told you they wouldn't approve that transfer you asked for. Well, they didn't."

Compare the tone of that statement with this way of saying the same thing: "I'm sorry, but the super won't approve that transfer right now. You recall, we thought it might have to be held up as long as we're short-handed here and they're full in the keypunch department. But you speak to me about it again in the spring, and we'll try it when we're slack in this department."

How can you be sure that people understand what you mean?

A very simple device is to ask an employee to repeat back to you what you have said. If the person can't do this, it's the signal for you to tell your story over again.

Another way is to get the employee to ask questions. What is queried will tip you off to areas of weak understanding. Once a conversation is established on a give-and-take basis, communications are always improved.

One reason for poor understanding is that words mean one thing in one relationship and something very different in other situations. Everyone has an idea, for instance, of what is meant by *faster, slower, harder, up a little, bear down*. To make the meaning clearer, be more specific. Say, "Go a little slower—down to 2,100 rpm." Or, "I want you to bear down a little harder on quality this month. Last month we had complaints about poor finishes on six of the cabinets you turned out. Will you be especially careful about the application of the 00 emery cloth in the future?" Said with this explanation, *bear down* has explicit meaning.

Should you keep personalities out of the picture?

Don't be impersonal or cold-blooded in your approach to people. In fact, you should tailor your presentation to best fit the person you're talking to. Some employees like rough language. Others feel it is a sign of disrespect. Some employees respond well to an informal request like, "When you've got time, will you sweep up the loading dock?" Others want you to be more formal, like, "Please get a broom and sweep the shipping platform. Start now and be sure it's done by three o'clock."

On the other hand, it's a good policy to deemphasize personalities in your communications. Think of communications as a process essential to the firm's organization. Try to avoid interference from personal factors that don't belong in the picture. Watch your tone so that it is objective and keeps emotional opinions out. There are helpful ways of rising above personalities. For instance:

"Now let's look at this from the point of view of company policy.

"This isn't between me and you. This is a question of whether office discipline will be maintained or not."

"Let's get back to the facts of the case."

"This is really a question of interpretation of the union contract. Let's see what they say in personnel."

It should go without saying, of course, that bias and prejudice should be held in check. You will arouse anger and resistance if you let your prejudices about sex, color, religion, handicaps, age, or national origin creep into your communications.

What will encourage employees to communicate with you?

Good faith, mutual confidence, appreciation for their ideas, and a friendly attitude are the foundations on which employees will build their trust and learn to talk to you. A more specific method is for you to develop the fine art of listening.

Real communication is two-way. In the long run people won't listen to you if you won't listen to them. But listening must be more than just a mechanical process. Many employees (in fact, most people) are poor communicators. This means that you have to be an extraordinary receiver to find out what workers may be trying to say. Here are a few suggestions that may improve your listening power.

Don't Assume Anything. Don't anticipate. Don't let an employee think that you know what is going to be said.

Don't Interrupt. Let the individual have a full say. The employee who is stopped may feel that there will never be an opportunity to unload the problem. If you don't have the time to hear the employee through just then, ask that the discussion stay within a time limit. Better still, make an appointment (for the same day, if at all possible) for a time when you can get the whole story.

Try to Understand the Need. Look for the real reason the employee wants your attention. Often this may be quite different from what appears to be the immediate purpose. For instance, the real reason for a request for a half-day off may be to test the employee's standing with you against another worker who has recently gotten a half-day off.

Don't React Too Quickly. We all tend to jump to conclusions. The employee may use a word that makes you see red, or may express the situation badly. Be patient in trying to make sure that you are both talking about the same thing. Above all, try to understand — not necessarily agree with — the other's viewpoint.

Can listening be overdone?

Listening should make up at least a third of your communications, but it shouldn't take the place of definite actions and answers on your part.

When an employee begins to ramble too far afield in discussions, return to the point with astute questioning. If an employee is clearly wrong on a point of fact, make that clear even if it means contradicting the individual. But watch your tone!

When conferences or group discussions tend to turn into purposeless rap sessions, it's time for you to set talk aside and take action.

Finally, when an employee comes to you with a problem, and its solution is clear to you, give a straightforward reply. It does help, if you have the time, to permit the employee to develop a solution. But when you have been approached because of your knowledge and experience, chances are a direct answer is wanted, not a session of hand holding.

Which kind of communications technique is the best?

For a supervisor nothing can beat face-to-face communications. With this method the common situation is shared with whomever you're talking to. You get a chance to see immediately where your timing, tone, or choice of words has misfired.

The biggest drawback to face-to-face communications is that it can be very time-consuming. You may feel at the end of some days that you've done nothing but talk. This can interefere with other work.

Because person-to-person communications, talking to one person at a time, is so time-consuming, you will want to consider some of the other effective ways for communicating to employees. There are many forms of communications and an almost infinite combination of them. Combinations are usually more effective than any particular technique used by itself. To aid in your choice of technique, think of employee communications in two ways—person-to-person or with groups of employees.

How can person-to-person communications be conducted effectively?

The maximum of "custom tailoring" for the individual is not only feasible but definitely in order. It becomes increasingly so as the relationship accumulates a common background. That's because an individual who is addressed singly, but like anyone else, is usually resentful in proportion to the degree of previously assumed familiarity.

Spoken. In spoken communications the immediate situation is shared, and the person addressed is aware of the conditions under which the message takes place. Therefore, haste, tone, mood, expression, gestures, or facial expression may seriously affect the way the person reacts.

1. *Informal Talks*. Still the most fundamental form of communications. They are suitable for day-to-day liaison, direction, exchange of information, conference, review, discipline, checking up, maintenance of effective personal relations. Even if brief, be sure they provide opportunity for two-way exchange.
   Face-to-face communications should always be used (in preference to the telephone) when the subject is of personal importance to either party.
2. *Planned Appointments*. Appropriate for regular review or liaison, recurring joint work sessions, and so forth. The parties should be adequately prepared to make such meetings complete and effective by being up to date, by providing adequate data and information, and by limiting interruptions to the fewest possible.
   Many supervisors have regular planned appointments with each major subordinate—daily (brief), weekly (longer), and monthly (extensive). It's valuable to note the gist of the discussion, for future reference.
3. *Telephone Calls*. For quick checkup or for imparting or receiving information, instruction, or data. These play a part in the personal relationship of the individuals concerned, which is sometimes overlooked. Your telephone personality sometimes contradicts your real self. An occasional personal note can alle-

viate the sometimes resented impersonality of routine calls, which may sound indifferent.

Written. All messages intended to be formal, official, or long-term or that affect several persons in a related way should be written. Be sure that you use only a written communication to amend any previous written communication. Oral changes will be forgotten or recalled indifferently.

4. *Interoffice Memos.* For recording informal inquiries or replies. They can be of value, too, if several people are to receive a message that is extensive, or when data are numerous or complex. The use of memos should not be overdone, or they will be ignored.
5. *Letters.* More individualized in effect than a memo and usually more formal. They are useful for official notices, formally recorded statements, or lengthy communications, even when the addressee is physically accessible. Letters are often valuable for communicating involved thoughts and ideas for future discussion and development, or as part of a continuing consideration of problems.
6. *Reports.* More impersonal than a letter and usually more formal. Reports are used to convey information associated with evaluation, analysis, or recommendations to superiors or colleagues. They are most effective when based on conferences, visits, inspections, surveys, research, or studies. Reports should carefully distinguish objectively determined facts from estimates, guesses, opinions, impressions, or generalizations.

How can you communicate most effectively with groups of employees?

Groups that are uniform in status, age, sex, compensation level, occupation, and length of service provide a valid basis for highly pointed messages. This approach helps avoid the gradually numbing stream of form letters, memos, and announcements that really have meaning for only a few of the recipients. Establishment of such groups on a continuing basis helps to build a sense of unity and group coherence that fosters favorable group reaction and group response, especially where there is routine personal contact among the members.

Spoken. Effective spoken communications with groups calls for special skills. Those that are effective in a committee of equals may be inadequate in a mass meeting. Ability to conduct a conference of your own staff doesn't mean you will have equal ability to participate effectively as a staff member in a conference called by your superior. Conflicts of interest need more tactful handling than a discussion of factual topics.

1. *Informal Staff Meeting*. This provides an opportunity for development of strong group cohesiveness and response. Properly supplemented with individual face-to-face contacts, it offers the outstanding means of coordinating activities and building mutual understanding. Hold such brief, informal staff meetings daily (if your schedule permits) — early in the morning, at the end of the day, or at lunch.
2. *Planned Conferences*. A relatively formal affair. The commonest error is for the person calling the conference to set up the agenda without previous consultation with those who will attend. It is usually desirable to check with most of the prospective participants in advance; provide time for preparing and assembling needed data, information, reports, and recommendations; allow opportunity for suggestions as to agenda and conduct of the meeting.

    Properly conducted, a planned conference can be extremely useful. If improperly managed, participation will be limited or misdirected. As a result it can be not only wasteful of time but even harmful in effect.
3. *Mass Meetings*. Of large numbers of employees or management. The meetings can be a valuable means of celebrating occasions, building morale, changing attitudes, meeting emergencies, introducing new policies or key personnel, or making special announcements. Mass meetings can also be used to clarify confused situations, resolve misunderstandings, or identify dissident elements. But such procedures require that the presiding individual has great skill and a forceful personality, and there is always the danger of interference or interruption.

Written. The effect of a single, isolated written communication to a group of employees is generally unpredictable. But a carefully planned program of written communications can develop a desirable cumulative effect.

4. *Bulletin Board Notices*. For lengthy or formal announcements. These notices can be used for a series of illustrated messages and are most effective when readership is constantly attracted by changes and by careful control of content, including prompt removal of out-of-date material. Most bulletin board announcements should be supplemented by other forms.
5. *Posters*. Small or large, at suitable locations, used in series, and changed frequently, they can do much to supplement your other communications media. The usual and most effective subjects are safety and good housekeeping.
6. *Exhibits and Displays*. Can serve a useful purpose when appropriate space is available and when they can be properly pre-

pared. Such preparation is often expensive. The commonest subjects are company products, advertising, promoting quality production, increasing safety, cutting waste and costs, and stimulating suggestions.

7. *Visual Aids.* Films, filmstrips, easel presentations, audio cassettes, and other special visual materials have great potential value but are only as good as the way they are used. Few are self-administering. A good film will be far more effective, for instance, if presented with a soundly planned introduction and follow-up. Much material that could be of considerable value will be relatively worthless if not presented appropriately. Careful, competent preparation, planning, and utilization procedures should be applied to all visual materials.

Review Questions

1. Why is communication needed in an organization in the first place?
2. Of the wheel and the web communications networks, which is more restricted and which is more open? What are some advantages and disadvantages of each?
3. Discuss the shortcomings of the grapevine.
3. How can the credibility gap be narrowed between a supervisor and the employees?
5. Should a supervisor who finds that the department cannot deliver an important order on schedule tell the boss about it immediately or wait until the order is finally shipped? Why?
6. Is it ever possible for a supervisor to overcommunicate? If so, is it harmful? How?
7. Why shouldn't a supervisor who is quick at getting the gist of an employee complaint cut off the conversation right away to give a reaction or a decision?
8. Discuss the pros and cons of a supervisor's holding a mass meeting with everybody in the department.

A Case in Point: The Case of the Changing Ledger Entries

Norma Brooks supervises 35 clerks in the collections department of a large California insurance company. Since the advent of computer postings to central accounts, the controller has on a number of occasions changed the prescribed methods for making ledger entries. While this has created difficulties for Norma, each time she has carefully instructed her employees in the new method. Nevertheless, the number of incorrect postings has risen. Lately, Norma's boss has made a practice of visiting the collections department to observe the entry operation. On several occasions the boss has told employees to make the entries differently from the way Norma had told them. As a result, there is an increasing state of confusion about how the entries should be made.

If you were Norma Brooks, what would you do? Five alternative approaches are listed below. Rank them in the order in which they appeal to you (1 most attractive, 5 least). You may add another approach in the space provided, if you wish. In any event be prepared to justify your rankings.

_____**A.** Post a notice advising employees that no changes in procedures should be made without your prior approval.

_____**B.** Informally advise employees to disregard any instructions they may get from your boss.

_____**C.** Ask your boss to meet with the employees in the collections department to explain the new procedures.

_____**D.** Request that your boss stay out of the department entirely.

_____**E.** Ask your boss to route all changes in instructions or corrections in procedure through you and not to communicate these directly to employees.

If you have another approach, write it here. _____
_____
_____

Action Summary Checklist		Action Needed Yes No	Date Completed
	1. Minimum of "noise" in your communications system: employees ready to listen, absence of conflicting instructions, employees and supervisors talking about the same thing.	____ ____	_____
	2. Expertise in, and reliance on, many methods rather than a single method of communications.	____ ____	_____
	3. Your department's communications network plugged into the company management information system.	____ ____	_____
	4. Choice of the kind of communications system—open (web) or restricted (wheel)—that best suits your operations.	____ ____	_____
	5. Knowledge of, but avoidance of, the grapevine as a method of supervisory communications; rumors spiked as soon as possible.	____ ____	_____

Action Summary Checklist (continued)

	Action Needed Yes No	Date Completed

6. Emphasis on the free flow of information up, down, and across your department. ____ ____ _____
7. Willingness to track down and retrieve job-related information for employees who request it. ____ ____ _____
8. Guard against overcommunicating and sensitive subjects. ____ ____ _____
9. Your boss kept regularly informed of accountable, controversial matters and the department's attitudes toward policy. ____ ____ _____
10. Personal actions that back up your words. ____ ____ _____
11. Sensitivity to employees' feelings with a minimum of emphasis on personalities and with avoidance of prejudices. ____ ____ _____
12. Willingness to listen without taking offense and with an emphasis on face-to-face communications. ____ ____ _____
13. Recognition that words mean different things to different people; dependence on hard facts rather than vague generalities. ____ ____ _____
14. Development of your person-to-person communications skills: spoken—informal talks, planned appointments, telephone calls; written—interoffice memos, letters, and reports. ____ ____ _____
15. Development of your group communications skills: spoken—informal staff meetings, planned conferences, mass meetings; written—bulletin board notices, posters, displays, and visual aids. ____ ____ _____

Chapter 11
Giving Orders and Instructions

Key Concepts

- Supervision implies the need to exercise authority—the need to direct and control the activities of subordinate employees. To discharge this responsibility, supervisors must regularly issue orders, instructions, directions, and, occasionally, commands.

- In a free society an employee's reaction to the exercise of authority tends to be highly individualistic. While one person responds readily to a preemptory order, another may cooperate only when a direction implies the prerogative to accept it or not. Accordingly, it is essential that successful supervisors understand and anticipate the response pattern of each employee who works for them.

- Issuance of orders is an act of communications. As such, orders are susceptible to the shortcomings and misfires that obscure, distort, or otherwise interfere with the exchange of information. Therefore, clarity, consistency, restatement, and rapport are essential to the order-giving process.

- Manner and tone as well as sensitivity and empathy provide a basis for the employee's understanding and acceptance of a supervisor's orders and instructions—even the most arbitrary commands. When employees can be helped to grasp the reason for, and the rationality of, the directions they are expected to follow, they are likely to accept the directions more readily and carry them out with great alacrity and enthusiasm.

- Effective order giving is based on effective communications; techniques like active listening can improve communications and thus help identify and overcome resistance and encourage cooperation. Following proved guidelines can increase a supervisor's chances for success in getting employees to understand and accept orders and instructions.

How can you get better results from the instructions and orders you issue?

By being sure your order is the right one for the particular situation at hand and by being specific about what the employee is to do and what kind of results you expect.

Your orders are even more effective when you use care in selecting the person most likely to carry them out well. You add power to your orders by being confident (not arrogant) and calm as you deliver them. Finally, your orders will stand the best chance of accomplishing what you intend if you make a practice of checking to be sure they are carried out at the time and in the manner you prescribe.

Should you repeat an order?

Yes, by all means. Repeat your instructions to be certain the employee understands them clearly. All of us are expert at misunderstanding. So give a worker an opportunity to ask questions if there seems to be doubt about what you want. In fact, it's a good practice to ask the employee to repeat your instructions back to you. In that way you can readily find out where the stumbling blocks might be.

When should you "request" an employee to do something?

As often as possible. It used to be thought that order giving was a one-way street, that all a supervisor had to say was, "I tell you. You do it." Such an attitude gets you nowhere. Today's employees want and deserve more consideration, and many of them have unions to back up this desire. In addition we now know lots more about employees' attitudes. For instance, psychologists who study employee behavior tell us that most workers will rate a boss high, and will cooperate more willingly as a result, if the boss gives orders pleasantly. We know, too, that employees like to feel they are offered some say in decisions that affect them and will work harder when they have had a chance to participate.

There's nothing wrong and much good in saying, "Will you try to get that machine cleaned up before quitting time?" or, "Won't you please make an effort to get to work on time Monday?"

Generally speaking, a request carries the same weight as a direct order. But it does impart a feeling that workers have some freedom of action, that they can question any part that bothers them. It's especially useful with thin-skinned employees who tend to see every boss as a dictator.

When should you "command" an employee to do something?

Although commands are dangerous, they may be necessary in emergencies. In case of accident or fire, for instance, your instructions should be direct, clear, and unequivocal to avoid conflicting actions.

Orders should be specific and firm, too, in operating situations that demand active leadership. It's desirable to be especially decisive, for instance, in directing a crew that requires rapid coordination on an unfamiliar job—like supervising workers who are lowering a 100-ton machine onto its foundations, or starting up a new and complex machine.

But in general, commands cause resentment. It's best to avoid them until you need them. If you use commands only occasionally, your employees will know that you're not being bossy for the sake of showing your authority. They will recognize that your change in approach is necessary and will snap to accordingly.

Is it your fault if an employee misses an order?

Not necessarily. In fact, the employee may be the one who goofed. This points up the wisdom of seeing order giving as a two-way street.

Look at it this way: An order is given only to get something done. You see a situation. You see what the situation calls for. Your job as an order giver is to make sure the person who is to do the job sees the situation the same way you do.

For example, say you're supervisor of the packaging department in a soap flake plant. You come by the discharge end of a packaging machine that fills and seals boxes of soap flakes. You test-weigh a box and find that it is overweight. From your experience you know that an adjustment of the filling mechanism will correct the situation. The only reason you will give an order is to help the package machine operator see the situation, and the action it calls for, as you do.

How would you give your order? "Wake up, Joe! Shut down your machine and get it fixed." That's not too bad, but it doesn't tell Joe what's wrong or recognize that Joe might know what to do without your telling him. This is better: "Joe, your machine's running overweight. Better shut down until I send the repairman up." Even better, if you have confidence in Joe, is just to hold up a box to get his attention. Then say, "Overweight!" Let Joe take over from there.

Try to look at your orders as solutions to action-demanding situations that both you and your employees must see in the same light if orders are to be carried out willingly and well.

What should you do when employees willfully refuse to do what you tell them?

The first piece of advice and the toughest to follow is: Don't fly off the handle. Count to 100 if subordination makes you want to blow your top. Then ask yourself whether the order was a fair one and whether you've chosen the proper person to follow it. Have you made yourself understood?

If you think you've done your part, next try to find out what the employee objects to. Ask for specifics: "Well, what is it that you object to? Why do you think it's unreasonable?" An employee who is willfully disobedient is probably looking for an excuse to blow off steam. It may be that if you listen for a couple of minutes, the resentment will pass. For that reason it's smart not to talk about your authority or threaten with discipline, not then, anyway.

But if an employee is stubborn and can't or won't be cooled off or have a change of mind about doing what you say, you're faced with a disciplinary problem. You still have alternative choices of what to do, so don't be quick about firing, penalizing, or suspending. You may find it wise not to insist—at that moment—that the order be carried out. Or you may want to modify the order so that it will be accepted. If you choose to do either of the latter, don't let the matter drop there.

Find an early opportunity to talk calmly, constructively, and privately. Don't permit the employee to think that you were soft or that there's no penalty. Let it be known that you will take disciplinary steps if the employee doesn't straighten up and fly right and that you've made a note about the incident in your records. (See Chapter 14 for more information on discipline.)

Your other choice is to take whatever disciplinary action your company permits—that same day, while the incident is fresh in everyone's mind. But this is a choice supervisors should avoid if possible. Punishment is a last resort only. That's why it's unwise to force a showdown—especially if other employees are watching or listening and especially if you might like to change your mind later.

When should you put an order in writing?

Whenever you change an order that was previously in writing, put the new order in writing, too. Or if you give an order that must be carried over into another shift, it's wise to jot it down in writing—on the bulletin board, in the department logbook, or as a note to be passed on to the employees concerned. This is much more reliable than word of mouth.

When instructions are complex and contain variations from normal in amounts and sequence, it's wise to write them down, too. On the other hand, don't depend too much on written orders. Not everyone follows written instructions easily. In fact, if you do write

CHAPTER 11: GIVING ORDERS AND INSTRUCTIONS

down instructions, look for an opportunity to review them orally with employees to see if they understand them. The written orders thus serve as a reference.

It is wise to let employees use their own judgment in following your instructions?

Sometimes it's a good idea just to suggest what you want. Then let the employees use their own discretion in carrying it out. This leaves it up to the employees whether or not anything will be done and how it will be done. For instance, "I wonder if there's anything you can do to get this job finished by quitting time." Or, "It looks as if our scrap record will be off this month. Is there something you can do to get it back on the beam?"

Such an implied order stimulates initiative and cooperation among more responsible workers. It's a form of delegation, and it helps develop your employees' judgment.

The suggestion approach is risky to try with inexperienced or unreliable people. You shouldn't use it when you have decided in advance exactly what you want done and how. After all, you can't expect your workers to be mind readers.

Should you let anyone else give instructions to your employees?

Unless you have expressly asked someone else to pass along orders to people who work directly under you (and this should be done only infrequently), it's best to see that you're the only one who gives orders to your employees. Otherwise, your employees will find themselves working for two bosses, and your status and effectiveness will be weakened.

You were hired to direct your employees. That's your responsibility. If someone else tries to take over this part of your job, it's up to you to hold on politely, but firmly, to your rights. If your boss makes a habit of bypassing you in issuing instructions to your employees, you should speak to your boss at once about it. Be tactful, of course, but be convincing that what the boss is doing works against department morale and efficiency; otherwise, you're in for trouble.

Employees are paid to work, aren't they? Why, then, should you handle them with kid gloves?

Because in the long run it's easier on the supervisor. Actually, giving orders pleasantly and thoughtfully isn't babying employees. It's just common sense to make it as easy as possible for them to say yes to what you ask them to do. It's an old adage that a willing worker does better work.

One reason old-fashioned supervisors had trouble with order giving (and consequently cost their companies lots of money by having to fire disobedient workers) was that they overlooked one and sometimes two of the three important ingredients of order giving. It may be obvious that you should tell workers what to do. But it's easy to forget that they may not know how to do it—that you must take time out to show or tell how to go about the job. The biggest error of all is not to tell them why.

Telling employees why something must be done gives them a reason for wanting to do it. There's a world of difference, for instance, between "Starting tomorrow I want you to show me personally each piece of off-quality raw material you charge for credit" and "The purchasing department wants a report on how well our new supplier is meeting specifications with our raw material. For a couple of weeks I'll have to furnish them with a detailed report. So will you set aside for me each piece of off-quality stock so that I may inspect it? I have to tell the purchasing department exactly what's wrong with it."

Should you give an order when you're angry?

If you can avoid it, don't give orders when you're uptight. There's always the possibility that you'll make a threat you can't, or won't want to, carry out.

You probably know of a case similar to this one: Ralph, the machine-shop supervisor, has just been reprimanded by his boss for the number of damaged hand tools charged to his department. As soon as the boss leaves, Ralph blows his stack to his employees. "Next one who turns in a damaged tool, no matter what the reason, you'll pay for it out of your own pocket." What happens? That afternoon Sylvia, who has been with the company 15 years and who is as conscientious as can be, accidentally ruins a micrometer. Who is on the spot? Nobody but Ralph!

How is your tone of voice important?

Remember the story of the cowboy who said, "When you call me that, smile." Employees feel the same way. They'll read your voice like a book to hear whether you're trying to throw your weight around, whether you mean what you say or are just talking through your hat. When you give an order that's going to be hard to carry out, smile to indicate that you know what you ask isn't easy; but let the tone of your voice show that you expect it to be done regardless.

Should you ask an employee to do anything you wouldn't do?

You don't have to do everything you ask others to do, but, in principle, you should show that you'd be willing to do it if you had to.

Giving orders is a test of your leadership courage. General Patton used to say that an army was like a piece of cooked spaghetti. You can't push it, you can only pull it. You might not have to lead an army, but you should always imply your willingness to stand up where the shots are being received.

If there's a dirty or unpleasant job, be sure you expose yourself to the same conditions your workers do. If they must work in the rain or cold, get out there with them. If they have to get in the muck under a machine, show that you're not above getting your hands dirty either.

Shouldn't each person be handled differently?

Yes, if you can find time. Some people like their bosses to be specific about what they want done. Others want only an opportunity to raise a question or make a suggestion. Still other people work best when given a free hand. To assign orders accordingly, you'll want to improve your ability to size up people. Then improve your leadership by tailoring each order to fit the individual.

Do you issue group orders differently?

Many people believe that orders given to groups of people are ineffective unless the group is permitted to discuss them and decide how the group can best carry them out. This isn't always practical or desirable, of course. But when you issue orders to groups, keep in mind that getting across to groups is many times harder than reaching one person. It's always better if you can find a suitable time and place to discuss the reasons behind the order and to get suggestions from the group as to how it might best be carried out.

One rule to follow in group instructions is to pin down who is to do what. If you don't, you're likely to find each person waiting for someone else to carry the ball.

How can active listening help gain acceptance for your orders?

A supervisor who actively listens to an employee's negative reaction to an order, for example, may hear the reason for that resistance. Usually, however, we tend to put our minds into neutral when others resist us. We engage in passive listening, hardly hearing what the other person says, and we are ready to attack again. Compare these two examples:

Passive listening

Employee: What does the scheduling office think I am, Rose—a miracle worker? There is no way this job can be finished today.

Supervisor: That's the order, whether you like it or not. Just make sure you've finished it by 5 p.m.

Employee: I'm already behind schedule because of the press breakdown this week. Doesn't anybody understand what kind of pressure that puts on me?

Supervisor: Look, I don't make up the schedules here. It's my job to see that they get carried out. We're all under pressure this week. So, like it or not, you've got to get hopping right away so that we meet the deadline.

Employee: I'll do it, but this is the last time you're going to treat me like dirt.

Active listening

Employee: What does the scheduling office think I am, Rose—a miracle worker? There is no way this job can be finished today.

Supervisor: Sounds like you're really angry about it, Joe.

Employee: You're darned right I am. I've been working all week to catch up after that press broke down. Now that I'm about on schedule, this lousy order comes in.

Supervisor: As if you didn't have enough to do already. Seems as if you're shoveling sand against the tide.

Employee: Yeah. It's all uphill around here. I can hardly catch a breath.

Supervisor: You feel like it's unfair to unload a rush job on you when you've been trying so hard to get back on schedule.

Employee: That's right. I'm willing to pull my share of the load, Rose, but it's discouraging to feel that you're being dumped on all the time.

Supervisor: You feel that we have been asking more than you can handle?

Employee: Not more than I can handle. I can get this job out today. But it sure puts me near my breaking point.

Supervisor: I understand how you feel. Actually, Joe, we haven't been picking on you. The whole department is in a bind this week. But I appreciate your taking on what seems like an unjustified overload.

The difference between the two examples is that the supervisor is actively listening in the second one. Joe is, in effect, saying that he is being misused. Rose is listening and responding to make it clear to Joe that she appreciates the feeling he is expressing. Active listening won't solve all order-giving problems, but it does provide a good base for acceptance. It helps to show that the supervisor is not just mechanically passing on instructions and that the supervisor views the employee as a human being with very personal feelings and problems.

What can a supervisor do to detect a hidden resistance?

Try to put yourself in the employee's shoes. When you are giving an order, it is only natural for you to see the need only from the top down. If you turn yourself around mentally, you may begin to see what the need is from the bottom up. One good way to get this turned-about feeling is to answer an employee's challenge with a response that reflects what the employee has said. For example:

Employee's challenge: Just who is eligible for those filing cabinets, anyway?
Supervisor's response: Do you feel that someone is trying to take over your authority for them?

Employee's challenge: Isn't it about time that younger, more able people get a shot at a promotion before the older guys do?
Supervisor's response: It seems to you that younger people should get a chance now.

Employee's challenge: How does the company think I'm going to turn out clean letters on this broken-down typewriter?
Supervisor's response: You really are fed up with this machine, aren't you?

Employee's challenge: Don't you think my work has gotten better over the last few months?
Supervisor's response: Sounds as if you feel that your work has picked up since last we talked about it.

Responses like this are not sweet talk. Their purpose is to keep open the flow of communications from the employee. Kept talking to a sympathetic ear, the employee may expose the real source of irritation. If so, the supervisor may be better able to shape the order or instruction to the employee's preference. At the very least, the supervisor may be able to take the sting out of the assignment.

Technically speaking, this approach provides empathy, which is defined as understanding of, not necessarily sympathy for, another's feelings. This, in turn, helps to establish rapport (harmony, closeness, and confidence) between supervisor and employee.

What can be done to avoid ambiguity in instructions?

Many words and phrases have a double, or at least an unclear, meaning. Here is a list of troublemakers. Avoid words or terms like these when handing out assignments. Instead, try to add clarifying details to make them more specific.

Quality Factors. Avoid words like *good, smooth, well-done,* or *clean.* Try instead: *fewer than three rejects per day; so smooth that* *a dust cloth won't catch on the surface; a steak without a trace of red in it; completely free of the grease that protected it when shipped.*

Quantity Factors. Avoid words like *large, small, heavy,* or *tight.* Try instead: *over ten inches; smaller than a ten-cent piece; over two ounces; as tight as a 20-psi wrench can make it.*

Time Factors. Avoid terms like *quickly, as soon as possible, in a few days.* Try instead: *25 per minute; within 24 hours; by Thursday at 2 p.m.*

Which particular guidelines may keep a supervisor out of trouble when directing, ordering, assigning, or instructing?

There are no assurances that employees won't get hung up about a particular assignment, but there are 11 guidelines that should minimize trouble:

1. Don't make it a struggle for power. If you approach too many order-giving situations in an I'll-show-you-who's-boss frame of mind, you'll soon be fighting the whole department. Try to focus your attention—and the worker's—on the goal that must be met. The idea to project is that the situation, not a whim of the supervisor, demands the order.
2. Avoid an offhand manner. If you want employees to take instructions seriously, deliver them that way. It's all right to have fun, but be firm about those matters that are important.
3. Watch out for your words. As you have seen, words can be unreliable messengers of your thoughts. Watch the tone of your voice, too. Few people like to feel that they are being taken for granted or pushed around. Most employees accept the fact that it is the supervisor's job to hand out orders and instructions. Their quarrel is more likely to be with the way these are made.
4. Don't assume that the worker understands. Give the employee a chance to ask questions and to raise objections. Have the employee confirm an understanding by repeating what you've said.
5. Be sure to get feedback right away. Give the employee who wants to complain about the assignment a chance to do so at the time. It's better to iron out resistance and misunderstanding before the job begins than afterward.
6. Don't give too many orders. This is an area where a communications overload will be self-defeating. Be selective in issuing instructions. Keep them brief and to the point. Wait until an employee has finished one job before asking that another be started.
7. Provide just enough detail. Some jobs require more information than less complex ones. Some workers need more detailed instruction than others. Think about the information needs of the

person you're speaking to. For an old hand there's nothing more tiresome than having to listen to familiar details.

8. Watch out for conflicting instructions. Check to make sure that you're not telling your employees one thing while supervisors in adjoining departments are telling their people another.
9. Don't choose only the willing worker. Some people are naturally cooperative. Others make it difficult for you to ask them to do anything. Be sure that you don't overwork the willing person. Make sure the hard-to-handle employees get their share of the rough jobs, too.
10. Try not to pick on anyone. It is a temptation to punish a person by handing out an unpleasant assignment. Resist this temptation if you can. Employees have the right to expect the work to be distributed fairly. So if you have a grudge against an employee, don't use a disagreeable job assignment to get even.
11. Above all, don't play the big shot. New supervisors are sometimes guilty of flaunting their authority. Older supervisors are more confident. They know that you don't have to crack the whip to gain employees' cooperation and respect.

Review Questions

1. When should a supervisor be expected to repeat an order?
2. Under what circumstances might a supervisor command an employee to carry out an order?
3. Contrast a request that something be done and a suggestion that it might be done.
4. When you give orders, why is it important to try to get the employee to understand the situation in the same way you do?
5. Suggest at least two ways a supervisor can call an employee's attention to a misread order.
6. In an instance of an employee's apparent willful disobedience, what recourses are open to the supervisor?
7. What are some disadvantages of passing orders through other people?
8. Why should supervisors try to develop the ability to listen actively when giving orders?

A Case in Point: The Case of the Refused Overtime

One day in June a machine-shop supervisor asked a number of employees in the department to work a few hours overtime. All agreed to stay except Tony.

"You'll have to get someone else," said Tony. "I'm painting my house after work these days. Besides, I don't need the overtime money."

"That's got nothing to do with it," replied the supervisor. "We have an order to get out tonight. And whether you like it or not, you'll have to stay and help."

"Nothing doing," said Tony, starting to get angry. "My personal time is my own. I work 40 hours every week here. If you want me to work overtime, you'll have to let me know in advance so I can plan for it."

"This is an emergency that couldn't have been foreseen," said the supervisor. "You'll work tonight or regret it."

"You can't fire me for not working overtime. The union had a grievance on this and cleared it up last year. See you tomorrow." With that Tony put on his jacket and punched out.

If you were the machine-shop supervisor, what would you do? Five alternative approaches are listed below. Rank them in the order in which they appeal to you (1 most attractive, 5 least). You may add another approach in the space provided, if you wish. In any event, be prepared to justify your ranking.

_____**A.** Forget about this incident and try to avoid such a situation in the future.

_____**B.** Call Tony back to find out if there isn't some way he can rearrange his off-duty work to handle tonight's overtime.

_____**C.** Tomorrow tell Tony that he will have to work his share of overtime, but that you will try to let him know at least a day in advance.

_____**D.** Suspend Tony for refusing suitable work.

_____**E.** Take Tony off the overtime list so that he does not get a chance to work overtime in the future, whether he wants it or not.

If you have another approach, write it here. _____
_____
_____
_____

Action Summary Checklist		Action Needed Yes No	Date Completed
	1. Regular and candid assessment of whether your orders and instructions are getting through to employees and being carried out effectively.	___ ___	_____
	2. Willinginess to repeat an instruction to make sure that it is clearly understood.	___ ___	_____
	3. Immediate search for feedback from an employee to assure that there has been no misunderstanding about required details.	___ ___	_____

Action Summary Checklist (continued)

	Action Needed Yes No	Date Completed

4. Care in the choice of words so as to make instructions clearer, especially in terms of their quality, quantity, and time factors. ____ ____ _____
5. Use of the request approach as often as possible. ____ ____ _____
6. Avoidance of any semblance of a power struggle when issuing orders; use of the situation as the basis for the order that is issued. ____ ____ _____
7. Commands reserved for emergencies or for situations where a high degree of immediate coordination is needed. ____ ____ _____
8. Selective use of the suggestion approach, reserving it for employees who have shown that they respond well to it. ____ ____ _____
9. Selective use of written orders and instructions, mainly to amend those already in writing or where the work is especially complex and varies from normal in terms of sequence, timing, or quantities or quality required. ____ ____ _____
10. Curb on your anger and concern for your tone of voice. ____ ____ _____
11. Regular demonstration of your willingness to share unpleasant working conditions with your employees. ____ ____ _____
12. Precision in group orders to make sure that all concerned know who is to do what. ____ ____ _____
13. Development of your skill as an active listener, using your responses to establish empathy and rapport. ____ ____ _____
14. Rein on any compulsion you may have to give too many orders or to give more details than the job or the individual really needs. ____ ____ _____
15. Fairness in making assignments, with an objective of spreading the unpleasant as well as the attractive assignments equitably among willing and unwilling workers. ____ ____ _____

Self-Check for Part 3

Test your comprehension of material in Chapters 7, 8, 9, 10, and 11. Correct answers are in the Appendix.

True-False Indicate whether each of the following statements is true or false by writing *T* or *F* in the answer column.

1. A supervisor should develop a uniform way of dealing with people so that he or she is certain to treat everybody exactly alike.   1. _____
2. A supervisor should use caution in drawing conclusions.   2. _____
3. Because two employees come from the same neighborhood, you can expect them to have the same reactions to supervision.   3. _____
4. Some people do strange things under stress because they know they can get away with this kind of behavior.   4. _____
5. Above all else, a supervisor should see that the work crew is a happy one.   5. _____
6. Good human relations are built on mutual respect between employee and supervisor.   6. _____
7. Every employee who has ever known poverty will always place the highest priority on how much money can be made.   7. _____
8. Herzberg says that a feature like a good company insurance plan is not a positive motivator, but can only create dissatisfaction when it is lacking.   8. _____
9. As a general rule, a supervisor should concentrate on formal work groups and need have little concern for informal groups.   9. _____
10. Supervisors might as well accept the fact that individual and group goals and interests will always conflict with organization goals.   10. _____
11. Loyalty to a work group can make employees resist the direction of a supervisor.   11. _____
12. A supervisor who is aware of the feelings of others is more likely to anticipate their behavior in a particular set of circumstances.   12. _____

13. A supervisor who is sensitive to what's going on among the people in the department recognizes that a group as a whole exerts considerable influence on the attitudes and performance in the department. 13. _____
14. If the goals of one person or group interfere with the goals of another person or group, conflict is almost sure to occur. 14. _____
15. An employee's behavior may be a visible demonstration of a hidden attitude. 15. _____
16. A supervisor should use the grapevine mainly as a means of dispersing information rather than receiving it. 16. _____
17. The greatest advantage of a wheel communications network is that it distributes ideas very quickly. 17. _____
18. Noise is any extraneous distraction that interferes with communications. 18. _____
19. A supervisor who serves mainly to facilitate and verify information flow probably functions in an open (or web) communications network. 19. _____
20. A good supervisor can often help to improve output in his or her section just by listening to the employees. 20. _____
21. Orders should never be repeated because this will cause resentment and resistance. 21. _____
22. An important key to giving group orders is to make it especially clear who is to do what. 22. _____
23. Because emotions play so great a role in supervisor-employee relations, it doesn't take much to distort what appears to be a reasonable request. 23. _____
24. Understanding the reason for what sounds like a difficult assignment may be all that is needed for an employee to accept it. 24. _____
25. A request is the most autocratic way to issue an order; a command is probably the most democratic way to approach it. 25. _____

Multiple Choice Choose the response that best completes each statement below. Write the letter of the response in the space provided.

26. Which of these supervisors is least likely to encounter excessive conflict? 26. _____
    a. One who is unpredictable and can keep employees off balance.
    b. One who tells employees what to do and doesn't take any back talk.
    c. One who gives up all responsibility to the group.
    d. One who encourages employees to talk to the supervisor about their gripes.

27. The general goal of a supervisor in dealing with   27. _____
    conflicts is to:
    a. See that conflicts never occur.
    b. Resolve them in such a way that work objectives can be met.
    c. Use any means necessary to avoid confrontations.
    d. Get the people involved in the conflict to shut up and get back to work.
28. The main thing wrong with hidden agendas is that   28. _____
    they:
    a. Interfere with a group's progress toward meeting mutual goals.
    b. Allow individuals to satisfy personal needs in group situations.
    c. Make group meetings too orderly and not creative enough.
    d. Are always based on untrue beliefs.
29. Management can improve attitudes among employees by: 29. _____
    a. Giving occasional pep talks.
    b. Setting examples of good attitudes themselves.
    c. Tightening discipline.
    d. Weeding out malcontents.
30. A supervisor with an authoritarian, parental point   30. _____
    of view would be likely to feel:
    a. I'm not okay; you're not okay.
    b. I'm not okay; you're okay.
    c. I'm okay; you're not okay.
    d. I'm okay; you're okay.

PART 4
HANDLING SENSITIVE PROBLEMS

Some interpersonal relationships at the supervisory level are undeniably difficult, if not downright unpleasant. Supervisors face their most challenging tasks as they handle problems of poorly adjusted employees, try to adjust to complaints and grievances, and mete out discipline.

Chapter 12 helps supervisors to become more keenly aware of ways to counsel employees whose performance or attendance is adversely affected by mental illness, drugs, or alcohol.

Chapter 13 encourages supervisors to develop a sensitivity to employee complaints and grievances and outlines methods for handling grievances effectively.

Chapter 14 deals with the need to think of discipline in a positive as well as a negative fashion and suggests ways for firmly administering it.

Chapter 12
Counseling Problem People

Key Concepts

- Problem employees are those people who, for one reason or another, have not found a way to adjust satisfactorily to the hardships of life or work. Their failure to cope causes them to behave unproductively or erratically on the job and to interrupt regularly the harmony of the work group.

- Problem employees can be recognized by such disharmonious conduct as sudden changes in behavior, preoccupation, irritability, increased accidents or absences, unusual fatigue, irrational anger or hostility, heavy drinking, or symptoms of drug abuse.

- Constructive counseling by supervisors can help many problem employees to improve or control their behavior, provided that the degree of their maladjustment is slight and the underlying causes are not intense.

- Counseling requires that supervisors themselves are well adjusted; that they are willing to listen understandingly, even to hostility directed toward them; that they permit the employee to dominate the interview; and that they refrain from offering judgments or advice.

- It is absolutely critical, morally as well as medically, that supervisors realize the limits of their ability to counsel and the incapacity of many problem employees to accept or respond to nonprofessional counseling. In these instances (and they are frequent), supervisors should confine their efforts either to suggesting professional counsel or to referring the employee to the company personnel office.

Who are the problem employees?

The chronic absentee, the rule breaker, the boss hater, the psychosomatic, the malingerer, the person who's lost self-confidence, the heavy drinker, the alcoholic, the pill popper, the troublemaker, and, yes, even the work-obsessed.

Why worry so much about them?

Simply because there are so many of them. Authoritative estimates place the number of potential mentally disturbed employees at one out of every four or five American workers.

There are many sociological and humanitarian reasons for being concerned about problem workers. One big reason is that a problem employee is also probably a problem husband, son, daughter, or wife. But industry's concern, admittedly, is primarily one of economics. Problem employees are expensive to have on the payroll. They are characterized by excessive tardiness and absences. They are difficult to supervise, and they have a tendency to upset the morale of the work group. Consequently, a supervisor should worry about (1) hiring problem employees in the first place, (2) handling them on the job so that they reach maximum productivity with the least disruption of the company's overall performance, and (3) determining whether problem employees have become so seriously maladjusted that they need professional attention.

How can you recognize an employee with an emotional problem?

There are problem employees, and then there are employees who are really problems. The most serious problem employees are those who are emotionally disturbed, and it is very difficult to tell when an employee has crossed over the line into the more serious category. Generally speaking, the symptoms of employees with emotional problems are similar. These people tend to run away from reality. They do this by going on sick leave or by too frequent visits to the dispensary; they believe that their supervisors are against them and blame their failures on other people and other things rather than accept any blame themselves.

Many problem employees fall into these categories: They are perpetually dissatisfied, are given to baseless worries, tire easily, are suspicious, are sure that superiors withhold promotions, and believe their associates gossip maliciously about them. Some are characterized by drinking sprees, are given to drug abuse, are insubordinate, or have ungovernable tempers.

Among themselves problem employees differ widely, just as normal people do; but within the framework of their symptoms, they are surprisingly alike in their reactions.

Are emotionally disturbed employees insane?

Most emotionally disturbed employees definitely are not insane. In fact, a psychological consultant for Eastman Kodak Company, Ralph Collins, said, "One out of four workers is subject to emotional upsets that visibly disturb his or her work." Such employees' behavior under certain kinds of stress is not normal. When goaded by fear (such as the threat of a bill collector) or by anger (because of being refused a day off), they may act in a way that you would describe as "crazy." But they are not (except for a very few) insane or even abnormal.

What about psychotic and neurotic employees?

Both terms sound pretty ominous, but only the employee with a *psychosis* is seriously ill. The most common type of psychosis is schizophrenia, or split personality. Schizophrenics live partly in a world of imagination. Especially when the world seems threatening to them, they withdraw. They may be able to adjust to life and even have a successful career. But when they lose their grip, their problem is beyond the scope of a lay person.

On the other hand, most people are *neurotic* to a degree. People who have exaggerated fears, who feel the need to prove themselves, or who are irritable, hostile, opinionated, timid, or aggressive (which somewhere along the line describes most of us) have the seeds of neurosis in them. It's when this condition becomes exaggerated that a neurotic employee becomes a problem to associates and to the supervisor.

Here are examples of neurotic employees: the lift-truck operator who boasts about drinking and sexual prowess; the supervisor who gets pleasure from reprimanding an employee in front of others; the secretary who visits the nurse every other day with some minor ailment; the punch press operator who meticulously arranges the workplace in the same manner every day and who can't begin the job unless everything is exactly right.

What makes problem people problems?

The key lies in the word *adjustment*. Most problems of neurotic employees are trivial, and the employees can adjust to them readily. But for months or years they may keep their disturbed feelings hidden, even from themselves, and then be stricken by fear that is so great they can't control it. They may then do something that can't be explained, even to themselves. They have lost, perhaps temporarily, the ability to adjust.

What sort of management action can put pressure on employees with emotional problems?

All human problems are the result of cause and effect. A supervisor does something and an employee can't adjust. The result is a human explosion. Typical of some managers who unthinkingly put pressure on workers are:

The supervisor who thinks it's smart psychology to set production and quality goals just a little higher than an employee can reach. What could be more frustrating?

The supervisor who thinks it's poor psychology to praise an employee for doing a good job. Is there anything so damaging to a person's morale than to do something well and have it taken for granted?

The supervisor and management who think that employee relations are better whenever the threat of a layoff hangs over employees' heads.

What are the signs of a worried worker—the employee who is about to become a problem?

Until now we've been discussing the general symptoms of problem employees. You'll be more interested in pinning down the specific kinds of behavior that make employees a problem in your company. You'll then be able to know what to do to aid them. Some specific signs of a worried worker are:

Sudden Change of Behavior. Pete used to whistle on the job. He hasn't lately. Wonder what's wrong?

Preoccupation. Judy doesn't hear you when you speak to her. She seems off in a fog. When you do get her attention, she says she must have been daydreaming. Is something serious bothering her?

Irritability. Albert is as cross as a bear these days. Even his old buddies are steering clear of him. He didn't used to be that way.

Increased Accidents. Bob knocked his knuckles on the job again today. This is unusual. Until a couple of months ago, he hadn't had even a scratch in five years.

More Absences. Sara is getting to be a headache. She wasn't in this morning again. She never was extra dependable, but now we'll have to do something to get her back on the ball.

Increased Fatigue. Mary seems to live a clean life and keep good hours, but she complains about being tired all the time. Is it something physical, or is she worried about something?

Too Much Drinking. Ralph was so jittery at his desk this afternoon, I felt sorry for him. He had a breath that would knock you over. I know he used to like going on the town, but this is different.

What can you do about problem workers?

Let's make this clear: We are not talking here about psychotic persons or the ones with serious neurotic disorders. We'll talk about them later.

You can help problem employees toward better adjustment only after you have reassured them that you are trying to help them keep their jobs — not looking for an excuse to get rid of them. No approach does more harm with persons who have problems than the better-get-yourself-straightened-out-or-you-will-lose-your-job attitude on a supervisor's part. You have to believe, and make them believe, that your intentions are good, that you want to help them. Then, you must give them every opportunity to help themselves. This approach is called *counseling*.

How do you counsel an employee?

The researchers in this field suggest that a supervisor can best counsel an employee if these five rules are followed for each interview:

1. Listen patiently to what the employee has to say before making any comment of your own.
2. Refrain from criticizing or offering hasty advice on the employee's problem.
3. Never argue with an employee while you are counseling.
4. Give your undivided attention while the employee is talking.
5. Look beyond the mere words of what the employee says; listen to determine if the person is trying to tell you something deeper than what appears on the surface.

What results should you expect from counseling?

Recognize why you are counseling an employee, and don't look for immediate results. Never mix the counseling interview with some other action you may want to take, such as discipline.

Suppose Tom has been late for the fourth time this month. The company rules say he must be suspended for three days. When talking to Tom about his penalty, try to keep the conversation impersonal. Your purpose at that point is to show him the connection between what he's done and what is happening to him.

In the long run you may wish to rehabilitate Tom because he's potentially a good worker. This calls for a counseling interview. It's better to hold the interview with Tom at a separate time. (Of course. it would have been better to hold the interview before Tom had to be disciplined.)

A counseling interview is aimed at helping employees to unburden themselves. Whether or not the conversation is related to the problem they create for you at work is not important. The payoff comes as they get confidence in you, and consequently don't vent their resistance and frustrations on the job. Experience seems to show that this will happen if you are patient. It won't work with every problem employee, of course, but it will with most of them.

How do you start a counseling session?

Find a reasonably quiet place where you're sure you won't be interrupted and won't be overheard. Try to put the employee at ease. Don't jump into a cross-examination. Saying absolutely nothing is better than that. If Ruth has become a problem because of spotty work, you can lead into the discussion by saying something like this: "Ruth, have you noticed the increase in the orders we're getting on the new model? This is going to mean a lot of work for the company for a long while ahead. I guess it has meant some changes, too. How is it affecting your operations? What sort of problems has it created?"

In this case, you are trying to give Ruth an opportunity to talk about something specific and mechanical. If you listen to her ideas, she may begin to loosen up and talk about her emotional problems or her worries.

Another approach is simply to talk to Ruth casually about things she would be interested in that have no connection with her work. Then let her lead the conversation to the subject that is uppermost in her mind. This "hang loose" approach, which lets the employee set the course of the interview, is called *nondirective counseling*.

How many counseling interviews should you have with a problem employee? How long should a counseling interview last?

These are difficult questions for clear-cut answers. For a less serious case, one interview might clear the air for a long time. For employees whose emotional problems are more serious, it may take five or ten 15- to 30-minute conversations just to gain confidence. For still other employees, the counseling will have to become a regular part of your supervisory chores with them.

CHAPTER 12: COUNSELING PROBLEM PEOPLE

You can readily see that counseling can be time-consuming. That's why it's so important to spot worried workers early and take corrective action while you can help them, with minimum drag on your time.

As to how long an interview should last—you can't accomplish much in 15 minutes, but if that's all you can spare, it's a lot better than nothing. At the very least, it shows the employee you're interested in the problem. Ideally, an interview should last between three-quarters of an hour and an hour.

How can you best handle these touchy problems objectively?

Make no mistake: Handling an employee who has become a problem isn't easy. Sometimes it can become downright unpleasant, and it's only natural to want to evade this responsibility. But the solace you can extract from it is that the sooner you face up to this key supervisory responsibility, the sooner the problems get solved. To be objective, you must:

Recognize that this is your job and you can't run away from it.

Look at your task as a fact-finding one, just as in handling grievances.

Control your own emotions and opinions while dealing with the employee.

Be absolutely sold on the value of listening rather than preaching.

Finally, as a word of caution: Be aware of your own limits in handling these situations.

How can you recognize when an employee needs emotional first aid?

Dr. Harry Levinson, a nationally recognized authority and founder of the Levinson Institute, recommends the following basic steps for you to take in administering emotional first aid (Figure 12-1):

1. Recognize the emotional disturbance.
2. Relieve acute distress by listening (counseling).
3. Refer cases beyond your limits to professional help.

To recognize the employee who needs counseling help, says Dr. Levinson, look for three major signs:

Extremes. The ordinarily shy person goes even deeper into a shell. The hail-fellow-well-met steps up social activities to a fever pitch.

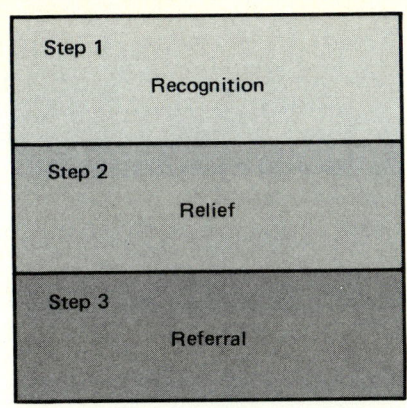

Figure 12-1. Levinson's three-phase guideline for supervisors to use in counseling problem employees.

Anxiety. If withdrawal or activity brings no relief, the employee may become panicky or jittery, show extreme tension, flush in the face, or perspire heavily.

Breakdown. If still unable to cope with the anxiety, the problem employee may break down altogether and be unable to control thoughts, feelings, or actions. Thinking becomes irrational. The person doesn't make sense to others. Emotions may become irrational. The tidy person may become slovenly, the quiet person noisy.

How can you provide relief for the emotionally troubled employee?

Dr. Levinson suggests you may help simply by letting the emotionally disturbed employee know how much the current distress is affecting the job—and how much of this the company will tolerate. Above all, a person under strain may add to it materially with fears of what the company might do if and when it discovers the condition. If you can offer some rule of thumb ("We appreciate the fact that you have something bothering you, and we're willing to go along with your present performance for a couple of weeks or so; but if it doesn't improve after that, we'll have to find a solution"), even if it's not entirely sympathetic, you at least provide something concrete to guide the employee's actions.

If the employee voluntarily brings the problem to you, you can help most by listening, advises Dr. Levinson. This is more difficult than it appears, he cautions. Listening must mean truly nonevaluative listening—no interruptions, advice, prescriptions, solutions, pontifications, or preaching.

When should you call for professional help?

Dr. Levinson offers this rule: *If after two listening sessions you seem to be making little headway in establishing confidence, you should report the case (in confidence, of course) to the company nurse or the company physician.*

Dr. Levinson also advises that your approach in referral should be that of opening another door for additional help. Don't ever suggest by action or word that the employee is mentally unsound, hopeless, or unworthy of attention.

Is an accident-prone employee likely to be emotionally disturbed?

Dr. Gerald Gordon, of Du Pont, which has one of the best safety records of any company in the world, had this to say:

> Our studies have revealed a small group of individuals around whom occupational injuries seem to cluster in disproportionate numbers. Obviously there is something more than hard luck plaguing a man whose career shows a long series of injuries. What's back of his trouble? The answer is that the accident maker is suffering from a form of mental illness so widespread that it may be found to some degree in most of us. . . . It is the failure of the employee as a whole person that is the core of his problem. He tends to evade the rules, both of working and of living. . . . In most cases the potential accident victim has a long service record and is well trained for his job. But all too often he's a victim of his own bottled-up emotions, which he turns against himself.

What can a supervisor do about an accident-prone employee?

Du Pont's Dr. Gordon advises that so-called accident-prone employees can be helped fairly easily if they are discovered early enough and something is done to help them:

> A basic approach involves requiring employees to follow safety rules and develop sound work habits. In my opinion, the fact that a worker violates a safety rule is more important than why he violates it. Pampering the emotionally disturbed individual only serves to increase his demands and, at the same time, aggravates the severity of his illness. If a supervisor openly and honestly exercises his authority to obtain good performance, he is helping both the employee and the company for which they both work. On the other hand, a supervisor who evades responsibility for the safety of his men becomes mentally ill himself and spreads this illness to others.

Absentees are a special kind of problem. How lenient should you be with them?

It depends on the reasons for absence. Professor P. J. Taylor of London University, who was formerly medical director of Shell (UK) Ltd., observed that 60 percent of all absences are due to serious or chronic illness and 20 percent to acute, short-term illnesses like the flu; 10 percent feel unwell because of a minor illness like a cold and they do or don't report to work according to their attitude about their jobs; and the final 10 percent are completely well but feign illness to enjoy a day off.

It is the group of absentees who make up the bottom 20 percent who are suspect. Industrial psychologists call their virus "voluntary absence" or, more ominously, "motivation morbidity." In many employees this is deeply rooted. The Puritan ethic of work does not apply to them. There is an inevitable conflict between the desire for more leisure and more work. This tug is especially evident among the younger workers.

Many authorities, however, still contend that an employee who is chronically absent from work is mentally ill. They reason that the reality of work must be so unbearable to these emotionally disturbed employees that they literally escape from reality by staying away from work. Regardless of the reason, you can help reduce absenteeism by:

Firming up your rules about it.
Being consistent in applying penalties.
Trying to find out why an employee is often absent.

The last method requires the counseling technique. Widespread absenteeism is cured by getting one person to come to work, then another, and so on. Consequently it's important that each individual case be followed up promptly. In your discussion of the problem with employees, be sure to permit them to explain their reactions to the job itself, the people they work with, the working conditions, their tools and equipment, the kind of training they receive. You thus avoid their feeling that you are placing all the blame on them. If they are specific in their reactions, you then have specific complaints rather than vague dissatisfactions to deal with.

Don't overlook, however, the power of job satisfaction in luring absence-prone workers back to the job. Surprisingly, however, working conditions seem to have little effect. In company after company, attendance figures show little variation between the dirty, unpleasant tasks and those that are clean and well lighted. Even most incentive schemes to reduce absences are relatively ineffective. Closeness of the work team, its homogeneity, and the state of its morale seem to have the greatest effect.

How effective is counseling in reducing absenteeism?

Success depends on the root cause of individual absences. See how the patterns and the motivations differ.

Chronic Absentees. People who have little capacity for pressure, either on the job or off, may be prime candidates for counseling. But first, they must be made fully aware of the consequences of poor attendance. Theirs is a habit, usually of long standing, and correction requires pressure to attend, as well as handholding.

Vacationing Absentees. People who work only so long as they need the cash, and who then treat themselves to a day or two off, are difficult cases. These employees are often extremely capable on the job, but they feel no deep responsibility for it. Vacationers make a conscious choice to be absent and are rarely helped by counseling.

Directionless Absentees. Younger employees who have as yet found no real purpose in work may simply follow the lead of the vacationer, who appears to lead a footloose, exciting life. A Dutch-uncle talk with the directionless absentee may be more effective than counseling.

Aggressive Absentees. Persons who willfully stay away from work, in the hope that their absence will cause an inconvenience for you, are probably emotionally disturbed. This kind of behavior, however, requires professional counseling to correct — not the kind of counseling the ordinary supervisor can provide.

Moonlighters. Persons who hold more than one job are often either too tired to come to work or are faced with conflicting schedules. Straight talk, rather than counseling, is prescribed. When attendance is affected, the moonlighter must be forced to make a choice between jobs.

Occasional Absentees. Persons who seem to have slightly more absences than the rest of your staff are probably prime candidates for counseling. Their absences are legitimate, and their illnesses are real. Their problems are often temporarily insurmountable. These people deserve a mixture of sympathy, understanding, and sometimes outright advice.

In summary, you can probably help people who are absent for the following reasons: (1) Getting to work is a problem, real or imagined. (2) Off-the-job pressures are so strong that they weaken the employee's resolve to get to work. (3) The employee is imitative and easily led or misled. (4) The work appears boring, disagreeable, or unattractive. (5) Working relationships are unpleasant. (6) There are in fact off-the-job problems—child care, serious illness, court appearances—that need immediate attention. (7) Absence or lateness has become a habit.

You will have difficulty helping people who are absent for these reasons: (1) Work or the pay associated with it hold no strong attraction. (2) Off-the-job pleasures have a greater appeal than work. (3) The employee is willfully absent in order to disrupt or inconvenience the organization.

What can you do for alcoholic employees?

Whatever you attempt, proceed slowly and cautiously. Not all heavy drinkers are alcoholics, and the more they drink, the less likely they are to admit to anyone (even themselves) that their ability to handle liquor is out of control.

An alcoholic employee is really just another kind of problem employee—only the case is an aggravated one and may need the help of a professional (see later question). Nevertheless, many alcoholic workers have rescued themselves with the aid of Alcoholics Anonymous, an association of ex-alcoholics who, because they don't preach and because they emphasize the individual's need to face weaknesses, have perfected the art of listening without being either sympathetic or critical.

Your best bet, however, is to recognize an alcoholic in the early stages. Then use the same techniques to gain the person's confidence that you would with any other problem employee. Your objective is to provide security at work and to help with talking out problems. If these employees can be helped to recognize that excessive drinking is a problem they are not handling, then you can refer them to the company doctor or nurse, who in turn may be able to persuade them to look into Alcoholics Anonymous or to visit a psychiatrist or a special clinic for alcoholics.

To guide you in recognizing alcoholic employees, Prof. Harrison M. Trice of Cornell University advises that you look first to the employee's absence record. A sharp rise in overall rate of absences almost always accompanies the development of drinking problems, he says. In a study of 200 cases of alcoholism in industry, Trice also noted three differences from the normal conception of absences among problem drinkers:

Absences are spread out through the week. Neither Monday nor Friday absences predominate (probably because the alcoholic is trying to be careful not to draw attention to the condition).

Partial absenteeism is frequent. A worker often reports in the morning but leaves before the day is over.

Tardiness is not a marked feature of alcoholism. The widespread notion that a problem drinker comes to work late, was not substantiated by Professor Trice's study.

How should you approach counseling an employee you believe to be an alcoholic?

Alcoholism requires a special form of counseling, say those who have coped most effectively with it. For example, the U.S. Department of Health, Education, and Welfare in its *Supervisors' Guide on Alcohol Abuse* offers the following suggestions to supervisors who are faced with this problem among their employees:

1. Don't apologize for confronting the troubled employee about the situation. Your responsibility is to maintain acceptable performance for all your employees.
2. Do encourage this employee to explain why work performance, behavior, or attendance is deteriorating. This can provide an opportunity to question the use of alcohol.
3. Don't discuss a person's right to drink; it is best not to make a moral issue of it. Alcoholism is viewed by HEW as a progressive and debilitating illness that, if untreated, can eventually lead to insanity, custodial care, or death.
4. Don't suggest that the employee use moderation or change his or her drinking habits. A person who is an alcoholic cannot, at the start, voluntarily control drinking habits.
5. Don't be distracted by the individual's excuses for drinking—a difficult spouse, problem children, or financial troubles. The problem as far as you are concerned is the employee's drinking and how it affects work, behavior, and attendance on the job.
6. Don't be put off by the drinker's assertion that he or she is already seeing a physician or a psychologist. The employee may claim that the doctor thinks the drinking is no problem, or that the use of alcohol will subside once the "problems" are worked out. Tell your worker that a doctor who knew the employee's job was in jeopardy because of alcohol abuse would attach a new importance to the drinking habits.
7. Do remember that the alcoholic, like any other person with an illness, should be given the opportunity for treatment and rehabilitation.
8. Do emphasize that your major concern as a supervisor is the employee's poor work performance or behavior. You can firmly state that if there is not improvement, administrative action—such as suspension or discharge—will be taken.
9. Do state that the decision to accept rehabilitative assistance is the employee's responsibility.
10. Ann St. Louis, personnel counselor for Canada's Department of National Revenue, whose program maintains a 90 percent recovery rate among alcoholic government workers, adds this

thought: An employer, far better than spouse, parent, religious adviser, or social agency, "can lead an alcoholic to treatment by 'constructive coercion.' Give an employee every chance to take treatment, but make it clear that [the employee] must cooperate or lose the job. This has proven to be more effective than loss of friends or family."

How widespread is drug addiction among employees?

It is not so pervasive as you might think. Because regular drug use is incompatible with regular attendance, drug users tend not to select regular or demanding kinds of employment. Attempts by a company to screen out hard drug users before employment have not been particularly successful. Dismissal afterward can be difficult because drug users are good at hiding the tools of their habit even if they cannot conceal its symptoms.

Symptoms of drug use are well known. At work they manifest themselves objectively in terms of poor or erratic performance, tardiness, absenteeism, requests to leave early, forgetfulness, indifference to deadlines and safety, and in many instances theft of company property.

Treatment and rehabilitation of drug users are as difficult and complicated as for alcoholics, and the treatments are somewhat similar. Policies of companies against drug addiction, however, tend to be firmer than against drinking and alcoholism. For one thing, the addict is different from the alcoholic because many addicts try to involve other people in drugs. The danger of an alcoholic's inducing another employee to begin alcoholism is slight. Then, too, drug use is illegal; in most instances, use of alcohol is not.

Here again, a supervisor's responsibility should be limited to detecting drug addiction, preventing drug use or sale on company property, and counseling and referral (if indicated) of drug users to the appropriate company authority.

What makes some people overwork to the point of sickness?

A great many people suffer from work addiction. To mask deep emotional problems, and sometimes very real difficulties in their economic or home lives, they burrow into their work. It is a form of retreat from reality. It helps them forget what seem like insurmountable problems. The difficulty from a supervisor's point of view is that the work of workaholics tends to be nonproductive. Paradoxically, as these work-obsessed individuals intensify their diligence, it impedes their output. Furthermore, they often stir up such waves in the office or company that they cut down the output of their associates.

It is difficult for a supervisor to do much other than to recognize the work addict. These compulsive individuals are usually highly moral, ambitious, intelligent, honest, and intensely loyal to their employers. At higher levels, they are the persons who stuff the briefcase for what is often needless work in the evening or weekends. They suffer from anxieties and depressions and generally will not respond to advice to take it easy. They need professional therapy that aims at improving self-understanding, flexibility, and creativity.

What do the professionals do for problem employees that the supervisors can't?

Two kinds of industrial professionals usually work with mentally disturbed employees who are beyond the supervisor's limits to help adjust:

The psychiatrist is a fully qualified physician who has practiced medicine before qualifying for this specialty. An industrial psychiatrist, because of specialized training and experience, can diagnose more closely what an individual's trouble is and prescribe the kind of treatment required. No supervisor should try to do either.

The counselor, or industrial psychologist, works with the great majority of emotionally disturbed employees who do not need full-scale psychiatric treatment. Because of specialized training, the counselor's biggest asset is the ability to listen understandingly to an employee's account of problems. The professional counselor has an advantage over the line supervisor, since the counselor doesn't have the authority to discipline, promote, or fire the employee and therefore has a greater chance of winning the employee's confidence.

Review Questions

1. List at least five symptoms of an employee with an emotional problem.
2. Differentiate between a neurotic employee and a psychotic employee.
3. Which kinds of problem employees is a supervisor likely to be able to help, and which kinds should a supervisor refer to a more highly qualified counselor?
4. What symptoms characterize an extremely disturbed employee who ought to receive professional help without delay?
5. In what ways are the accident-prone employee, the alcoholic employee, and the drug-addicted worker similar?
6. Discuss the difference between valid absences due to a bona fide illness and those absences that psychologists describe as voluntary absences. What is the supervisor's role in minimizing the latter?

7. What should a supervisor stress when counseling an employee who has shown signs of being an alcoholic?
8. Why are professionals, such as psychiatrists and industrial psychologists, able to handle seriously disturbed employees better than a supervisor can?

A Case in Point: The Case of Mary Smith's Irrational Behavior

Mary Smith reported to work as a clerk-typist for the first time at the Ploughers Power and Light Company five years ago. Mary was neat, quiet, and reasonably proficient. During the next four and a half years Mary's performance continued this way. While not outstanding, her work was good, her attendance regular, and her manner pleasant but reserved. Beginning about six months ago, however, Mary's manner has become increasingly less reserved. At first her associates applauded. "Mary is finally coming out of her shell," they said. But as time passed, Mary became more and more shrill. She would hear an off-color joke and then laugh almost hysterically about it for long after the humor had passed. A couple of weeks ago her conduct in the office became even more bizarre. She would sit at her desk and begin laughing aloud to herself. Then, just as suddenly, she'd sit staring at nothing, with tears running down her face. A couple of times one of the women with whom she worked asked her if anything was wrong, but Mary would just shake her head.

During this period, of course, her work also deteriorated. Her typing was sloppy and often contained errors. Her output fell off markedly. Finally, her supervisor called her into the office. First the supervisor spoke to her about her performance and showed her some examples of her poor typing. Then, quite gently, the supervisor said, "Mary, I know something has been bothering you for several months now. I hesitated to speak to you about it before because I felt that it was a private matter. But now it is affecting your work to the point where we can't tolerate it any longer. Would you like to talk to me about it? I'm ready to listen and to see if together we can work out a satisfactory solution."

At that Mary flared up. She threw back her head and laughed uncontrollably. Then suddenly she turned with scorn and heaped on the supervisor what seemed to be completely irrelevant abuse. She began shouting, so the supervisor closed the door in order that others in the office might not hear it. Mary then leaped to her feet and screamed, "Don't lock me in here! I'm going to leave." But when she reached the door, she turned around and slumped to the floor and began to sob.

If you were Mary's supervisor, what would you do? Five alternative approaches are listed below. Rank them in the order in which they appeal to you (1 most attractive, 5 least). You may add another approach in the space provided, if you wish. In any event, be prepared to justify your rankings.

_____**A.** Help Mary to her feet and tell her that is a good start and that you will counsel her again tomorrow.

_____**B.** Ask one of the older women in the office to come in and take Mary to the employees' lounge.

_____**C.** Call the company doctor for advice.

_____**D.** Urge Mary to stay in your office until she's gained her composure, and then suggest that she see her own doctor before coming to work tomorrow.

_____**E.** Ask Mary to stay on and to really let her hair down with you this afternoon so that she can get this out of her system.

If you have another approach, write it here. _____
_____
_____
_____

Action Summary Checklist	Action Needed Yes / No	Date Completed
1. Astuteness in trying to avoid hiring potentially problem employees during the selection process.	____ ____	_____
2. Awareness of, and sensitivity to, employees who display emotional problems, without overreacting to them.	____ ____	_____
3. Recognition that all of us, including the supervisor, have soft spots in our emotional armor and that this does not make us "crazy."	____ ____	_____
4. Ability to distinguish between evidence of neurotic behavior (which may be tolerated) and psychotic behavior (which is bizarre and may become threatening to the individual or to others in the workplace).	____ ____	_____
5. Attitude of wanting to help employees to adjust to their emotional problems, rather than to ridicule or punish them for these problems or to minimize their importance to the individual.	____ ____	_____

Action Summary Checklist (continued)

	Action Needed Yes No	Date Completed

6. Recognition of the signs of poor emotional adjustment: sudden changes in behavior, preoccupation, irritability, increased accidents or absences, fatigue, too much drinking, or drug abuse. ____ ____ _____

7. Development of your skill as a listener, especially a nonevaluative one, a person who does not pass judgment on what is heard. ____ ____ _____

8. Conduct of your counseling sessions in a nonthreatening way, with emphasis on nondirective interviewing rather than cross-examination. ____ ____ _____

9. Time set aside in your schedule to counsel employees who need attention. ____ ____ _____

10. Readiness to refer to an emotionally disturbed employee to your company nurse, doctor, or psychologist for professional advice and treatment whenever your efforts are not fruitful. ____ ____ _____

11. Combination of firmness and empathy when counseling employees with problems of absenteeism, alcoholism, or drug abuse. ____ ____ _____

12. Separation of your approach to the willful absentees (vacationers, directionless workers, moonlighters, and aggressive persons) from the chronic and occasional absentees. ____ ____ _____

13. Alert to early warning signs of alcoholism among your employees: a sharp rise in absences, absences spread throughout the week, and part-day absences. ____ ____ _____

14. Willingness to confront the alcoholic employee with the choice of stopping drinking or losing the job. ____ ____ _____

15. Tolerance for the work-addicted individual, with your guard up to prevent this from happening to you. ____ ____ _____

CHAPTER 12: COUNSELING PROBLEM PEOPLE

Chapter 13
Handling Complaints and Avoiding Grievances

Key Concepts

- A vigilance toward those conditions that induce employee grievances, combined with (1) an attitude that invites rather than turns employees away and (2) a cheerful readiness to deal with them justly and harmoniously, has inestimable value in creating and maintaining good morale.

- A grievance, even when trivial, unjustified, or fancied, can be very real to the employee who raises it; consequently, it deserves serious and emphatic consideration by the supervisor.

- Unless objectivity, consistency, and absolute fairness characterize a supervisor's handling of grievances, the supervisor's rulings are unlikely to gain the acceptance by employees that is needed to maintain harmony and discipline.

- A careful and thorough examination of all the specific facts, events, and attitudes that make up the circumstances of a grievance is a fundamental step that must be taken for its eventual resolution.

- Grievance discussions should be conducted by the supervisor in a businesslike manner, the settlement concluded without undue delay, and corrective action discharged promptly without future prejudice toward the complainant.

How much attention should supervisors pay to employee complaints?

Just as much as is necessary to remove the employees' complaints as obstacles to their doing a willing, productive job. That's the main reason supervisors should act as soon as they even sense a complaint, gripe, or grievance. A gripe, imagined or real, spoken or held within, blocks an employee's will to cooperate. Until you've examined the grievance and its underlying causes, an employee isn't likely to work very hard for you. If the complaint has merit, the only way for you to get the employee back on your team 100 percent is to correct the situation.

Can you settle every grievance to an employee's satisfaction?

No. It's natural for people sometimes to want more than they deserve. When an employee complains about a condition that the facts don't support, the best you can do is to demonstrate that the settlement is a just one—even if it isn't exactly what the employee would like.

Jake may want the company to provide him with work clothing on a job he considers dirty. Suppose you are able to show Jake that the working conditions are normal for the kind of work being done, that other workers in the company doing the same kind of work provide their own coveralls, and that this practice is common in the industry. Jake should be satisfied with this answer. He's getting equal treatment, but there's nothing to prevent Jake from still feeling dissatisfied with the settlement of his complaint. He may still believe the company should provide work clothing.

Look at it this way, though. You didn't give Jake the brush-off. You listened to his argument attentively. You didn't give him a snap answer. You checked with other supervisors and with the manager to see what the company practice is. You found out that the company practice conforms with that of the industry. All this adds up to something of value in you that Jake can see. He can take his troubles to you and get a straight answer. That's good leadership.

Is there danger in trying to talk an employee out of a complaint?

Talk if you will. But don't try to outsmart an employee—even if that's what the employee may be trying to do to you. Grievances are caused by facts—or what an employee believes to be facts. Clever use of words and sharp debating tactics won't change these facts or dissolve the grievance.

Patience and sincerity are the two biggest keys to settling a grievance. In many cases, just listening patiently to an explanation will result in the employee's forgetting the grievance.

What is meant by an imagined grievance? If it's a figment of a worker's imagination, why give it serious attention?

Marie, an unskilled machine operator, files a grievance saying that you've been picking on her, accusing her of doing substandard work. As far as you're concerned, she's off her rocker. In fact, you've hardly paid any attention to what she's been doing. Where did she ever get a notion like that?

Well, where did she? Your department has been pretty rushed lately—that's why you haven't seen much of Marie. You've been spending a good deal of your time with two new apprentices that have just been turned over to you for assignment. You knew that their presence had nothing to do with Marie or her job. But did Marie?

Here's how Marie looked at the situation: "I've been here four years working hard for Joe. So what does he do when they send up a couple of bright young boys? He puts me on the blacklist. He thinks he's going to freeze me out of my job by not speaking to me for two weeks. Then when he does, he tells me that the last batch of fasteners I turned out have to be reworked. And first thing this morning he jumps me for breaking a drill. Next thing I know he'll have one of those apprentices showing me how to do a job I've done for four years, or taking my job on some phony pretext and bumping me back to the foundry. I'll squawk now before it's too late."

Marie has imagined this grievance, hasn't she? She has the situation all wrong, too. But if you don't take time out right now to get to the bottom of this complaint, you will have a real problem on your hands. You will make a good beginning by saying, "Marie, if I've been picking on you, it certainly wasn't personal. In fact, if I thought you had any complaint, it was that I hadn't been giving you enough attention. For the last couple of weeks, I've let you pretty much alone because you're an older hand here. I feel I can trust you to go ahead without my standing over your shoulder. But somewhere maybe I've gotten off the track. Can you tell me what you mean by 'picking on you'? I certainly want to get this matter straightened out."

What's the most important thing you can do when handling grievances?

It can't be said too often: Above all, be fair. Get the employees' point of view clear in your mind. If they have an opportunity to make themselves understood, the grievance may turn out to be something different from what appears on the surface.

To be really fair, you must be prepared to accept the logical conclusion that flows from the facts you uncover in the process.

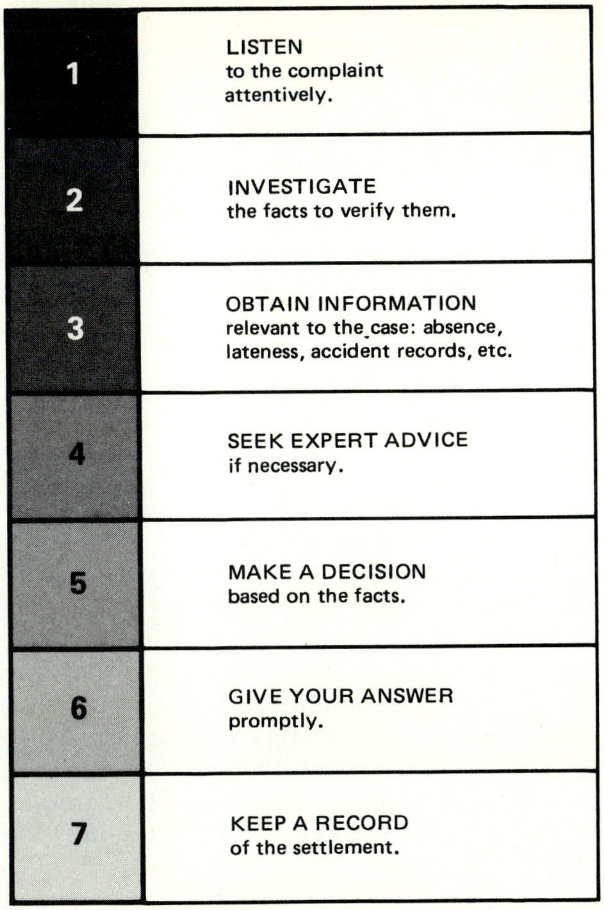

1	**LISTEN** to the complaint attentively.
2	**INVESTIGATE** the facts to verify them.
3	**OBTAIN INFORMATION** relevant to the case: absence, lateness, accident records, etc.
4	**SEEK EXPERT ADVICE** if necessary.
5	**MAKE A DECISION** based on the facts.
6	**GIVE YOUR ANSWER** promptly.
7	**KEEP A RECORD** of the settlement.

Figure 13-1. Grievance Handling Process.

(See Figure 13-1.) This may mean making concessions. But if the facts warrant it, you often have to change your mind or your way of doing things if you are to gain a reputation for fair dealing.

If you find you've made a mistake, admit it. A supervisor isn't expected to be right all the time. But your employees expect you to be honest in every instance — even if it means your eating crow on occasion.

Should a supervisor bargain on grievances?

No. Be like a good baseball umpire: Call each one as you see it. Umpires who blow a decision are really in for trouble if they try to make up for it on the next call. It should be the same with grievances. An employee either has a case or hasn't a case. Consider each case on its merits, and don't let the grievances become political issues.

Should supervisors change their stories if they find the facts won't support their original conclusions?

Supervisors have no other choice if on investigation they find their actions or decisions have been wrong. But they should avoid this embarrassing situation in the first place. Just be sure to get the facts —all the facts. Get them straight to begin with—before you give the employee or a shop steward your decision. It costs you nothing to say, "Give me a couple of hours (or a couple of days) to look into this matter thoroughly. Just as soon as I know all the facts, I'll be able to discuss this grievance so that we come up with the fairest solution."

In trying to round up the facts of a case, explore further than just the obvious places. For example if the grievance involves a dispute over pay, look beyond just the time-card and payroll data. Ask yourself: Has the worker been upset about the jobs assigned? Has the worker had a fair share of easier jobs? Have we had occasion to turn the worker down on a bid for a better job? Does the worker know how to fill in a time card properly? Does the worker know the procedure for getting credit for machine breakdown time? Have the worker's materials and tools been up to standard?

All these factors could affect a person's pay and should be examined before you commit yourself.

Records are especially useful in assembling the facts and backing you when you present your decision to the employee or the union. If your complaint is that someone's output has been below par, you'll need the worker's records and the records of others to prove it.

Isn't there a danger that if you attach importance to a grievance, you'll encourage the employee to think it's more legitimate than it really is?

There's that chance, but you have to risk it. In the long run, treating each grievance with care and consideration pays off. That's different, of course, from giving in on a grievance. That might lead employees to believe you're soft and that you'll make concessions just to avoid arguments.

It is best to follow this rule for handling grievances: Be businesslike in your discussions. Talk with an employee someplace where you'll be free from distractions and interruptions. By all means treat the grievance as a private matter; discuss it away from other employees. Once the employee refers the grievance to the union for handling (if there is a union in your organization), don't attempt to settle it except in the presence of the union representative.

When you have made your own investigation and are ready to discuss how the grievance should be settled, advise the union steward. Ask the steward to invite the employee to be present. After all, your reply is to the employee as well as to the union. Even though the employee has gone to the union for representation, you still want to maintain your personal relationship. The employee can observe that you maintained the initiative, that the steward didn't have to tell you off.

As in any business situation, handle all your discussions in a civil tone. Avoid discussing personalities. Keep the steward's focus, as well as your own, on the grievance situation. Show the steward you, too, wish to settle it fairly. Keep control of your temper, even if the employee or steward loses control. Resist the temptation to blow your top. It's all too easy to permit a grievance to fall to the level of a personal squabble between you, the employee, and the steward. Avoid this at all cost.

When you give your decision on a grievance, how specific should you be? Should you leave yourself a loophole?

A supervisor is paid to make decisions. When the grievance has been fully investigated and you've talked it over with the parties involved, make your decision as promptly as possible. Be definite in your answer. State your decision so that there's no mistake about what you mean. If it involves a warning rather than a more serious penalty, for breaking a safety rule, for instance, don't give this kind of reply: "I'll withhold the warning this time, but next time it happens it won't be so easy for you."

Instead, use this clear-cut approach: "There appears to be good reason to believe that you misunderstood what I expected of you. So I'll tear up the warning and throw it away. Next time you'll get a written warning. And if it happens a second time, it will cost you a week off without pay."

It is also a good idea to make sure that the worker understands the reasons for your decisions. For instance, in the safety warning case above, the supervisor might have said: "Ordinarily, ignorance of the rule is no excuse. The rule is in the employee handbook and has been posted conspicuously in the department. Your case seems to be different because you asked me about this rule last week, and you misunderstood what I told you about it. I told you that you were to report any injury, no matter how minor, to me before going to the company nurse. You seem to have thought that you didn't have to report the injury so long as you didn't go to the nurse—which you didn't. I've explained now that I want to know about every injury—and I'll decide whether we treat it here or send you to the dispensary."

Must you give your decision right away?

No, but don't sit on it forever. Nothing breaks down the grievance procedure like procrastination. If you can't make up your mind on the spot, or need to check even further than you did originally, tell the employee and the steward that you'll give a definite answer "this afternoon" or "tomorrow." Stick to this promise. If you run into an unexpected delay, let them know about it. Like: "Sorry I can't let you know this afternoon as I'd hoped, because the paymaster has been tied up all morning. I won't be able to check the time sheets until late this afternoon. But I will let you know first thing in the morning."

Incidentally, where union stewards are involved, get your answer back to them directly. It ruins the stewards' prestige in the company if your decision leaks out before you've had a chance to speak to them in person.

Suppose your boss or your boss's superior asks you to hand down a grievance decision that you don't agree with. Should you accept responsibility for it?

This is that old supervisor-in-the-middle situation. It's bound to come up from time to time. Sometimes you'll find that company practice is easier on the employee than you think it should be. Sometimes just the reverse—it's tougher than what you'd do if you had no one but yourself to answer to. In either case, don't pass the buck. If you as a supervisor say that you agree with the employee but that the company manager can't see it your way, you destroy the whole management teamwork. If you don't agree with company policy, try to adjust your own thinking. In any event, and hard as it may be to swallow, you should pass the decision along as your own.

Should a supervisor help employees save face if they have a grievance go against them?

It seems as if it's asking too much for a supervisor to be noble about winning a grievance—especially when the employee or the union has been nasty or aggressive in pursuing it. But here again, it's a bad practice in the long run to make the employee eat humble pie. If you help employees save face, they may be considerate to you when the tables are turned. If you rub in the decision, you may irk them so much that they will be on the lookout for a gripe they can't lose.

This shouldn't be interpreted to mean that you must be so downright nice as to appear sorry you were right. Try saying something like this: "I've checked your complaint from every angle, but it still looks like no to me. You made two comparisons when you stated that I was playing favorites. In each case the facts show that both employees you referred to outranked you both in output and quality of production. On my scorecard they deserve the better assignments. I'm far from glad that I had to say no to you. But I am glad that you brought your position out into the open. Perhaps now that I know how you feel, I can give you some help to improve your performance so you can do some of the jobs requiring greater skill."

What is the best way to wind up a grievance settlement?

Carry out your part of the bargain and see that the employee does, too. Once an agreement has been made, follow through on corrective action promptly. You may lose all the good will you've built in settling the grievance if you delay in taking action.

Is there a standard grievance procedure set down by law?

No. A company may choose to establish its own procedure voluntarily. If a union or other organization represents employees, however, the procedure will be based on an agreement between management and the labor union or employee association. This agreement will be written into your labor contract or whatever contractual document exists.

Why is there a grievance procedure? Wouldn't it be better to settle gripes informally without all the red tape?

Most union contracts (and many nonunion shops) establish a step-by-step grievance procedure. Experience has shown both management and labor that it's best to have a systematic method of handling complaints. Without a formalized procedure in dealing with unionized employees, management would find it difficult to coordinate labor and personnel practices from department to department.

The formal procedure provides an easy and open channel of communications for employees to bring complaints to the attention of supervisors, and it guarantees that these complaints won't be sidetracked or allowed to ferment without corrective action being taken. Good supervisors and wise managements know that an unsettled grievance, real or imaginary, expressed or hidden, is always a potential source of trouble. The grievance machinery helps uncover the causes and gets the grievance out into the open.

What happens to grievances that go unsettled?

They continue to fester. Frequently a supervisor may feel that he or she has taken care of a complaint just by soft-soaping the aggrieved employee. This is a mistake. The grievance will continue to simmer in the employee's mind, even if nothing more is said about it to the supervisor; and dissatisfaction is contagious.

TABLE 13-1

Common Grievances and Their Causes

Grievances (listed in order of their frequency)	Typical Causes (as an employee sees it)
Wages and Salary	
1. Demand for individual wage adjustment	I'm not getting what I'm worth. I get less than other people doing work that requires no more skill.
2. Complaints about job classifications	My job is worth more than it pays and it should be reclassified.
3. Complaints about incentive systems	The method used to figure my pay is so complicated that I don't really know what the rate is. My piece rate is too low. You cut my rate when my production went up.
4. Miscellaneous wage complaints	You made a mistake in figuring my pay. The wages here are too low for what you ask me to do.
Supervision	
1. Complaints about discipline	My supervisor doesn't like me and has it in for me. Any mistakes that I made were because my boss didn't instruct me properly. My supervisor plays favorites.
2. Objections to general methods of supervision	There are too many rules and regulations. The rules are not posted clearly.
Seniority and Related Matters	
1. Loss of seniority	I was unfairly deprived of seniority when the department was reorganized.

An unsettled grievance is like one rotten apple in a basket. It spoils the good ones; the good ones don't make a good apple of the rotten one. An offended or angry employee tends to make other employees lose confidence in the supervisor. The co-workers may encourage the dissatisfied employee to pursue the matter if it appears that you have been evasive.

When does a grievance go to arbitration?

Most union-management contract agreements call for a grievance to go to arbitration if the grievance cannot be settled at any of the steps of the authorized procedure. Once the complaint has been

TABLE 13-1

Common Grievances and Their Causes (continued)

Grievances (listed in order of their frequency)	Typical Causes (as an employee sees it)
2. Calculation of seniority	I didn't get all the seniority due me.
3. Interpretation of seniority	You didn't apply my seniority the way it should have been when assigning overtime.
4. Layoffs	I was laid off out of sequence. You didn't recall me in sequence.
5. Promotions	There is no chance to get ahead in this job. You promoted the other person ahead of my seniority.
6. Disciplinary discharge	The company has been unfair. What I did didn't warrant this severe a penalty. You were just looking for an excuse to get rid of me.
7. Transfers	I've had more than my share of dirty work. I don't want to work in the mixing department. Will you get me off the midnight shift?
General Working Conditions	
1. Safety and health	The lockers are too crowded. This place is unsafe because it is too damp, too noisy, and there are dangerous fumes.
2. Miscellaneous	I lose time waiting for materials. Overtime is unnecessary. The company should pay for my work clothing. You can't do the job right without better tools than you provide.

turned over to an impartial arbitrator, the arbitrator acts somewhat like a judge by listening to the facts presented by both parties and then making a decision. The arbitrator does not mediate, that is, try to reopen the discussions between the company and the union. Both parties agree to abide by the decision.

Where are grievances most likely to occur?

It's hard to pinpoint just what situations are most likely to breed grievances, but there are some indicators for you to follow:

First, don't lose sight of the fact that grievances are symptoms of something wrong with employees, or with working conditions, or with immediate supervision.

Second, employees are most likely to be worried about situations that threaten their security: promotions, transfers, work assignments, layoffs, the supervisor's evaluation of their performance, mechanization or elimination of their jobs, and so forth.

For an indication of situations that stir up grievances, together with some ideas of how employees are likely to feel about them, see Table 13-1, which is based on (and updated from) studies made by the U.S. Bureau of Labor Statistics.

It's easy to see that it would be better to prevent grievances in the first place. How can you do that?

The trick lies in detecting situations that breed grievances and then correcting these situations. Don't make the mistake of planting seeds of trouble where it doesn't exist, though. A perfectly happy worker may be able to find something to complain about if you ask directly, "What is there about your job that you don't like?" Better leave that type of open-ended prospecting to company-directed attitude surveys, which are discussed in Chapter 9.

As a rule of thumb, however, you can reduce the number of grievances by applying common sense to your relationhips with your staff. For example:

1. Give employees prompt and regular feedback about how well they are doing their jobs. Uncertainty in this area is a major source of employee dissatisfaction.
2. Remove, or try to ease, minor irritations as they arise. The presence of unnecessary aggravations tends to magnify the more serious complaints when they occur.
3. Listen to and encourage constructive suggestions. Take action whenever it is reasonable and nondisruptive.
4. Make certain of your authority before making a commitment to an employee. Then be sure to keep your promises.
5. When you make changes, take special care to explain the reasons—and as far in advance as possible.
6. Assign work impartially. Try to balance the distribution of attractive and disagreeable work so that employees share it equally.
7. Be consistent in your standards of performance and the way in which you reward those who comply or punish those who fail to measure up.
8. Render your decisions as soon as possible when responding to employee requests. A prompt no is often more welcome than a long-delayed yes.

9. If you must criticize or take disciplinary action, do not make a public display of it. Keep it a private matter between you and the employee.

Review Questions

1. Contrast a real grievance with an imagined one.
2. Why should every complaint be treated as if it were important?
3. For supervisors to be fair in settling a grievance, they must expect that occasionally they will "lose" one. Why should they resist the temptation to give in on one grievance so that they can "win" on another?
4. In the search for facts that contribute to a grievance, what are some of the places where a supervisor should look?
5. How specific and conclusive should a supervisor's settlement of a grievance be?
6. Is it wise for a supervisor to refer an employee's complaint to a staff department rather than first trying to deal with it alone? Why?
7. To what extent are grievances handled differently when there is a formal grievance procedure prescribed by the labor contract?
8. Name several administrative procedures and situations from which grievances are likely to arise.

A Case in Point: The Case of the Typist Who Got No Raise

Work in the typing pool of the Cascade Underwriting Company is sporadic. Two or three days a week, the five typists are under heavy pressure. But rarely a week goes by without one day when the slack is so great the typists have to work very hard to look busy. Janice, one of the newer typists, simply sits at her desk staring out the window when there is nothing to do. The other typists spend a great deal of time in the employees' lounge or keep a paper in their typewriter to type on whenever Ms. Tender, the office manager, comes by. In fact, one of the older typists can do this so well she can look busy while she is reading a magazine hidden in her desk drawer. However, when time for annual merit reviews came around, Ms. Tender recommended all but Janice for a raise.

When the other typists got their paychecks with increases and Janice found none in hers, she asked Ms. Tender for the reason. "I couldn't give you a good rating," Ms. Tender said, "because you waste too much time."

"I do not," said Janice. "The only time I'm not working hard is when I have nothing to do."

"When you run out of work," replied Ms. Tender, "it's your responsibility to let me know, and I'll find something for you to do."

"That's unfair," said Janice. "I'm as entitled to a good review and a raise as any of the other typists. If I don't get it, I'll ask to see Bob Dunne, the chief clerk."

"Go ahead," said Ms. Tender.

Later that week Bob Dunne invited Janice and Ms. Tender into his office to talk about Janice's grievance. Janice told her story to him very much as she had to Ms. Tender. Ms. Tender, however, insisted that Janice did not show the initiative in seeking work during slack periods that the other typists did. Furthermore, she said that she had to keep after Janice regularly to make sure that she kept busy. After hearing both these women out, Bob told Janice that he had to agree with Ms. Tender's decision, and that he considered the matter concluded.

Rank the following conclusions in the order in which you think they are most valid (1 most valid, 5 least). If you wish to add another conclusion, write it in the space provided. In any event, be prepared to justify your ranking.

_____**A.** Bob Dunne failed to ascertain properly the facts of the situation before making his decision. This was unfair to Janice.

_____**B.** Dunne gave Janice as fair a hearing as she deserved.

_____**C.** It was Janice's fault that she hadn't learned to follow the practices in her department or to show initiative in seeking out work when she wasn't busy.

_____**D.** Ms. Tender's recommendation for no increase was correct regardless of what the other typists may or may not have been doing.

_____**E.** Ms. Tender is not a very perceptive supervisor, and she certainly might have helped Janice get a better hearing if she had conscientiously reviewed the situation.

If you have another conclusion, write it here. _____
_____
_____

Action Summary Checklist		Action Needed Yes No	Date Completed
	1. Sensitivity to sources and symptoms of employee discontent: wages, nature of supervision, seniority, assignments, transfers and promotions, discipline, safety and health, and general working conditions.	____ ____	_____

Action Summary Checklist (continued)		Action Needed Yes No	Date Completed

2. Respect for, and attention given to, all grievances, real or imagined.
3. Desire to resolve the issue or grievance clearly, whether or not the solution is one that fully satisfies the employee.
4. Decisions based on facts, which have been thoroughly gathered and carefully examined.
5. Unwavering standard of fairness in judging the merit of complaints and grievances.
6. Candidness and the absence of trickery in discussing grievances with employees.
7. All discussions, with employees or union representatives, conducted in a businesslike manner and in a civil tone with personalities set aside.
8. Decisions carefully explored beforehand, but made as quickly as possible.
9. Grievances with companywide implications discussed first with your superior or with the personnel department before the decision is given.
10. Willingness to pass along and support as your own the rulings on grievances made by higher authorities.
11. Decisions rendered in clear-cut terms with full explanation of your reasoning.
12. Opportunity for employees to save face when the ruling on a grievance goes against them.
13. Follow-up on decisions to make sure that promised corrective action actually takes place.
14. Strict adherence to your company's grievance procedure, if one has been established.
15. As much as possible, handling of grievances as confidential matters between you and the employees involved.

CHAPTER 13: HANDLING COMPLAINTS AND AVOIDING GRIEVANCES

Chapter 14
How and When to Discipline

Key Concepts

- Only a relatively small percentage of any work force ever becomes involved in disciplinary problems to any great extent. These persons tend to be the more poorly adjusted individuals, who find it difficult to accept the regulations and conformity imposed on them by an organized activity.

- The great majority in the work force usually exert the necessary self-control to keep themselves out of trouble. The state of their morale, however, is significantly influenced by the way in which their supervisor maintains discipline.

- To be effective for all members of the work force, discipline must be essentially a positive effort. It should be exercised as much to encourage and reward desirable employee behavior as to penalize and discourage undesirable conduct.

- There are two hallmarks of effective employee discipline: (1) Punishment should suit the importance of the offense and should become progressively severe only as offenses are repeated. (2) Discipline should follow the "hot-stove" rule—it should be given only if there has been adequate warning, and it should be immediate, consistent, and impartial.

- The supervisory role in maintaining discipline requires unusual objectivity and integrity. The supervisor not only must identify and apprehend transgressors; the supervisor must also determine the nature and extent of guilt and impose the penalties. Even then, the supervisor can never be sure that the decisions will not be modified or reversed by an appeal to higher authority.

What is the real purpose of discipline?

The real purpose of discipline is quite simple: It is to encourage employees to meet established standards of job performance and to behave sensibly and safely at work. Supervisors should think of discipline as a form of training. Those employees who observe the rules and standards are rewarded by praise, by security, and often by advancement. Those who cannot stay in line or measure up to performance standards are penalized in such a way that they can clearly learn what acceptable performance and behavior are. Most employees recognize this system as a legitimate means to preserve order and safety and to keep everyone working toward the same organizational goals and standards. For most employees self-discipline is the best discipline. As often as not, the need to impose penalties is a fault of management as well as the individual worker. For that reason alone a supervisor should resort to disciplinary action only after all else fails. Discipline should never be used as a show of authority or power on the supervisor's part.

Why do employees resent discipline?

Employees don't object to the idea of rules and regulations, but they frequently object to the way a supervisor metes out discipline. In civil life, if a person breaks the law, the police officer only makes the arrest. The person is tried before a jury of peers who are guided by the rulings of an impartial judge, who in turn determines the punishment.

Now compare the civil procedure for handling lawbreakers with what happens in your organization. As supervisor, you're often called on not only to put the finger on the wrongdoer, but also to hear the case and decide the penalty. To many employees this seems unfair because you've acted as police officer, judge, and jury.

So don't take your job as disciplinarian lightly. It's a great responsibility and requires impartiality, good judgment, and courage on your part.

Incidentally, when the work group thinks the rules are reasonable, the group itself will impose discipline to keep its members in line.

Why do employees break rules?

As in most personnel problems, only a small percentage of workers cause disciplinary problems. People who break rules do so for a number of reasons—most of them because they are not well adjusted. Contributing personal characteristics include carelessness, lack of cooperation, laziness, dishonesty, lack of initiative, lateness, and lack of effort. The supervisor's job is to help employees to be better adjusted.

People break rules less often when the supervisor is a good leader and shows a sincere interest in employees and when employees get more enjoyment from their work. After all, if an employee finds the work uninteresting and the boss unpleasant, is it surprising that the employee will find reasons for being late or for staying away from work altogether?

If the supervisor gives employees little or no chance to show initiative on the job or to discuss ways the work should be done, the supervisor shouldn't be surprised that employees talk back or shirk their responsibilities. That's what some people do who can't express themselves any other way.

Sometimes the real reason an employee breaks rules or seems lazy on the job has nothing to do with working conditions. The employee may be having worries at home—money problems or a nagging spouse—or may be physically sick. You might ask, "What concern is that of the supervisor?" It isn't—unless the supervisor wants that employee to be more cooperative and productive at work. If you're smart enough to see the connection, you can do much to improve this worker's performance. Don't snoop in personal affairs, but do offer a willing and uncritical ear. Let the employee know that you're an understanding person, that the boss is someone to talk to without getting a short answer or a lot of false advice.

So when an employee breaks a rule, make discipline your last resort. Instead, search hard for the reason the employee acts that way. Then try to see what you can do to remove the reason.

What kind of handling do employees expect from a supervisor in the way of discipline?

Justice and equal treatment. Being soft, overlooking nonstandard performance, or giving chance after chance to wrongdoers does not win popularity among most employees. In fact, it works the other way to destroy morale. That's because most people who work hard and stay in line are frustrated and disappointed when they see others get away with things. No one likes to be punished, but everyone likes to be assured that the punishment received is in line with the error. ("Let the punishment fit the crime" is the advice given in Gilbert and Sullivan's *Mikado*.) The treatment should be neither better nor worse than that given anyone else for the same fault.

Some people talk about negative discipline and say positive discipline is better. What does this mean?

When you have to penalize someone, that's negative. If you can get an employee to do what you wish through constructive criticism or discussion, that's positive.

Supervisors, more so than employees, understand that disciplining is an unpleasant task. All a supervisor wants is to run the department in peace and harmony, to see that things get done right, and that no one gets hurt. The supervisor who can establish discipline through good leadership won't have to exercise negative discipline through scoldings, suspensions, or discharges.

What is meant by progressive discipline?

The penalties for substandard performance or broken rules become increasingly harsh as the condition continues or the infraction is repeated. Typically, a first offense may be excused, or the worker is given an oral warning. A second offense receives a written warning. A third infraction may bring a temporary layoff or suspension. The final step occurs when an employee is discharged for the fourth (or very serious) infraction.

What is the "hot-stove" rule of discipline?

The hot-stove rule, shown in Figure 14-1, is used to illustrate four essentials of a good disciplinary policy. If the stove is red-hot, you

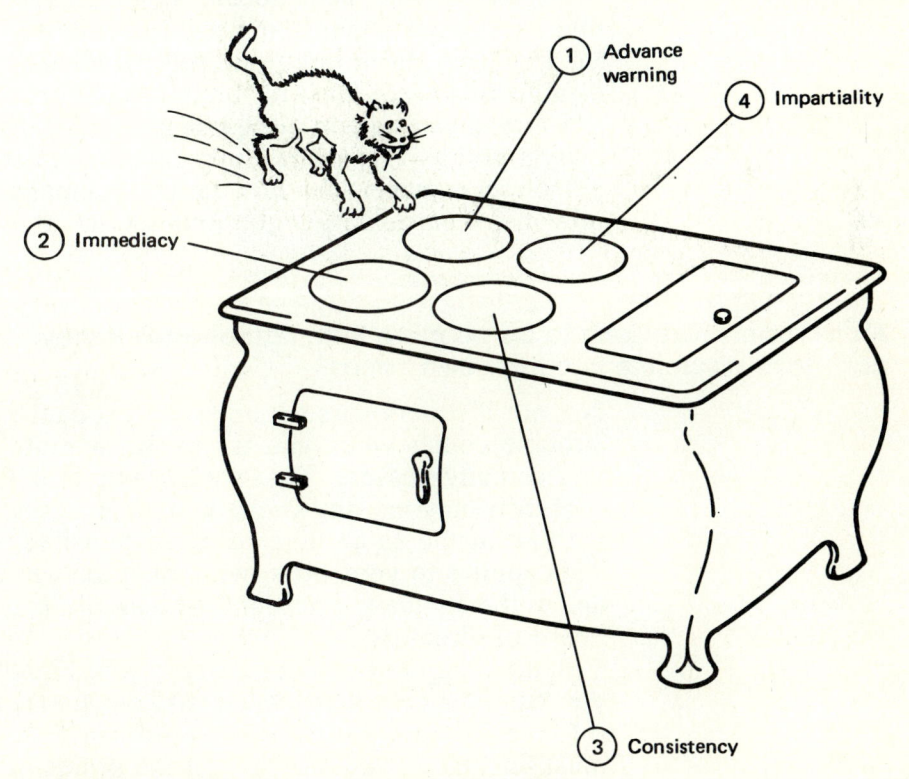

Figure 14-1. "Hot-Stove" Rule of Discipline.

CHAPTER 14: HOW AND WHEN TO DISCIPLINE

ought to be able to see it and know that if you touch it, you will be burned; that is the principle of *advance warning*. If you touch the hot stove, you get burned (penalized) right away; that is the principle of *immediacy*. Every time you touch a hot stove, you will get burned; that is the principle of *consistency*. Everyone who touches a hot stove will get burned because it plays no favorites; that is the principle of *impartiality*.

How far can a supervisor go in handling discipline?

That depends on your company's management policy and on the labor agreement, if your company has a union.

Legally, a supervisor can hire and fire. But firing is a costly action. To break in a new employee can cost from $250 to several thousand dollars for a skilled mechanic, for example. So most companies have tried to approach discipline from a positive direction. Since discipline puts a supervisor in such a responsible position, many companies have carefully spelled out just how far a supervisor can go before having to check with the boss.

Labor unions, in their desire to provide the maximum protection from injustice and unfair treatment, maintain that discipline shouldn't be handled by management alone. Unions contend that they, too, should help decide an employee's punishment. How much say a particular union will have depends on how successful the union has been in writing this privilege into the contract or in establishing precedents for its participation.

So tread carefully in discipline matters. Find out from your company's policy-level management (your immediate superior or the personnel manager) just how far the company wants you to go and how much participation you must permit the union.

Aren't supervisors likely to be no more than figureheads if they can't take discipline into their own hands?

No, not if supervisors act only in accordance with their authority. Trouble comes when you try to throw more weight around than you actually possess. That's when you look foolish!

Hardly anyone anywhere can take action that affects others without at the same time being responsible to still other people. This applies to your boss, who must answer to higher executives and to the company president, who in turn may have to answer to a board of directors.

Being a supervisor isn't an easy job. Handling discipline when you know that if you make a mistake you may be reversed or overruled makes the job even more difficult. To make it easier, you must become a "legal eagle" on the points of how far you can go before it's wise to check with your superior.

Should you act when you're angry?

It's a very unusual person who can think and act sensibly when angry. For that reason it's a good idea for a supervisor not to take any disciplinary action while boiling over. How can this be accomplished? Try one of these:

Count to 100. An oldie, but it works.

Take a walk. Ask the employee to walk over to the window or to your office—anything that takes time. This is especially good, since it gets the person away from other employees and from familiar surroundings, where you may be resisted.

See the employee later. Simply tell the employee you'll speak about the matter in a couple of hours. This gives you a chance to cool off, to think the matter through, and to check with your boss, if necessary.

How do you decide what to do?

No one can make a decision without all the facts. If a situation arises that looks as if you have to take disciplinary action, look hard before you leap. Take time to investigate. Let the employee tell the full story—without interruptions. Check with witnesses for their observations. Look in the company records to see what other supervisors have done in the past. Speak to your boss or the personnel manager to get their advice.

For instance, someone tips you off that Alice Jones is going to take home a baby Stillson wrench in her lunch box tonight. You stop Alice at the time clock. Sure enough, there's the wrench tucked underneath a wad of sandwich wrappers. Your first reaction is to fire Alice on the spot for stealing. But should you?

Suppose, on checking, you found any of these circumstances:

Alice had asked the toolroom supervisor for the wrench and received permission to borrow it overnight for a home-repair job.

Two of Alice's co-workers tell you Alice had said she was just borrowing the wrench overnight and planned to return it in the morning.

Alice could prove that the wrench was one she actually had bought herself to use on her job.

When checking with the personnel department, you found that the company had agreed with the union not to fire any ten-year employee for petty thefts, that the most Alice's penalty could be for a first offense would be one day off without pay.

Wouldn't any of these facts change your decision?

CHAPTER 14: HOW AND WHEN TO DISCIPLINE

When should you consult the union on disciplinary problems?

Practices vary from company to company. Some supervisors, however, have found it helps to inform the union immediately of any planned disciplinary action. The supervisor who sees that a disciplinary problem has arisen holds an informal hearing with the employee, with the shop steward standing by. The shop steward is a witness to the situation from the beginning and can observe that the supervisor's handling of the case is fair. It also makes it harder for the employee to change the story later on and avoids the shop steward's saying to you, "That's not what I was told."

Unless your company has a practice to the contrary, you should avoid asking the union or the shop steward what you should do or what penalty is appropriate. You should make it clear that the union representative has been invited only for the purpose of keeping him or her informed. Keeping order in the department is your job, not the union's, although you may welcome the union's cooperation.

How much good are warnings?

Warnings do a lot of good if you make them more than idle threats. Your warnings put employees on notice that their performance isn't up to standard. You have a chance to explain a rule that they may have taken only lightly before and to make the penalty clear to them. When you warn employees, that's the perfect time for you to be constructive, to offer help, to practice positive discipline.

To make a warning a valuable piece of evidence in a union grievance, you should always make a written record of it. You'd be surprised how much weight arbitrators and union officials give to notations that you have written in your pocket notebook or the department logbook, or have inserted in the employee's personnel file.

Some companies make this written notation a formal practice by requiring supervisors to fill out a form to be filed by the personnel department. These notations are called written reprimands, and copies of the reprimand are sent to the employee and the union.

When should you fire an employee?

As mentioned previously, the supervisor's authority is limited by the company's policy and by its agreements with the labor union, if one exists.

Speaking generally, however, some employee offenses are worse than others. Drinking or sleeping on the job, smoking in restricted areas, willfully destroying property, and falsifying time cards are charges that often result in discharge. It is easier to generalize about offenses like fighting on company property and gross insubordination. But all these wrongdoings have one thing in common — they are single incidents rather than an accumulation of minor offenses, and many of these single acts require immediate action by the supervisor.

To handle any of these serious offenses and still leave yourself free from reversal later, there's an effective action you can take. It's short of discharge, but it gets the culprit out of the company quickly and legally. This action is called suspension. It follows the advice arbitrators give employees: "Obey first — argue later."

To suspend an employee, you merely say something like this: "You've come to work in an unfit condition. I think you're under the influence of liquor right now and are unfit to do your job. You could be subject for dismissal for being in this shape. I haven't made up my mind yet whether that's what I'll do. But in the meantime, you're suspended. Punch out your time card and don't come back to work until I call you. I'll try to let you know definitely tomorrow."

By suspending the employee, you have demonstrated your willingness to enforce your authority when needed. Yet you have protected yourself and the company from looking weak, foolish, or indecisive. If tomorrow, in the opinion of your superior, the personnel manager, or the company's lawyer, you can't make the discharge stick, you and the company are still in an effective position. It's when you cast the die — fire an employee and then have to take that person back — that you have to eat crow.

When can't you make disciplinary action stick?

Here are some famous last words: What's difficult about discharging a third-rate employee? Get rid of the person whose work is poor, who talks back or breaks a rule.

Many supervisors with that attitude have ended up behind the eight ball; and the company has been involved in an arbitration case, had to give back pay to a discharged worker, and even faced a charge of an unfair labor practice. Why? Because the situation that requires the most delicate handling is the provision for discipline and discharge. Dead beyond recall are the days when a supervisor could act and talk tough, when an employee had no recourse.

As difficult as the discipline problem is, many discharges or other penalties could be made to stick if the following mistakes weren't made:

No Clear-cut Breach of Rule. In one company a supervisor fired an employee for sleeping, only to see the decision reversed by the arbitrator. The union brought out the fact that the supervisor had made the observation from 60 feet away. The arbitrator ruled that at this distance the supervisor was "likely to see what was anticipated."

Inadequate Warning. Arbitrators frequently believe that workers are entitled to sufficient warning that their conduct won't be tolerated—even though the rules and penalties are in an employee manual. Typical is the case where an employee has had a record of poor attendance for months without having been disciplined. Suddenly the supervisor cracks down without warning and fires the employee.

Absence of Positive Evidence. Consider this case of loafing—always a difficult charge to make stick: The company went along with the supervisor and fired a worker caught loafing. The arbitrator reversed the company because (1) the supervisor had not been in the department continually but had popped in and out during one afternoon and (2) the employee's job entailed occasional waits for material. Furthermore, the company could produce no time sheets that showed reduced output in black and white. The arbitrator ruled that the supervisor might have come into the department at the times the employee had legitimately been waiting for materials.

Acting on Prejudices. Real or imagined discrimination or favoritism weakens a disciplinary ruling. If a supervisor has shown that she has it in for a worker and just waited for an opportunity to enforce a penalty, an arbitration case may bring this out. If the supervisor has let others get away unpunished with the same offense for which she punishes another, she will have a hard time justifying such unequal treatment.

Inadequate Records. The value of written records of warnings and reprimands can't be overemphasized. It's especially valuable for documenting action taken to correct an accumulation of minor offenses. You may not want to discharge a person who's been late the first time—or even the fifth. But when it gets to be a frequent and costly habit, you'll want to take action. Unless you've built up a record of warnings and kept a file of them that can be shown to the union and an arbitrator, if necessary, your case will be hard to prove.

Too Severe Punishment. Many arbitrators recommend "progressive punishment" and look unfavorably on too severe discipline, especially for first offenses. For instance, a supervisor in a can company noticed a worker away from his work station 10 minutes before the end of the shift. A look at the time card showed that the employee had punched out a half minute early. The man was fired because not long before that he had received a written reprimand for doing the same thing. He had been warned that the next time he'd be fired. An arbitrator ruled that a penalty was called for—but not such a tough one. Do it progressively, the arbitrator said—just a little tougher each time. A lighter penalty would keep an old (seven years' service) and valuable employee on the payroll.

What consideration should be given to an employee's good work record?

There's danger in carrying the rule book too far. Treating each offender equally does not mean that you should not weigh personal factors, too. For instance, what was the worker's attitude when the rule was broken? Was it done deliberately or accidentally? Was the worker emotionally upset by a circumstance beyond control (like worrying about a sick child at home)? How long has the employee worked for the community? What kind of work record has there been? Remember, it costs money to fire a good employee. Even civil courts occasionally suspend sentence or put on probation a guilty person who has been considered a good citizen in the past.

In many instances it is also good to wipe an employee's slate clean now and then. For example, an employee had a poor absence record two years ago, but has had almost perfect attendance since then; the past record should not be considered if at a later date the employee runs into an absence problem again.

How much should employees know about your discipline policy?

The more the better. Technically you can make your rules and penalties stick as long as they are posted on bulletin boards, written in union contracts, or expressed in employee manuals; but for rules to be really effective, employees should be reminded (not threatened) of them from time to time.

It's especially good if you tell them the purpose of the rules. A no-smoking rule, for example, would be much more effective if in addition to posting a sign, you told employees: "You can smoke most places in the company, but not in Department 29. We use a lot of solvents there. If you dropped a lighted match or butt in that department, we'd all blast off! And it would knock the department and maybe the company out of operation and jobs for a long time. So don't light up in Department 29—or even carry a cigarette in there accidentally. We'd hate to do it, but you might be fired on the spot."

When you've had to discharge an employee, be sure that the other employees know what the circumstances were and why that person was fired. Don't use the worker as an example, but do convince other employees that you were fair and impartial. Use this opportunity to emphasize that you don't want to discipline—that you want only to see that the department is run smoothly for the benefit of all concerned.

Review Questions

1. In what way does the enforcement of discipline in business differ from that in civil life?
2. What kind of people are most likely to break work rules regularly?
3. Distinguish between negative discipline and positive discipline.
4. What kind of restraints are placed on a supervisor's authority to handle discipline independently?
5. When Carlos saw Jane sneaking out early again, he fired her on the spot, even though he hadn't given her any prior warning. What should he have done to make discipline progressive?
6. The hot-stove rule is meant to help supervisors remember four important points about discipline. Briefly describe the four.
7. Explain the importance of making written notations of discussions held with employees regarding disciplinary matters.
8. Describe at least three reasons why a supervisor's decision to discharge an employee might not be upheld.

A Case in Point: The Case of the Sleeping Miner

Bob Medford is a recently discharged veteran working as a third-shift tailpiece man in a soft-coal mine in Virginia. His job is to clean up the coal that spills off a conveyer belt as it is loaded from the shuttle cars. It is hard, dirty, tiring work and must be performed in cramped quarters, as is characteristic of most of the work in this mine. Bob's job pays well, and the mines are about the only place in the area where a young man can earn a decent wage. Medford, however, spends a lot of his time talking about his $9,500 decorated Pontiac Trans Am, with its supercharger engine and Mag wheels. He is always going off somewhere, so that his crew chief has to hunt for him. While he is away from the tailpiece, the coal piles up on the floor and obstructs the shuttle cars so that the miners who operate them have to slow down their unloading. Bob's boss is intensely loyal to all the men in his crew, but one night when he went looking for Bob, he found him asleep under a pile of loose shale. When he woke Bob, Bob said, "Don't turn me in on your report. I was up all day hunting, and when I came on shift, I just couldn't keep my eyes open."

If you were Bob's boss, what would you do? Five alternative approaches are listed below. Rank them in the order in which they appeal to you (1 most attractive, 5 least). You may add another approach in the space provided, if you wish. In any event, be prepared to justify your rankings.

_____**A.** Say that sleeping on the job is carrying a good thing too far. Being away from the tailpiece occasionally is all right, but if he's caught sleeping, you won't cover up for him any longer.

_____ **B.** Tell him he's off the job as of that moment and put another employee in his place for the remainder of the shift.

_____ **C.** Tell him that this is the last time he can be away from the tailpiece for any reason at all. Next time he's away, you'll turn him in for discipline.

_____ **D.** Tell Bob that he's been letting the rest of the crew down and that he ought to think more about their interests.

_____ **E.** Ask one of the shuttle operators to have a heart-to-heart talk with Bob.

If you have another approach, write it here. _____
_____
_____

Action Summary Checklist	Action Needed Yes / No	Date Completed
1. Discipline considered as an ongoing training program device to encourage desired performance and to discourage undesirable behavior.	___ ___	___
2. Discipline used only for corrective purposes and never as a display of personal power or authority.	___ ___	___
3. Establishment of rules that are reasonable and generally regarded by the work group as mutually beneficial to them and the company.	___ ___	___
4. Understanding of the reasons why employees break rules: willfully by frustrated or disturbed employees and unthinkingly by untrained or misinformed workers or by employees distracted by personal problems.	___ ___	___
5. Standards of performance and departmental rules enforced fairly, neither too leniently nor vindictively.	___ ___	___
6. Discipline that stresses the positive rather than the negative, improvement rather than punishment.	___ ___	___

Action Summary Checklist (continued)

	Action Needed Yes	No	Date Completed

7. Approach to meting out corrective discipline that is progressive, with increasingly severe penalties for successive infractions. ____ ____ _____

8. Advance warnings of possible disciplinary action communicated to employees through training sessions and general information media such as bulletin boards, manuals, and face-to-face discussions. ____ ____ _____

9. Corrective discipline exercised without undue delay: the principle of immediacy. ____ ____ _____

10. Disciplinary action that is consistently applied in like situations and for similar failures to meet standards or to conform to established rules and regulations. ____ ____ _____

11. Discipline that is impartial and free from prejudice. ____ ____ _____

12. Knowledge of your company's policies, procedures, and regulations (and the influence of the labor contract if there is a trade union present) as they affect enforcement of performance standards and organizational discipline. ____ ____ _____

13. Determination to keep a cool head—and to be sure of all the facts and contributing influences—when administering negative discipline. ____ ____ _____

14. Care in making notations in your own records of oral or written warnings; maintenance of production, quality, safety, and absence records so that you can detect and correct off-standard performance before it gets out of control. ____ ____ _____

15. Double check of what it takes to make corrective discipline stick before taking action: clear-cut breach of a rule or standard, adequate warning, concrete evidence, impartiality, credible backup records, and appropriate penalties. ____ ____ _____

Self-Check for Part 4

Test your comprehension of material in Chapters 12, 13, and 14. Correct answers are in the Appendix.

True-False   Indicate whether each of the following statements is true or false by writing *T* or *F* in the answer column.

1. Most people will experience emotional disturbances some time in their life.   1. ____
2. Nearly all people who show poor behavioral adjustment at work need psychiatric help.   2. ____
3. Setting production and quality standards higher than employees can meet increases motivation and means that there will be fewer problem employees.   3. ____
4. Minor irritabilities and unusual preoccupations are symptoms of behavioral disturbance on which a supervisor could expect counseling to have a favorable effect.   4. ____
5. Listening is the essential element of constructive counseling.   5. ____
6. Counseling is always effective with excessive absenteeism regardless of the basic cause.   6. ____
7. A grievance should be investigated even if the supervisor believes it has no justification in reality.   7. ____
8. A complaint becomes a grievance when the employee seeks redress from management for the real or imagined injury.   8. ____
9. Mary's discipline is positive because the only reason she gives criticism or penalties is to help her employees work better and more safely.   9. ____
10. Immediacy is lacking if the punishment doesn't follow right after the offense.   10. ____

Multiple Choice   Choose the response that best completes each statement below. Write the letter of the response in the space provided.

11. Even if a grievance is found to be unjustified, the employee should be given: 11. ____
    a. An adjustment.
    b. Attention and an answer based on facts.
    c. The settlement he or she asked for.
    d. A chance to negotiate the settlement terms.

227

12. The reason employees make an issue over imagined injustices is that they:
    a. Have it in for someone, especially their supervisor.
    b. Live in an imaginary world, at home and at work.
    c. Believe the injustice to be real, no matter how others may see the facts.
    d. Don't understand the purpose of the grievance procedure.

13. After hearing a grievance, one of the first things a supervisor should do is to:
    a. Gather as much factual evidence as possible.
    b. Make an immediate decision.
    c. Report it to the shop steward.
    d. Report it to his or her superior.

14. If supervisors find that their first judgment in handling a grievance was incorrect, they should:
    a. Do nothing now, but give the employee with the grievance a break later.
    b. Admit it, make an adjustment, and do a better job of investigating in the future.
    c. Have the employee reassigned to a different department.
    d. Do nothing; everyone makes mistakes.

15. A good approach for avoiding grievances before they occur is to:
    a. Be sure employees know where they stand in regard to the quality of their performance.
    b. Encourage employees to make suggestions and act on them when possible.
    c. Explain proposed changes carefully and in advance.
    d. All the above help to avoid grievances.

16. The main reason for enforcing discipline is to:
    a. Get rid of misfits.
    b. Convince employees that they can't get away with anything.
    c. Establish the supervisor's authority.
    d. Maintain the necessary order in the conduct of work.

17. Gertrude's boss has called her into his office. He has noticed that of four of her subordinates who committed exactly the same first offense, she fired one, gave one an oral warning, and did nothing at all to the other two. The boss might tell Gertrude:
    a. "You're not being impartial."

b. "Stop using positive discipline."
　　　c. "You should have asked the union steward what punishment to give."
　　　d. "Don't worry about that rule; it's not important anyway."
18. If a supervisor excuses a habitual rule breaker:　　　18. ____
　　　a. It will probably improve that person's behavior in the future.
　　　b. It is likely to harm the general state of discipline in the department.
　　　c. It will be just between the two of them.
　　　d. It will probably improve morale in the department.
19. A good way to make sure that a disciplinary action　　19. ____
　　has a positive effect is for the supervisor to:
　　　a. Make the culprit an example to everyone else.
　　　b. Avoid giving any penalty.
　　　c. Use it as an opportunity to show an employee how to perform the work more effectively.
　　　d. Announce it at a general meeting of all employees.
20. A good rule to follow about giving warnings is:　　　20. ____
　　　a. Forget them; they don't work anyway.
　　　b. Use warnings as your exclusive means of maintaining discipline.
　　　c. Use warnings as an occasion for training and encouragement to bring about improvement.
　　　d. Never make records of warnings because that could cause trouble with the union.

CHAPTER 14: HOW AND WHEN TO DISCIPLINE

PART 5
IMPROVING EMPLOYEE PERFORMANCE

One of the most constructive aspects of supervisory management is the opportunity to help individuals make the most of their potential. This is accomplished by the supervisor through formal and informal appraisal systems and by informed training efforts.

Chapter 15 explains how to relate employee performance to job requirements and shows how to conduct performance appraisals in a positive way.

Chapter 16 emphasizes the supervisor's role in employee training and development and outlines a variety of useful techniques for breaking in new employees, training employees to be more skillful on their present jobs, and developing employees' potential for increased responsibilities.

Chapter 15
Appraisal of Employee Performance

Key Concepts

- The objective of performance rating is to help employees improve the caliber of their job performance. When made aware of those areas in which they are already doing a good job and of those in which there is room for improvement, employees can be encouraged to develop strengths and to overcome weaknesses.

- Just as employees consider themselves individuals who are valuable to the organization, they want to know how valuable the organization considers them. Because of this desire to have their work appreciated, employees welcome the chance to talk candidly with their supervisors about how well they are handling their jobs now and how they can improve their performance in the future.

- The careful and fair application of both objective and subjective factors in appraisals will help assure employees that their ratings are based on facts and not opinions. This assurance enables them to recognize criticism for what it is: helpful advice toward complete mastery of the job.

- An appraisal interview should first accentuate the positive by giving credit where credit is due. It may then shift to areas where performance can be improved by underlining goals called for by the job but not yet attained by the employee. When supervisor and employee meet in an appraisal interview, it should be on a two-way street highlighted by a mutual examination of job requirements, a mutual review of how adequately the requirements are being fulfilled, a mutual agreement on new targets, and a mutual responsibility for improvement.

- Carelessness and lack of effort are not the only causes of inadequate performance. Supervisors must be alert to other causes and remedy them when possible. Mismatches between jobs and workers, ineffective training, pressures from other employees, physical or emotional stress, poor supervision, or inadequate procedures may bring about poor performance despite employees' best efforts.

At its root, what is the true purpose of an appraisal?

There are four basic reasons for making an appraisal of employee performance:

1. To encourage good behavior or to correct and discourage off-standard performance. Good performers expect a reward, even if it is only praise. Poor performers should recognize that continued substandard behavior will at the very least stand in the way of advancement. At the most drastic, it may lead to separation.
2. To satisfy an individual's curiosity about how well he or she is doing. It is a fundamental drive in human nature for each of us to want to know how well we fit into the organization for which we work. An employee may dislike being judged, but the urge to know is very strong.
3. To provide a firm foundation for later judgments that concern an employee's career: pay raises, promotions, transfers, or separation. It is a cardinal mistake, however, to stress the relationship of pay raises during the appraisal period. It is only human for persons who have been told that their work is good to expect an increase in pay to follow. If your company's compensation plan doesn't work that way, you may suffer a very red face when an employee tells you later that "you told me my good work would bring a raise or a promotion."
4. To serve as a basis for an employee's training and development. A good appraisal identifies performance weaknesses that often can be improved by specific training programs. It also highlights the presence of individual potential that can be developed through proper assignments and advanced training.

What is the difference between a job evaluation and an employee performance appraisal?

In a job evaluation, only the job is considered. In an employee performance appraisal (sometimes called a merit rating), you measure how well an employee is doing on the job. Essentially, one technique evaluates a job; the other evaluates an individual.

How formal will the performance rating procedure be?

It varies. Some companies prescribe and carefully follow through on their appraisal programs. Others leave it pretty much up to the individual supervisor. Many formal programs use a "forced choice" form to record the supervisor's rating. Its purpose is to force the supervisor to make a decision as to whether an individual is, for example, "unsatisfactory," "satisfactory," "very good," or "superior" according to each of a number of factors. Typical rating factors include the following:

- Quantity of work output
- Quality of work performed
- Job knowledge
- General dependability
- Initiative
- Attitude toward cooperation
- Adaptability to changing conditions
- Safety and housekeeping
- Attendance and punctuality
- Potential for advancement
- Supervisory potential

Is it proper to ask an employee to help you make an appraisal of another employee's performance?

Evaluation of an individual's performance and ability is a definite management responsibility. You cannot properly share it or delegate it to someone else outside the managerial ranks. It's perfectly all right, however, and often helpful, to discuss your opinions with your superior or, occasionally, with your associates (like an assistant supervisor). But management alone can determine the relative value of individual employees and their place in the organization.

It should be added that a few organizations use peer ratings successfully; but unless this is an established part of the appraisal program in your company, peer ratings should be avoided. Without proper preparation, this method will cause far more problems than it will solve.

Doesn't an employee's rating represent only the supervisor's opinion?

A good performance rating includes more than just a supervisor's opinion. It should be based on facts, too. In the consideration of quality, does the employee's work meet your standards? As to quantity, what do the production records show? Dependability — what's the absence and lateness record? Can you cite actual incidents where you may have had to discipline the employee or speak about the quality or quantity of output? Answering these questions makes your rating less opinionated and consequently more valid and worthwhile.

Such documented incidents become critical examples (often called critical incidents) of an employee's performance. These incidents should undeniably represent the quality (good or bad) of an employee's work. It is a good practice to make notes of such occurrences and place them in the employee's file. At appraisal time they serve to illustrate what you consider good or subpar performance and to support the ratings you make.

What factors should you consider when appraising an employee?

These can vary from plan to plan. What you are trying to answer about an employee's performance, however, are these three questions:

What has the individual done since last appraised? How well has it been done? How much better could it be?

In what ways have strengths and weaknesses in the individual's job approach affected this performance? Could these factors be improved?

What is the individual's potential? How well could the employee do if really given a chance?

Factors that are judged in appraisal also tend to fall into two categories: objective judgments and subjective judgments. *Objective factors* focus on hard facts and measurable results such as quantities, quality, and attendance. *Subjective factors* are opinions such as those about attitude, personality, and adaptability. Distinguish between the two. Be firmer about appraisal of objective factors than you are about those involving opinion only. But even subjective factors can be rated with confidence if they are supported by documented incidents.

How often should you rate an employee?

Twice a year is a happy medium. If you rate too often, you're likely to be much too impressed by day-to-day occurrences. If you wait too long, you're likely to forget many of the incidents that ought to influence your appraisal. Even if your company has a plan that calls for rating only once a year, it's good practice on your part to make an informal appraisal more often.

How can you make sure your ratings are consistent from employee to employee?

One good way to make sure you rate each employee fairly is to make out a checklist with the name of each of your employees down one side of a sheet of paper and the factor to be rated across the top. Look at only one factor at a time. Take quality, for instance. If you have previously rated Tom only "fair" and Pete and Vera "good," decide whether Pete and Vera should still be rated "good" when compared with Tom's rating. Perhaps you'll want to drop Pete's rating to "fair" because Pete and Tom produce about the same quality of work, while Vera's quality is consistently better than either of the other two.

Another way to check your ratings for consistency is to see whether there is a variation of appraisals, or whether you have rated all your employees the same. In any group there should be a variety of performances. Roughly speaking, three-quarters of your employees should be in the middle ratings—"fair" to "good." About one-eighth will stand out at the top with "very good" to "exceptional." Another eighth will be at the bottom, rated from "fair" to "unsatisfactory."

How do you convert employee performance ratings to money?

This is strictly a matter of your company's policy. About the only generality that can be stated is that employees whose ratings are less than satisfactory should not be recommended for increases. If a company has a rate range (maximum and minimum wage rates) for each job, many people believe that only workers who are rated "very good" or "exceptional" should advance to the maximum rate for the job.

If you can't give an employee a raise, why rate the employee at all?

Because performance rating is so often associated with money, supervisors and employees alike lose sight of the other important benefits. Periodic performance reviews help a supervisor to:

Point out strengths and weaknesses to employees so that they can cultivate the former and correct the latter.

Provide a fair and unbiased method for determining qualifications for promotions, transfers, and rate increases.

Recognize those employees who have exceptional ability and deserve training for higher positions and responsibilities.

Weed out those who aren't qualified for the work they are doing and help assign them to more suitable work; or, if they are wholly unqualified, separate them from the company's payroll.

Why should you bother to tell employees where they stand?

People like to know how they shape up, as long as your evaluation is fair and constructive. Informal discussions of ratings with an employee will:

Give the employee a clear understanding of how well the boss thinks the job is being done.

Provide the employee with a chance to ask questions about your opinion and give his or her views on efforts made.

Clear up any misunderstandings about what you expect from the employee on the job.

Set a course for the employee to improve attitudes and job skills.

Build a strong relationship based on mutual confidence between supervisor and employee.

Don't employees resent being told?

The biggest fear in most supervisors' minds is that an employee will dislike being criticized. Surprisingly, this fear is unfounded if the appraisal is based on facts rather than opinion only and if you display a willingness to change the ratings if the employee can show you're wrong. People want to know where they stand, even if the appraisal isn't good. But don't interpret this to mean that appraisal interviews are easy, or that employees will make it easy for you. They probably won't.

Furthermore, do not let your discussion with the employee you are rating take on the nature of an "end-of-term" school report. Mature adults resist this. If this attitude prevails, subordinates can easily regard the performance appraisal as just another way for the company to increase its control over them.

How do you handle charges of discrimination or favoritism?

Unfavorable criticism stings an occasional employee so hard that it's not unusual for the person to react by charging you with favoritism. Don't try to argue the employee out of it. Your direct denial won't be accepted anyway. Instead, try acknowledging that possibly you have erred in making your rating.

For instance, say, "Tony, why do you think I might be favoring Fran? If I've given you that impression, perhaps you can help me see where I've been wrong." Tony says, "Well, you give Fran all the easy jobs, and I get all the junk that no one else wants."

Your reply ought to be along these lines: "I don't agree that I give Fran the easy jobs, but I do find that I ask her to do lots of jobs that need first-rate attention. She seems easier to get along with when I need something done in a hurry. On the other hand, I've been hesitating to ask you to do anything out of the ordinary. That's because you act as if I'm taking unfair advantage of you. Don't you agree that it's just human nature on my part to lean on people who show they want to cooperate? Maybe it's been my fault that you feel I've favored Fran. I'll watch that in the future. But how about your pitching in and taking your share of the load? Will you try it that way with me, Tony?"

How can you tell employees their work is way below par?

Don't be too harsh on poor performers. Be especially sure that your treatment has encouraged the best kind of performance. Otherwise they may feel that their poor showing is more your fault than their own.

Your guides should be these: Be firm. Nothing is to be gained by being soft. If work has been bad, say so.

Be specific. For example, say, "We've been over this before. During the last six months I've made a point of showing you exactly where you have fallen down on the job. Remember the rejects we had on the X-56 job? And the complaints on the motor shafts? Only last week you put the whole department in a bad light by the way you mishandled the shaft job again. It looks to me as if you just aren't cut out for machine shop work. So I'm recommending that you be transferred out of this department. If there's no other suitable work available, I guess you'll have to look for work elsewhere."

Don't rub it in, though. Leave the employee's self-respect. End the discussion by summarizing what you have found satisfactory as well as the things that are unsatisfactory.

Isn't it true that no matter how well some employees do their job, there's little chance of their getting a better job?

Yes. It's especially hard on a good worker who is bucking a seniority sequence and who knows that until the person ahead gets promoted or drops dead, there is little chance to move up. Suppose a number 2 operator on an oil still said to you, "Each time I get reviewed, you tell me I'm doing a good job. But this hasn't done me any good. I'm getting top dollar for the job I'm on, and until the number 1 operator changes job, I'm stuck. All the performance review does for me is to rub salt in the wound!"

A good way for you to handle this gripe is to admit the situation exists, but don't oversympathize. Try saying something like this: "Sure, I agree that it's hard waiting for your chance. But some workers make the mistake of depending entirely on seniority for their advancement. I don't want you to fall into that trap. When the next better job opens, I hope both of us can say that you're fully qualified. That's one of the good things about performance ratings. You can find out where your weak spots may be and correct them. For a person who has your ability and does as well on the job as you do, there's no reason why you have to limit your ambitions to the number 1 operator's job. Maybe you'll be able to jump from a number 2 job to a supervisor's spot."

Should you discuss one employee's rating with another employee?

Not if you can possibly help it. Avoid comparisons when you can, and be sure that each employee knows that you treat each rating as confidential. Try to establish the entire procedure on the basis of confidentiality.

What is the best way to handle the appraisal interview itself?

While there are any number of approaches you might use, the following seven steps are a good path toward understanding and acceptance of the appraisal:

Step 1. Prepare the employee, as well as yourself, to come to the meeting expecting to compare notes. You then have your facts at hand and the employee has the same opportunity to recall performance during the previous period.

Step 2. Compare accomplishments with specific targets. Don't be vague or resort to generalizations. Be specific about what was expected and how close the employee has come to meeting these expectations.

Step 3. Be sure to give adequate credit for what the employee has accomplished. It is a temptation to take for granted those things that have been done well and to concentrate on the deficiencies.

Step 4. Review those things that have not been accomplished. Emphasize where improvement is needed. Explore together how this can be done and why it is necessary for the employee to improve.

Step 5. Avoid the impression that you are sitting in judgment. If there is blame to be shared, acknowledge it. Don't talk in terms of mistakes, faults, or weaknesses. Never compare the employee with a third person. Stick to a mutual examination of the facts and what they imply to both of you.

Step 6. Agree on targets to be met during the period ahead. Be specific about them. Relate them to what has not been accomplished during the current period. This sets the stage for a more objective appraisal discussion next time around.

Step 7. Review what you can do to be of greater help. Improvement is almost always a mutually dependent activity. An employee who knows that you share responsibility for it will approach the task with greater confidence and enthusiasm.

Where should you carry on performance rating or appraisal interviews?

Do it privately, in your own office or in a private room. You'll want to be able to give the interview your undivided attention, and you won't want to be within earshot of other employees. Allow yourself enough time—at least a half hour. Otherwise the whole procedure will be too abrupt.

What is the "sandwich" technique for telling employees about unfavorable aspects of their work?

The sandwich technique, shown in Figure 15-1, means simply to sandwich unfavorable comments between favorable comments:

Begin With
recognition of work well done

Discuss
unsatisfactory area of performance

End With
summary of favorable as well as unfavorable performance

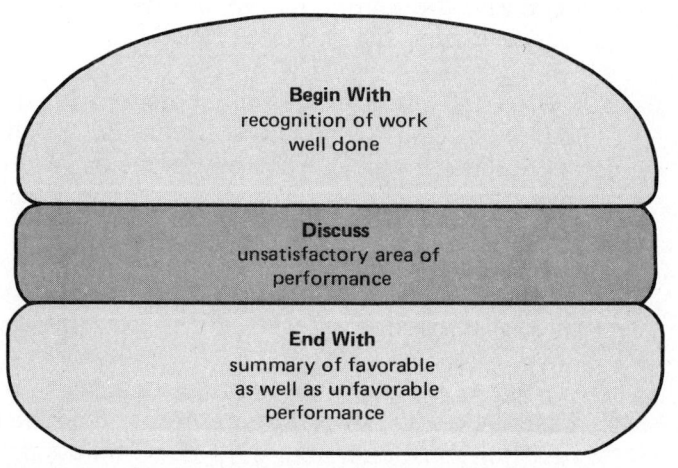

Figure 15-1. "Sandwich" Appraisal Technique.

"I've been pleased with the way you've stepped up your output. You've made real improvement there. I am a little disappointed, however, by the quality of what you produce. The records show that you're always near the bottom of the group on errors. So I hope you'll work as well to improve quality as you did quantity. I feel sure you will, since your attitude toward your work has been just fine."

The same technique is a helpful guide to the entire appraisal review discussion. Use it by starting the talk with a compliment. Then discuss the work that must be improved. Finish by finding something else good to say about the employee's work.

Should you leave room for employees to save face?

Call it what you want, but give employees every chance to tell you what obstacles stand in the way of their making good. Don't interrupt or say, "That's just an excuse." Instead, take your time. Let the person talk. Often the first reason given isn't the real one. Only if you listen carefully will you discover underlying causes for poor attitude or effort.

Confidence in you as a supervisor and in the appraisal system is important. So don't be too anxious to prove that the employee is wrong. Above all, don't show anger, regardless of what kind of remark the employee makes. That advice goes even if the employee becomes angry.

Isn't it dangerous to tell employees you've given a high rating? Won't they expect to get an immediate raise or promotion out of it?

Knowledge of where an individual stands with the boss is just as important to a top-notch performer as it is to a mediocre employee—maybe even more so. If you fail to show your recognition of a good job, the employee is likely to feel, "What's the use of doing a good job? No one appreciates it."

Good workers are hard to come by. They should know what you think about them, even when you can't show them an immediate reward. Remember, people work for lots more than what they get in the pay envelope.

What is the halo effect? How can you avoid it?

Nearly all of us have a tendency to let one favorable or unfavorable trait influence our judgment of an individual as a whole. This is called the *halo effect* (see Figure 15-2). You may feel that Carl is a hard person to socialize with, that his attitude is wrong. This

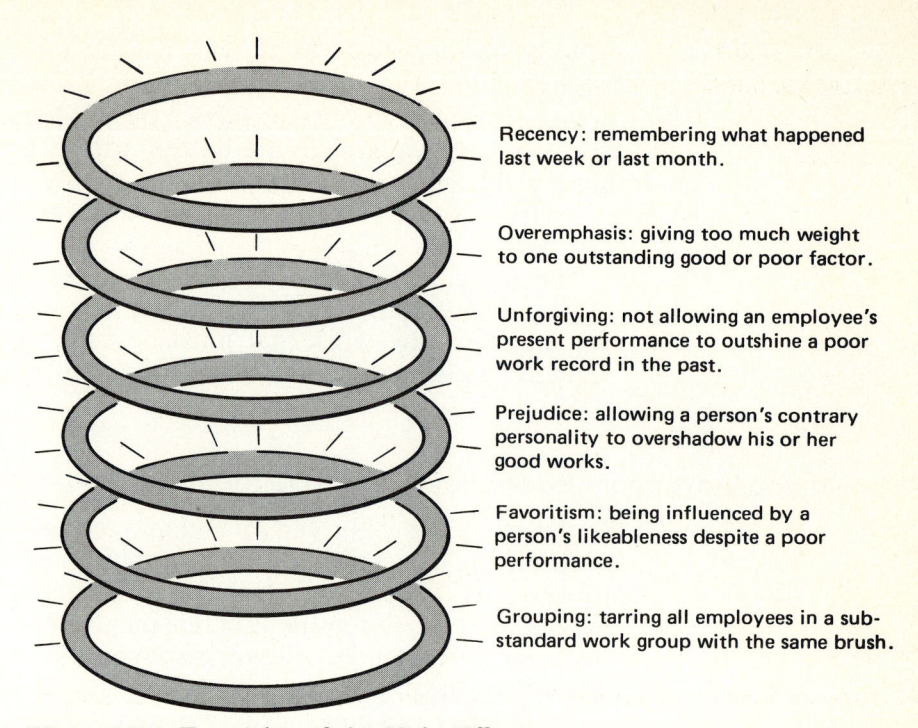

Recency: remembering what happened last week or last month.

Overemphasis: giving too much weight to one outstanding good or poor factor.

Unforgiving: not allowing an employee's present performance to outshine a poor work record in the past.

Prejudice: allowing a person's contrary personality to overshadow his or her good works.

Favoritism: being influenced by a person's likeableness despite a poor performance.

Grouping: tarring all employees in a substandard work group with the same brush.

Figure 15-2. Examples of the Halo Effect.

becomes a halo effect if you let this one trait color your whole judgment of Carl so that you forget that Carl's workmanship is outstanding or his attendance is good. In the other direction, you may be so impressed with a worker's loyalty that you may tend to overlook shortcomings. Either kind of halo effect is bad.

To avoid the halo effect, it's helpful to rate all employees on one of the rating factors before going on to the next factor.

What are some common errors a supervisor may make when appraising employee performance?

Plain old bias or prejudice will ruin an otherwise good appraisal unless you make a definite effort to avoid it. Ask yourself, "Am I measuring this person's performance only against the job? Or am I dragging in dress, accent, color or nationality, physical appearance?"

Overemphasizing a single incident will also distort your rating. Guard yourself against saying, "Merlin is one of the best employees we have. I remember three years ago when he saved our skin by turning out the Thompson job in six hours." Or, "Mary will never be any good. She proved that to me last year when she botched the Smith job."

What should be the supervisor's follow-up after the performance rating interview?

Appraisal isn't done today and finished. To be of lasting value to you and your employees, you should follow up the appraisal interview in the following ways:

Stick to Your Side of the Bargain. If you have promised to examine an employee's work more carefully to see if you've given a fair rating, do so. Check the past record and show the employee any data that's been questioned. If you must change your rating, do it promptly and let the employee know that his or her point of view has been supported.

Provide Techniques for the Employee's Development. An employee will need your help to improve—especially skills. Give the worker the kind of training your review indicated will help. If the employee needs more versatility, broaden the assignments by giving different and challenging jobs. If workmanship is inferior, study what the worker is doing wrong and show how it can be done right.

Continue to Show Interest in the Employee's Work. Drop by the workplace occasionally with a view toward letting employees know they have improved—or gone downhill—since the interview. If they are making progress, give them credit. If they are slipping, point out where you're dissatisfied.

Will the Management By Objectives (MBO) approach work with your employees?

Yes, if you don't carry it too far. At step 6 of the appraisal interview, described above, you can be very specific about performance goals for the next period. If you and the employee mutually agree on them, they become the employee's objectives. The employee can provide self-control (or self-management) in order to attain them. The MBO approach, described in Chapter 6, appeals to well-motivated, self-starting, responsible individuals. It is less attractive to, and less effective for, those employees who rely heavily on the supervisor for planning and control of their work.

Some employees try very hard, but their performance remains below par. What is the reason for this? What can be done about it?

If there is a weakness in performance appraisal programs, it is that management assumes the employees have only to try harder in order to measure up to standards. This is often not so. Many factors can contribute to employee performance:

1. Employees may be assigned to work that does not match their capabilities. It may be too easy or too difficult. One solution is a transfer to a more suitable job. Or the job might be redesigned to give the employee a better fit. An employee may not be able to handle the paperwork required. Perhaps it can be done by someone else. The job may require too little judgment for a highly intelligent person. Perhaps it can be rearranged to provide options that use this person's analytic ability.
2. Employees may not have received proper training. In any case of continued poor performance, the supervisor should first re-examine the training program and find a way to review the job procedure with the employee from start to finish. A key operating point may have been missed.
3. Employees may be victims of pressures from the work group. An employee may be trying to conform to your job standards, but co-workers give the person a hard time. To correct this situation, you may need to approach it from the group's point of view to change or modify their position.
4. Employees may not be up to the job requirements, physically or emotionally. A checkup by the company nurse or doctor may be in order. If there are persistent family problems—divorce, death, severe illness—you may try gentle counseling. Your objective should be to show that you are sympathetic, but that there is a limit to how long the related poor performance can be accepted.
5. Your own supervision may be at fault. It takes two to tango, and poor performance may be related to a supervisor's failure to provide clear-cut standards, to train employees effectively, or to help with problems and changes as they arise.
6. There is always the possibility, too, that there is some hitch in the operating process or a conflict in prescribed paperwork procedures. You may want to review these problems with your own boss or with the appropriate staff departments.

Review Questions

1. Distinguish between employee performance appraisal and job evaluation.
2. When you are rating an employee's performance, how important is it that you use the same yardstick you use with other employees?
3. Distinguish between merit rating for performance and merit rating for pay increases.
4. Under what circumstances will an employee accept criticism in an appraisal interview?
5. Should performance ratings be treated confidentially, or is it all right to show one person's rating to another? Why?
6. Contrast the sandwich technique with the halo effect.
7. Would it be better to go easy during interviews rather than risk hurting employees' feelings so that they can't save face? Why?

8. When the semiannual appraisal interview is over, why can't the supervisor forget about it for six months?

A Case in Point: The Case of the Revised Job Rating

Joe D. has worked for three years as a buyer in the purchasing department of the Barnwell Company. His supervisor, Beth Morgan, consistently rated his performance as "very good," with a point total of 85 out of a possible 100. Typically, Joe D. got top rating for his knowledge of the job and the quality and dependability of his work. The only reason his aggregate score did not move him into the "excellent" range was that his rating for quantity of work produced was never better than "fair." Six months ago Beth Morgan left the company and was replaced by dynamic young Bob Barnes. When the semiannual ratings were filed, Barnes judged Joe D.'s performance to be only "fair," with a score of 70 points. Yesterday Barnes called Joe D. into his office to discuss Joe's performance.

The news that his present rating was only "fair" upset Joe. "How can that be, Bob? I'm working as hard as I always have. My previous supervisor was always more than satisfied."

"I'm sorry, Joe," said Barnes. "That's not the way I see it. The amount of work you turn out is deplorable. If you can't pick up some speed, I'm going to have to put you on notice. As it is, I certainly won't recommend you for a raise at this time."

"That's unfair, Bob," said Joe. "I work on purchases that need very precise specifications and quotations. You can look at the record and see that I make hardly any mistakes. No one else in the department is as reliable as I am."

"You miss the point," said Barnes. "We've got to get more orders pushed through this department. You slow everything down with your nit-picking of every requisition. There is no need for it on 90 percent of what you handle; yet you triple-check every 5-cent item as if it were golden. Either you learn to step on the gas or you'll be looking for work elsewhere."

Obviously, there is something wrong in the past and present ratings of Joe D. Which of the following approaches best summarizes the situatoin? Rank them in the order in which they appeal to you (1 most attractive, 5 least). You may add another approach in the space provided, if you wish. In any event, be prepared to justify your rankings.

_____ **A.** Bob Barnes is out to "get" Joe D.

_____ **B.** Beth Morgan's standards for Joe's job emphasized quality and dependability rather than output, although even Beth had reservations about the quantity of what Joe produced.

_____ **C.** Joe D. is simply bucking Bob Barnes.

_____ **D.** Joe D. and Bob Barnes will have to have a meeting of their minds on the demands of the job before Joe's performance will change to fit them and his merit rating improves accordingly.

_____ **E.** Barnes's threats will serve to shift Joe's job emphasis to output rather than quality.

If you have another approach, write it here. _____
_____
_____

Comment on the way in which Bob Barnes handled the appraisal interview.
_____
_____
_____
_____

Action Summary Checklist		**Action Needed**		**Date Completed**
		Yes	No	
	1. Focus on the major goal of improving the individual's performance to match the job's requirements.	___	___	_____
	2. Recognition of which factors can be judged objectively and which tend to be subjective.	___	___	_____
	3. Desire to base as many judgments as possible on measurable, observable facts.	___	___	_____
	4. Maintenance of a file of critical incidents, or specific representative examples, of each employee's behavior to support the ratings you make.	___	___	_____
	5. Treatment of an individual's appraisal as confidential with respect to his or her associates or peers.	___	___	_____
	6. Conscious effort to apply the same standards to all so that your ratings are consistent from employee to employee.	___	___	_____
	7. Care in separating the discussion of an employee's rating from any talk or consideration of money.	___	___	_____

Action Summary Checklist (continued)

	Action Needed Yes / No	Date Completed

8. Establishment of a positive, constructive atmosphere during the appraisal interview so that the employee does not feel you believe yourself to be an infallible judge. ____ ____   _____
9. Willingness to listen to an employee's rebuttal of your ratings and to change that rating if the argument is sound. ____ ____   _____
10. Avoidance of use of the appraisal interview to scold or punish. ____ ____   _____
11. Proper preparation for, and conduct of, the appraisal interview: privacy, enough time, emphasis on job standards, credit where it is due, mutual examination of the facts supported by examples of critical incidents, focus on the future, and sharing by you of responsibility for the individual's performance. ____ ____   _____
12. Your guard up against the halo effect, which, based on a single incident or trait, discriminates for or against a person. ____ ____   _____
13. A continuing interest in, and appraisal of, the individual's performance so that your judgment isn't a one-time occurrence. ____ ____   _____
14. Your active assistance to the employee in helping to shore up weaknesses or develop skills. ____ ____   _____
15. Thoughtful reexamination of conditions beyond an employee's control that may be contributing to substandard performance: a poor match of skills and job, inadequate training, work-group pressure, physical or emotional problems, faulty supervision, problems in the process or procedures. ____ ____   _____

CHAPTER 15: APPRAISAL OF EMPLOYEE PERFORMANCE

Chapter 16
Training and Development of Employees

Key Concepts

- In the absence of a sound training effort, employees learn haphazardly and often inaccurately. Only by careful planning, systematic instruction, and responsible follow-up can a supervisor be certain that employees will learn how to perform their work accurately and in the most effective manner.

- Learning rarely can begin until trainees are properly prepared to learn. They must first be made aware of the value of the information they are expected to absorb—made aware in a way that arouses their interest and motivates them to provide their own initiative in making the training process productive.

- The process of instruction should use many techniques and appeal to many senses. Demonstration of a skill should (1) feature exercise and repetition, (2) include showing as well as telling how a job is correctly performed, and (3) make an impact on the eyes, the ears, and the senses of smell, touch, and motion.

- Trainees can absorb only a little at a time; this information ideally should be arranged in a sequence that advances the learning from the familiar to the unfamiliar, from the easy to the difficult, from the simple to the complex.

- Learning is accelerated to the degree that training provides the learner with insights—intellectual, sensory, and procedural—into the essentials that make the performance of a task successful or not.

When can you tell that training is needed?

Training needs are often the underlying cause of other problems. Be on the alert whenever you observe any of these conditions: too much rework, subpar production rates, operating costs that are out of line, a high accident rate, excessive overtime, and even a general state of poor morale. Any of these symptoms may respond better to a training program than to a crackdown on discipline, for example.

What are special rewards for a supervisor who does a good job of training workers?

In addition to making a better showing for your department in terms of better quality and quantity of output, training puts you in a favorable light in other ways. Effective employee instruction:

Helps you handle intradepartmental transfers better.
Allows you more time for planning and scheduling your work.
Provides a reserve of trained personnel in your department for emergencies.
Wins the confidence and cooperation of your workers.

Perhaps most important of all for a supervisor who wants to get ahead, training your employees makes you "available" for your own advancement.

When does good training begin?

When a new employee is hired. New workers who get off on the right foot are like members of a baseball team that gets off to a ten-run lead in the first inning. There's a good chance of eventual success.

Training recently hired workers, called induction training or orientation training, is a little like introducing friends at a club meeting where they are strangers. You'd want to introduce them around and try to make them feel at home. You'd show them where to hang their hats and coats. If you wanted them to think well of your club, you might tell something about its history and the good people who belong to it. If you had to leave them for a time to attend to some duty or other, you would come back occasionally to see how they were getting along. It's the same way with new employees who report to you. Treat them as persons you'd like to think well of you and to feel at home in your department.

What should you tell brand-new employees about their jobs?

An induction talk should cover the following subjects, where they apply:

Pay rates, pay periods, how employees are paid (by cash or by check), the day the first pay is received, and the pay deductions.

Hours of work, reporting and quitting time, lunch periods, rest breaks.

Overtime and overtime pay.

Shift premium pay.

Time cards and where they are located, how to punch in and out.

How to report sick.

What to do when late.

Location of lockers and rest rooms.

Location of first-aid facilities and how to report accidents.

Basic safety rules, employee's as well as company's responsibilities under the Occupational Safety and Health Act (OSHA).

Explanation of employee's options under company's benefits plans such as group life and health insurance.

Induction activities should include:

Tour of department or company.

Introduction to co-workers.

Assignment to work station.

This basic information is a lot for new employees to absorb, so don't be afraid to repeat what you tell them several times. Better still, give them some of the more detailed information in small doses: some today, a little more tomorrow, and as much as they can take a week from now.

Note that in many companies a new employee receives an induction talk from a central service, like the personnel or training department. As valuable as this talk may be, it won't help the new employee half so much as an informal, straight-from-the shoulder chat with you.

How do you get down to the real business of training employees to do a job the way you want them to?

Training can be either the simplest or the most difficult job in the world. If you can grasp just four fundamentals, you can be a superior trainer. If you don't buy this approach, you'll spend the rest of your life complaining that employees are stupid, willful, or not like workers used to be in the good old days.

The foundation of systematic, structured job training (also called Job Instruction Training) has four cornerstones:

Step 1. Get the Worker Ready to Learn. People who want to learn are the easiest to teach. Let trainees know why their job is important and why it must be done right. Find out something about the employees as individuals. Not only does this give them more confidence in you, but it reveals to you how much they already know about the job, the amount and quality of their experience, and what their attitude toward learning is. This familiarization period helps the trainees to get the feel of the job you want them to do.

Step 2. Demonstrate How the Job Should Be Done. Don't just tell the trainees how to go about it or say, "Watch how I do it." Do both —tell *and* show the correct procedure. Do this a little at a time, step by step. There's no point in going on to something new until the trainee has grasped the preceding step.

Step 3. Try the Workers Out by Letting Them Do the Job. Let the employees try the job—under your guidance. Stay with the trainees now to encourage them when they are doing right and to correct them when they are wrong. The mistakes made while you're watching are invaluable, because they show you where the trainee hasn't learned.

Step 4. Put the Trainees on Their Own, Gradually. Persons doing a new job have to fly alone sooner or late. So after the trainees have shown you they can do the work reasonably well while you're standing by, turn them loose for a while. Don't abandon them completely, though. Make a point of checking on their progress and workmanship regularly: perhaps three or four times the first day they are on their own, then once or twice a day for a week or two. But never think they are completely trained. There's always something an employee can learn to do, or learn to do better.

Training the four-step way is expensive, isn't it?

All training, structured or catch-as-catch-can, is costly. It is the results that count. You may obtain inexpensive training simply by having a new employee work along with an experienced one, and the costs won't show up immediately on the books. Or you can spend a little out-of-pocket money on a systematic plan like the four-step method.

How much should you teach at a time?

This depends on (1) the speed with which a trainee can learn and (2) how difficult the job is. Each learner is different. Some catch on fast, others are slow. It's better, therefore, to gauge your speed to the slow person. Try to find out why the person has trouble learning. With new employees it may simply be that they are nervous and trying so hard that they don't concentrate. So be patient. Give them a chance to relax, and when they complete even a small part of the task successfully, be sure to praise them.

Going ahead slowly is especially important at the start, since learning is like getting a stick-shift car into motion. You first warm up the engine, then start slowly in low gear. You shift into second only as the car picks up speed, and finally into high when it's rolling along under its own momentum.

What can you do to make the job easier to learn and to teach?

Jobs that seem simple to you because you're familiar with them may appear very hard to a person who has never performed them before. Experience has shown that the trick to making jobs easier to learn is to break them down into simple steps. The employee needs to learn only one step at a time and then add steps, rather than try to grasp the whole job in a single piece.

Breaking a job down for training purposes involves two elements:

First, you must observe the job as it is done and break it into its logical steps. For instance, if the job were to in-feed grind on a centerless grinder, the first step would be to place the piece on the plate against the regulating wheel. The second step is to lower the lever-feed and grind. The third step is to raise the lever-release, and so on until the job is finished.

Second, for each step in a job breakdown, you must now consider the second element—called the *key point*. A key point is anything at a particular step that might make or break a job or injure the worker. Essentially, it's the knack or know-how of experienced workers that makes the job go easier for them. The key point for the first step in the centerless grinding job in the previous paragraph would be to know the knack of not catching the workpiece on the wheel. For the second step it would be the knowledge of how to avoid tapering or oval surfaces.

Figure 16-1 shows how this centerless grinder job might be broken down into seven steps with their appropriate key points for

Job Breakdown Sheet for Training

Part: Shaft   Operation: In-feed grind on centerless grinder

IMPORTANT STEPS IN THE OPERATION Step: A logical segment of the operation when something happens to advance the work	KEY POINTS Key point: Anything in a step that might: Make or break the job Injure the worker Make the work easier to do i.e., knack, trick, special timing, bit of special information
1. Place piece on plate against regulating wheel	Knack—don't catch on wheel
2. Lower level-feed	Hold at end of stroke (count 1-2-3-4) Slow feed—where might taper Watch—no oval grinding
3. Raise lever-release	
4. Gauge pieces periodically	More often when approaching tolerance
5. Readjust regulating wheel as required	Watch—no backlash
6. Repeat above until finished	
7. Check	

Figure 16-1. Sample Job Instruction Breakdown. This illustrates steps that advance the work in an operation, together with the appropriate key points.

training purposes. Table 16-1 lists a number of factors that typically become key points for training purposes.

In what sequence must a job be taught?

The best way to teach a job is to start with the easiest part and proceed to the most difficult. This isn't always possible, of course; but if you can arrange your employee training in this sequence, learning will go more smoothly and teaching will be easier.

How soon should you expect an employee to acquire job skill?

This depends on the employee and on the job. It's wise, however, to set a timetable for learning. This can be very simple, as shown in Figure 16-2, or it can be as detailed as you like. The important

TABLE 16-1

Key-point Checklist

Key points are those things that should happen, or could happen, at each step of a job, which make it either go right or go wrong. Key points include any of the following:

1. **Feel.** Is there a special smoothness or roughness? Absence of vibration?
2. **Alignment.** Should the part be up or down? Which face forward? Label in which position?
3. **Fit.** Should it be loose or tight? How loose? How tight? Can you show the trainee? When can you tell that a part is jammed?
4. **Safety.** What can happen to injure a worker? How are the safety guards operated? What special glasses, gloves, switches, shoes are needed?
5. **Speed.** How fast must the operation proceed? Is speed critical? How can you tell if it's going too fast or too slow?
6. **Timing.** What must be synchronized with something else? How long must an operation remain idle—as with waiting for an adhesive to set?
7. **Smell.** Is there a right or wrong smell about anything—the material, the cooking or curing during the process, the overheating of a machine?
8. **Temperature.** Is temperature critical? How can you tell whether it is too hot or too cold? What can you do to change the temperature, if necessary?
9. **Sequence.** Is the specified order critical? Must one operation be performed before another, or doesn't it make any difference? How can the worker tell if he or she has gotten something out of order?
10. **Appearance.** Should surfaces be glossy or dull? Should the part be straight or bent? How can you correct an unsatisfactory condition?
11. **Heft.** Is weight important? Can you demonstrate how heavy or light a part or package should be?
12. **Noise.** Are certain noises expected (purring of a motor)? Unacceptable (grinding of gears)?
13. **Materials.** What is critical about their condition? How can the worker recognize that? When should the material be rejected? What should be done with rejected material?
14. **Tools.** What is critical about their condition? Sharpness? Absence of nicks or burrs? Positioning? Handling?
15. **Machinery.** What is critical about its operation? How is it shut down in emergencies? What will damage it? How can this be avoided?
16. **Trouble.** What should be done in the case of injury to persons, damage to materials, parts, products, tools, or machinery? How can damage be recognized?

	Answer telephone calls	File correspondence	File reports	Make logbook entries	File sales order forms	Prepare day-end report	Etc.	Etc.	Etc.
Garcia	√	√	√	√	√	√			
Nolan	√	√	√	11–10	–	–			
Smith	11–1	11–20	–	√	√	12–1			
Chan	–	–	√	11–15	12–1	12–8			
Etc.									

√ means the worker can already do the job.

– means the worker doesn't need to know the job.

11–1, 11–15, etc., indicate the dates the supervisor has set to have the workers *trained* to do the jobs required.

Figure 16-2. Sample Job Instruction Timetable, or Skills Inventory. This illustrates *(a)* jobs in which the employee has already been trained, *(b)* jobs in which the skill or knowledge is not necessary, and *(c)* dates for training various individuals in specific jobs or skills.

thing is to use the timetable to (1) record how much each worker already knows; (2) indicate what each worker doesn't need to know; (3) plan ahead for what each worker has to learn; and (4) set definite dates for completing training in each required phase of the job.

An analysis like that illustrated in Figure 16-2 is sometimes called a skills inventory because it tells you what skills each worker has already acquired as well as the total skills capability of your department.

Must supervisors do all the training themselves?

No. Instruction is a job that can be delegated—provided that the employee who is to conduct the training is a qualified trainer and that a job breakdown sheet with key points has been prepared. Just as you must know the ins and outs of teaching a job, any employees you appoint as instructors must also know how to train others. This means that they should have completed a course in Job Instruction Training (JIT) or have been thoroughly indoctrinated by you or by the company's training director in how to train. Nothing is worse than bringing a new employee over to an older employee and just turning that person loose. If the older worker doesn't know how to train, chances are 1,000 to 1 that the new employee will never learn the job correctly, and the training process itself will be slow and costly. So never depend on an older employee to show a new one the ropes.

Caution: Even if you have a qualified job instructor in your department, you can never completely delegate your training responsibility. It's up to you to show a personal interest in every trainee's progress and to supervise the training just as you supervise any of your other responsibilities.

Can you depend on an employee to learn a job by reading an equipment manufacturer's instruction manual?

Absolutely not. It's a very exceptional person who can solely on the basis of an instruction manual learn how to operate equipment. Instruction manuals are valuable training aids, however, and they will help you draw up job breakdown sheets. But they are not substitutes for personal instruction.

How much training can be accomplished through outside reading and by correspondence instruction?

If employees are ambitious to learn and to improve themselves — and if they are the rare persons who can absorb knowledge and skills through reading and self-help — they can learn much through reading or through correspondence courses. But make no mistake about it, this is the hard way! Few employees are up to it. And despite the claims of many advocates of correspondence courses, the percentage of workers who have learned their jobs this way is very small.

This is not to say, however, that outside reading combined with personalized instruction by the supervisor is not effective. It is, but the two must go hand in hand.

How good is group training?

Personalized training seems to be best for job skills, but it is expensive and time-consuming. Training employees in groups is obviously less expensive, and for many purposes it is just as effective as individualized training. Sometimes (for example, explaining the theory behind an operation) it's even better.

If you are working with disadvantaged employees under the Comprehensive Employment and Training Act (CETA) of 1973, the U.S. Department of Labor offers this advice: "Group instruction generally doesn't work; use the individualized approach. Find out exactly what the individual doesn't know and concentrate on teaching that rather than a rounded course of instruction. Use a frequent method of testing to provide feedback on learning progress. Instruction must be set for each individual at his or her own pace without peer group pressures or public disclosure of ignorance."

What is programmed instruction?

In 1912 Edward L. Thorndike, an educator, wrote: "If, by a miracle of mechanical ingenuity, a book could be so arranged that only to him who had done what was directed on page one would page two become visible and so on, much that now requires personal instruction could be managed by print."

Programmed instruction has achieved that miracle of mechanical ingenuity. In brief, it presents information in very small bits and then gives questions that must be answered correctly before the trainees go on to the next lesson. Answers are given immediately after the questions.

There are two techniques of programmed learning: linear and branching.

In *linear* programming the information is presented in a series of frames. Frame 1 presents a small bit of information, frame 2 reinforces frame 1 and adds another small bit, frame 3 reinforces frame 2 and adds another small bit, and so on.

In the *branching* technique the questions asked in each frame are multiple-choice. Then, if the trainees give one of the wrong answers, they are directed to information that clears up the specific misunderstanding. For example, they will be told that if they checked wrong answer *a*, they should see a certain page that explains why this was wrong. If they checked wrong answer *b*, they are directed to turn to a different set of instructions. If they checked the right answer, they go on to the next frame. Programmed instruction may be provided by a textbook, a series of pages, or a teaching machine.

What are teaching machines?

Recognize first that teaching machines cannot be used without programmed instruction. Typically, a teaching machine may require written answers, and as soon as the trainees have written their answers, they press a button or move a paper to see the correct answer. Or they may press a button to record the answer to a multiple-choice question. Usually, the machine is designed so that the trainees cannot move the machine to the right answer until they have given their own answers.

TABLE 16-2

Learning Retention Rates

Time Interval Since Learning	Percentage Forgotten	Percentage Retained
⅓ h	42	58
1 h	56	44
8¾ h	64	36
1 day	66	34
2 days	72	28
6 days	75	25

How quickly do people forget what they have learned?

According to the Research Institute of America, the startling figures in Table 16-2 indicate how fast our learning disappears unless we keep at it.

For employees to become expert at the job you're teaching, they must practice constantly, and you must keep repeating the important things that these figures show they are likely to forget. This is one reason why follow-up (step 4) in training is so vital.

What is the purpose of visual aids?

The classic Chinese proverb still tells the story best: One picture is worth 1,000 words. Any device that helps trainees visualize what you're telling them speeds up the learning process. After all, most of us use our eyes to pick up 80 percent of what we know. It's only natural for visual training to be more effective.

Visual aids may include a variety of devices such as transparencies, slides and filmstrips, motion pictures, and opaque projectors; charts and chart boards, posters, flannel and magnetic board presentations; simulated equipment and mock-ups, cutaway models of machines, and actual displays of products, materials, and so forth.

Visual aids may also be simple and obvious, such as writing on a blackboard or demonstrating a point on a machine. Practically nothing beats making the demonstration right on the equipment a worker will use.

How good is apprentice training?

Traditionally, the top-notch, all-around skilled artisans have been schooled through apprenticeship. This is a long, thorough, and expensive practice. It may take anywhere from twelve months to four years. People who have learned a trade through an approved apprenticeship program will be able to handle with skill almost any kind of job that occurs within that skill class. But as jobs have tended to become more and more standardized, much of what the person who has completed apprenticeship knows never gets used. For this reason the percentage of employees trained through apprentice programs gets smaller and smaller. Most employees today are trained for only one specific job at a time. As a result, the training is more to the point, is done faster, and costs less. But if you were to examine apprentice training, you'd find that it incorporates the four points of job training outlined previously. The main difference lies in the length of the training period and the variety of skills learned.

What is vestibule training?

When employees are trained by the company on the kind of work they are hired to perform before they begin to work on in-production materials, the training is called vestibule training. It gets its name from the fact that such training is often done outside the area — as if it were performed in the vestibule of the company before actual entry into the working area.

Can you teach old dogs new tricks?

Yes. Older workers can and do learn new methods and new jobs. While they may learn at a slower rate than younger workers, this is mainly because older workers frequently have to unlearn what was taught them in the past. Older workers often don't have the same incentive to learn that younger ones do. They tend to feel more secure in their jobs and have less interest in advancement. For these reasons, step 1 — getting the worker ready to learn — is of prime importance when teaching older workers.

How do you get employees to want to learn?

Employees must see how training will pay off before they pitch into training with a will. So show the younger employees how training helped others to get ahead — how it built job security for them and increased their incomes. For older workers stress the prestige that skill gives them with other workers. Show them how learning new jobs or better methods makes the work more interesting.

Telling workers why a job is done a certain way is often the key to securing their interest. To see the necessity for training, an employee needs to know not only what to do and how to do it, but why it needs to be done. This process may be compared with a technical problem in transmitting color television. As you may know, the picture is broken down into three separate channels, one of which carries the red, another the green, and the third the blue part of the picture. Unless all three are transmitted in harmony, the picture is blurred and distorted. So, too, unless all three requisites of training are transmitted to the employees, it makes little sense to them.

How smoothly should the training process proceed?

The learning process doesn't go smoothly for most people. We all have our ups and downs. Expect trainees to learn quickly for a while, then taper off on a plateau temporarily. They may even backslide a little. That's the time to reassure them that their halt in progress is normal. Don't let them become discouraged. If necessary, go through the demonstration again so that they can get a fresh start. And pile on the encouragement.

If supervisors are responsible for training, what's the purpose of a company's training department?

The function of a company training department will vary from organization to organization. But almost all training directors are agreed that unless supervisors are sold on training as their responsibility, the efforts of the training department won't be very effective.

Generally, the training department people are experts in teaching methods. They won't lay claim to technical skill about the job (except in cases where technical specialists are employed for certain types of instruction, such as blueprint reading). The training department serves best as an aid and a guide to their supervisors in improving the skills of workers.

For example, training directors can be of real help in determining specific training needs. They can help you recognize and interpret the training symptoms mentioned previously. You'll want their help, too, in learning how to be a good instructor and in training some of your key employees to be trainers. The training department is invaluable in getting you started in making job breakdowns and training timetables.

Certain employee training is best done by a central training group. Such general subjects as company history and products, economics, and human relations are naturals for them. Other classroom-type instruction (like arithmetic and work simplification) lends itself to centralized training, too. But when the training department does these jobs for you, you must still assume the responsibility for requesting this training for your employees and for making sure they apply what they learn to their work.

Review Questions

1. In what ways can a training specialist supplement the efforts made by supervisors to train their employees?
2. Contrast vestibule training with induction training.
3. Explain why a high accident rate in a machine shop might be related to the absence of, or an inadequate program for, employee training.
4. Would it be wise for a supervisor to let an employee try a new job before the supervisor got around to showing how it is done?
5. Compare the preparing-to-learn phase of training with the identification of a key point.
6. Why is individual rather than group training usually preferred for disadvantaged people (like those trained under CETA) and for specific job skills training?
7. Would it be a good idea to let an employee learn all about the operation of a new machine by reading the manufacturer's instruction manual?
8. In what way should the training of an older worker differ from that of a younger worker?

A Case in Point: The Case of the Lost Letter

Teddy, an employee in the mail room of a bank, has recently completed a short training course conducted by the bank's training staff in how to file a tracer with the U.S. Postal Service. At Teddy's very first attempt to file a tracer, however, the form was returned because it was not filled out correctly. Teddy's boss, Brenda Roberts, was irritated because this error further delayed the location of an important piece of mail for which the chief cashier was waiting. "What kind of muscleheads are teaching those courses now?" fumed Brenda. "You've missed the most important point about the information needed on these tracers. Next time I'll show you how to fill them out. And don't release any until you've first checked with me."

Five alternative conclusions are listed below. Rank them in the order in which they appeal to you (1 most attractive, 5 least). You may add another approach in the space provided, if you wish. In any event, be prepared to justify your rankings.

_____**A.** Teddy and his associates are liable to be gun-shy of future training offered by the bank's central training department.

_____**B.** Teddy didn't pay much attention in class.

_____**C.** Brenda will have to do all the training herself if her employees are to learn the proper way to place tracers.

_____**D.** Training in the mail room would improve if Brenda became more closely involved with the central training staff's planning and then coordinated her views and efforts with theirs.

_____ **E.** Programmed instruction would probably eliminate this kind of problem.

If you have another approach, write it here. _____
_____
_____

Action Summary Checklist

	Action Needed Yes / No	Date Completed
1. Continuing alert for symptoms of training needs—such as lowered output, off-standard quality, higher costs, accidents, or poor morale.	____ ____	_____
2. Care in orienting each new employee to your department by using the checklist for the induction talk recommended earlier in this chapter.	____ ____	_____
3. A systematic rather than a hit-or-miss approach to each and all training problems in your department.	____ ____	_____
4. Preparation of a simple job breakdown sheet with key points identified before you begin the training on a particular job.	____ ____	_____
5. Proper employee preparation and motivation provided before you begin the demonstration of a job.	____ ____	_____
6. Training demonstrations that emphasize both telling and showing.	____ ____	_____
7. Emphasis on identification and demonstration of key points that make or break a job.	____ ____	_____
8. Breaking the training material into easily learned pieces, not attempting too much during any one session.	____ ____	_____
9. Arranging the training sequence so that the learner begins with the least difficult and progresses to the most difficult phases.	____ ____	_____
10. Allowing trainees to try out the job under your watchful eye before turning them loose on their own.	____ ____	_____

Action Summary Checklist (continued)

	Action Needed Yes No	Date Completed

11. Regular feedback to the trainee regarding how well—or how incorrectly—the employee is learning the job.   ___ ___   _____
12. Encouragement of questions throughout the entire training process.   ___ ___   _____
13. Remaining available to trainees for help and guidance after they have been put on their own.   ___ ___   _____
14. Training in your department based on an analysis of skills needed (Figure 16-2 in the text) and a planned timetable for completion.   ___ ___   _____
15. Your training approaches tailored to fit the needs and learning capabilities of each individual, drawing on whatever resources you can muster (visual aids, operating manuals, and so forth) and the advice and assistance of your company's training department when one exists.   ___ ___   _____

Self-Check for Part 5

Test your comprehension of material in Chapters 15 and 16. Correct answers are in the Appendix.

True-False Indicate whether each of the following statements is true or false by writing *T* or *F* in the answer column.

1. Preceding and following criticisms with positive comments on an employee's performance is known as the halo effect. 1. ____
2. A desirable result of an appraisal interview is for the individual to have clear goals for future improvement. 2. ____
3. As much as possible, merit rating of an employee should be free of bias; use of objective factors aids in this direction. 3. ____
4. To give a fully rounded estimate of an employee's performance, a supervisor often is forced to be subjective about qualities that are hard to measure. 4. ____
5. A critical incident is a particular piece of behavior that represents an employee's overall job performance. 5. ____
6. "Show" and "tell" are the two main elements in an effective demonstration of the way a job is performed. 6. ____
7. A skills inventory shows the jobs or parts of jobs each employee can handle and the total skills capability of a department. 7. ____
8. A company that trains employees in the actual operations, machinery, and skills they will use, before putting them in the real workplace, is using programmed learning. 9. ____
9. A particular skill or item of knowledge that is critical in succeeding or failing in carrying out a job segment is a key point. 9. ____
10. A good training program should begin the very first day an employee is on the job. 10. ____
11. The accuracy and value of what an employee learns can be assured only through a well-planned and supervised training effort. 11. ____

12. A trainer should avoid actually carrying out any of the job steps when training because this will only confuse new employees. 12. ____
13. Since the difficult segments of a job always take longer to learn, they should be presented first. 13. ____
14. Back in grade school, many of us learned our arithmetic tables by frequent, repetitive drill. This technique is one of many supervisors can use to advantage. 14. ____
15. It helps an employee to learn the smaller segments of a particular task if he or she can first see the big picture into which these segments fit. 15. ____

Multiple Choice Choose the response that best completes each statement below. Write the letter of the response in the space provided.

16. Performance appraisals serve a purpose, even when raises in pay are not based on them, because the appraisals are: 16. ____
    a. Useful for selecting new employees.
    b. A way of punishing employees for poor performance.
    c. The supervisor's main way of communicating with employees.
    d. One way of getting employees to strive to improve performance.
17. In an appraisal interview it is important that a supervisor: 17. ____
    a. Show how much the employee is to blame for poor performance.
    b. Give credit for good performance as well as criticism for bad.
    c. Not extend too much praise for exceptional performance.
    d. Connect the rating to the employee's next payroll review.
18. What most employees probably want above all in an evaluation of their performance is: 18. ____
    a. Praise.
    b. Candidness.
    c. Kindness.
    d. Fairness.
19. A supervisor in a loan company makes a practice of beginning appraisal interviews with a summary of those things that an employee has been doing well. This is: 19. ____

a. A misleading way to begin the interview.
b. A fairly good way to open the session.
c. All right, provided the employee's performance is above average.
d. Dangerous because the employee may come away from the interview remembering only what was said first.

20. A supervisor who runs a tautly controlled pattern-making department in an aluminum foundry is candid, objective, and honest in talking to an employee in an appraisal interview, but does not allow the employee to offer explanations or opinions in return. This practice: 20. _____
a. Would be improved by inviting discussion, but it is better than one in which the supervisor is vague or soft-soaps the employee.
b. Does no good because the employee doesn't have a chance to refute mistaken judgments.
c. Makes sense because the supervisor keeps control of the session.
d. Simply inflates the ego of the supervisor.

Appendix

A Case in Point: The Case of the Complaining Keypunch Operator (Chapter 1)

The point of this case is to illustrate that supervisors must balance their concern for the technical side of their work with a genuine concern for people. Here are the preferred rankings:

____3____ **A.** Ruth has a good knowledge of the work to be done. On the other hand, she treats employees as machines rather than people. Her handling of the facts and clearly stated consequences of continued poor workmanship was good. On the bad side, however, she brushed aside Woodie's seemingly justified explanation of his poor work. She made little effort to counsel him or to indicate any true sympathy with what is obviously a deeply disturbing problem. Woodie has already shown that he has a hard time coping with personal problems and that they affect his work; threatening him with discharge may weaken his ability to cope even more. The chances are that his work and his attitude will continue to deteriorate.

____2____ **B.** A genuine show of interest on Ruth's part might help Woodie to separate his behavior at work from his problems at home. Employees look to their supervisors for understanding and support. Technical competence is not enough, although Ruth's fairness and courtesy are steps in the right direction. On the other hand, Ruth must continue to insist that all members of her department meet company standards.

____5____ **C.** This is a poor choice. Woodie is Ruth's problem. Although she might consult with her boss for advice, she is the one who should deal with Woodie.

____1____ **D.** This is the best approach. Ruth should devote a larger part of her time to getting to know her employees better and to establishing a greater degree of understanding. It is fitting for her to require that employees meet work standards, but she must learn to temper her approach with human kindness.

____4____ **E.** This is not a good choice. Just letting matters drift often lets them get even further out of hand. Without attention, Woodie's performance may get worse rather than better.

A Case in Point: The Case of the Worst Job in the Department (Chapter 2)

This case illustrates the need to identify the true causes of a problem, to evaluate the pros and cons of alternative solutions, and then to commit yourself to a choice (decision) of one of them. Here are the preferred rankings:

___3___ **A.** Technically, additional equipment would relieve the situation, but it does not seem justified economically, nor does it deal with the human side of the problem.

___2___ **B.** Upgrading the shaper's job is a viable solution, since the job appears to be underrated and status is an important factor in retaining operators.

___1___ **C.** Equipment and environmental conditions are badly in need of improvement; therefore, this is a very good suggestion.

___4___ **D.** Jason needs respect from his associates, but he won't get it by ignoring them. Giving Jason extra privileges will only make the situation worse.

___5___ **E.** Testing a person's mettle by giving that person an outrageous assignment is completely at odds with modern practices, let alone the expectations of present-day employees.

A Case in Point: The Case of the Nurses' New Supervisor (Chapter 3)

This case illustrates the points that leadership styles must fit the situation and the individuals involved, that leadership does not necessarily mean popularity, and that leadership (or followership) must be earned. Here are the preferred rankings:

___3___ **A.** It is good to insist on what she believes is right, but it is a little early to start cleaning house.

___5___ **B.** This is not good; her new rules are the best means for unifying the staff at this time.

___4___ **C.** Some modifications may be beneficial, but in this instance they may be interpreted as a sign that Molly will give in on other demands, too.

___1___ **D.** This is the most positive approach. It combines Molly's sense of mission with a realization that she must provide appropriate leadership for each individual.

___2___ **E.** This is also a worthwhile thing to do, but it won't necessarily guarantee that Molly's leadership will be accepted.

A Case in Point: The Case of the Forgotten Price Change (Chapter 4)

This case illustrates the need for flexibility and judgment in carrying out and interpreting policy. Here are the preferred rankings:

___5___ **A.** Regardless of why the problem occurred, the store manager is responsible for implementing policy properly.

___3___ **B.** Expecting perfection is unreasonable; errors are bound to crop up.

_____4_____ **C.** The manager appears to be the weakest link, not the stock clerk.

_____1_____ **D.** This is true.

_____2_____ **E.** This is true in that the manager was willing to carry out the company policy to the letter only if challenged.

A Case in Point: The Case of the Backposted Overtime (Chapter 5)

This case illustrates the need to match the organization's staff with the organization's goals and work loads, even temporary or occasional ones. It also points out the value of training and delegation. Here are the preferred rankings:

_____2_____ **A.** This may have to be done, but it is an expensive stopgap solution for what appears to be a temporary overload.

_____4_____ **B.** This seems to be a time-taking and expensive solution for what appears to be a temporary problem.

_____1_____ **C.** This approach makes the most sense because it accomplishes two things: It gets the job at hand done and it develops Fred as a potential supervisor. It also demonstrates to Tim the value of delegation.

_____3_____ **D.** For the long run, this is a good move, but it does not solve the immediate problem.

_____5_____ **E.** This, like **B**, is a costly way to solve a temporary problem.

A Case in Point: The Case of the Overheated Copying Machine (Chapter 6)

This sticky situation shows why it is necessary for supervisors to balance formal, procedural controls with a realistic acceptance of employees' attitudes and behavior when confronted with unpopular regulations. Here are the preferred rankings:

_____6_____ **A.** Because Cora has to do all this time-consuming work, it is a very costly control system and therefore a poor choice.

_____4_____ **B.** This passes the buck to the regional headquarters, which will probably reject such a request. It is a poor choice.

_____3_____ **C.** This makes the standards known to all, and everyone has a chance to see how well the department is doing. It relies, however, on everyone's exerting self-control, which is doubtful. It is a fair choice.

_____2_____ **D.** If the atmosphere is right, this could work. But Cora's history of threatening and taking over all the responsibility herself makes this solution doubtful. It might work if done in connection with **C**, however. It is a fair choice.

_____5_____ **E.** Cora still retains all the control responsibility herself. This is an expensive way of controlling, and on the basis of her history, Cora has cried wolf too often. This is a poor choice.

_____1_____ **F.** This is a sound way to establish standards. Combined with **D** and perhaps **C,** this is a good approach.

A Case in Point: The Case of the Conflicting Coffee Breaks (Chapter 7)

The case of Janet and Martha illustrates the degree to which individual desires in even very simple matters can become serious problems in human relations; a supervisor must follow through on the problems until they are solved. Your comments when discussing the suggested courses of action can be guided by the following preferred rankings and opinions:

_____5_____ **A.** This ignores Martha's right to express her opinions and preferences without having a judgment made about her motives. While supervisors are entitled to hand down the decision they think best, even if it isn't a popular one, they have no psychological right to pass value judgments on the behavior of others.

_____4_____ **B.** This implies that Janet's reason isn't as valid as Martha's, and then asks her to make a concession without asking Martha to make one. This kind of judgment initiates other complaints as employees try to even the score.

_____3_____ **C.** Logic has its place, but the solutions to most human relations problems turn more on emotional considerations. It's better to try to find out the underlying reasons for the complaint than to put it down too soon with facts.

_____1_____ **D.** Little can be lost by letting Martha and Janet find a solution that's mutually acceptable so long as it satisfies the job objectives, too. It should be noted that such mutual agreement is not always reached.

_____2_____ **E.** This is an equitable solution, but it may leave both Janet and Martha only half satisfied. In general, the better solutions come from patient listening by the supervisor, plus a willingness to let employees resolve their own differences when they can do so without disrupting company or department routines and provided that their performance meets required standards.

A Case in Point: The Case of the Sixteen Draftsmen (Chapter 8)

The case of Tony C. illustrates the power of group influence and the need for a supervisor to find a way to accommodate it. Here are the preferred rankings:

_____5_____ **A.** This is in direct conflict with the expressed wishes of the group and tends to confirm their charge of favoritism.

____3____ **B.** This is a step in the right direction, but it still tends to confirm the group's belief that favorites get the choice work.

____4____ **C.** This puts George dangerously on the spot, both with his supervisor and with his associates.

____2____ **D.** The weakness here is that the supervisor is doing all the problem solving without digging deep enough to find out the group's true reason for making this an issue.

____1____ **E.** This is a good way to get to the heart of the matter, and it will keep the department functioning in the interim. It concedes the right of the group to challenge practices that affect them and to make their views known without prejudice. Yet this approach retains for the supervisors the decision-making prerogative.

A Case in Point: The Case of the Unhappy Mixer Operator (Chapter 9)

This case typifies employees' reactions to disappointment or frustration. Understanding offered by the supervisor is far more effective than force in reducing conflict. Here are the preferred rankings:

____5____ **A.** Attitudinal changes cannot be coerced.

____2____ **B.** It is a good approach to bring Pete's attitude back to a neutral point. There is some danger, however, in holding out hopes that may not be fulfilled.

____4____ **C.** Do this only as a last resort. Pete is a good man, and his supervisor ought to retain him if possible.

____3____ **D.** A reasonable approach, it redirects Pete's attention to his present assignment.

____1____ **E.** This is a good approach in that Pete gains understanding and learns that his work is judged as valuable in some quarters, at least.

Case in Point: The Case of the Changing Ledger Entries (Chapter 10)

This case illustrates the problem of "noise" in communications. Conflicting instructions cause distractions that must be removed. Here are the preferred rankings:

____4____ **A.** This will cause difficulties because it places employees in the untenable position of refusing to follow directions from presumed authority. It is not a good choice.

____3____ **B.** Because this will eventually undermine Norma's relations with her boss, it is a poor choice.

___2___ **C.** This is not effective by itself, but it would be beneficial if combined with **E**. It is a fair choice.

___5___ **D.** It is difficult to make this request stick; a more constructive approach is needed. This is a poor choice.

___1___ **E.** This is a reasonable request provided Norma accepts full responsibility for communicating instructions accurately to employees. It is a good choice, especially if combined with **C**.

A Case in Point: The Case of the Refused Overtime (Chapter 11)

This case illustrates the point that orders should be reasonable and conform to established policy. The more insistent supervisors become, the more difficult it is for them to extract themselves. Here are the preferred rankings:

___2___ **A.** This may be a good approach. The supervisor should reconsider the whole method of handling overtime. It may be best to make it a request that can be refused; or it may be that a policy of advance notice is the most suitable. At any rate, this particular situation seems past rescuing.

___4___ **B.** Since the incident got off to such a bad start, it is unlikely that much rapport can be established right now; it would be better to let Tony go home. This is a poor choice.

___1___ **C.** This is a reasonable approach and allows Tony to get used to the idea that he must arrange his home schedule to accommodate overtime. It is a good choice.

___3___ **D.** If Tony is right that there is a precedent to support his position, or even if he only thinks there is, this is a questionable order to make an issue over. The supervisor should at the least make sure of backing by the personnel department. It is a poor choice.

___5___ **E.** This is a poor choice because it uses the withholding of what may sometimes be an attractive work assignment to punish an employee for failing to cooperate when the supervisor needed the cooperation.

A Case in Point: The Case of Mary Smith's Irrational Behavior (Chapter 12)

This case illustrates the need for supervisors to recognize symptoms of mental illness in an employee and to seek professional assistance as soon as possible. Here are the preferred rankings:

___4___ **A.** No; Mary needs professional help. For the supervisor to continue is dangerous.

___3___ **B.** The supervisor who stops there is dodging the issue and is letting another, possibly unqualified, person deal with a serious emotional disorder.

___2___ **C.** This is a good approach, provided the doctor is available and can respond by seeing her directly or making an appointment for her to see a psychologist or a psychiatrist.

___1___ **D.** This is a good approach and about all that the supervisor might be expected to do without professional advice.

___5___ **E.** Absolutely not; at this point she should not be pressed by a nonprofessional counselor.

A Case in Point: The Case of the Typist Who Got No Raise (Chapter 13)

This situation dramatizes the way in which an employee's sense of injustice can rise to the surface, requiring that the supervisor recognize it and attempt to reconcile it before it reaches critical proportions. Here are the preferred rankings:

___1___ **A.** True. Gathering and analyzing facts, rather than opinions, is the only sure way to lay the foundation for a just decision.

___3___ **B.** No. Confronting her with Ms. Tender wasn't exactly the best way to get at the real truth of the situation.

___5___ **C.** Asking a newcomer to buck the system is not realistic.

___4___ **D.** No. She appears to have used different standards in evaluating Janice.

___2___ **E.** Yes. Even when a supervisor hasn't been perceptive, a confrontation ought to waken her to her shortsightedness.

A Case in Point: The Case of the Sleeping Miner (Chapter 14)

Here is a case in which the supervisor can no longer dodge the responsibility for establishing and enforcing rules and regulations, even though carrying out discipline may be an unpleasant experience. Here are the preferred rankings:

___3___ **A.** This is a lax and probably ineffective way of handling a deteriorating situation. Differentiating between acceptable and unacceptable reasons for being away from the job is difficult at best. On the other hand, the edict on sleeping is clear and unequivocal, which has merit.

___2___ **B.** If Bob has been properly warned, this no-nonsense approach is all right. If he has not been warned, this action may backfire.

___1___ **C.** If the boss has not made a clear-cut issue about Bob's behavior in the past, this is about the best way to begin.

___4___ **D.** This leaves the matter entirely up to Bob's discretion, and there is little evidence that he will be responsive to the concerns of others.

___5___ **E.** Passing the buck to another employee not only won't work, it will also weaken the supervisor's ability to handle discipline in other instances and with other employees.

A Case in Point: The Case of the Revised Job Rating (Chapter 15)

This case illustrates the reason supervisors must first establish for their employees clear-cut standards of expected performance before they can conduct effective appraisal interviews that will lead to improved employee performance. Here are the preferred rankings:

___5___ **A.** No, but Barnes will insist on a change in standards.

___1___ **B.** True. The best conclusion.

___5___ **C.** No; Joe is honestly puzzled by the change in expectations.

___2___ **D.** Yes; unless Joe sees the job the way Barnes does, there is little hope that Joe will improve the way Barnes wants him to.

___5___ **E.** Support, not punishment, is what Joe needs. **A, C,** and **E** are unacceptable.

Comment
Barnes's objectives (to develop new performance standards) are his prerogative, and his rating of Joe was probably correct. But Barnes failed to use the interview to establish new performance targets mutually and to provide support for their attainment.

A Case in Point: The Case of the Lost Letter (Chapter 16)

This case illustrates the need for supervisors to accept responsibility for employee training and development and to become intimately involved in the process. Here are the preferred rankings:

___2___ **A.** A supervisor's negative attitude toward training has a broad impact.

___4___ **B.** Perhaps, but his supervisor should not have turned him loose on his own so soon.

___3___ **C.** True, unless Brenda develops a wiser attitude toward her training problems.

___1___ **D.** Training is most effective when it is a joint effort and the supervisor takes the final responsibility for it.

___5___ **E.** This dodges the basic problem and suggests only a long-term, probably costly and nonfeasible solution.

Key to Self-Check 1
1. c
2. b
3. d
4. a
5. d
6. a
7. c
8. c
9. a
10. b
11. T
12. T
13. T
14. F
15. T
16. F
17. T
18. T
19. T
20. T

Problem: a. Tom protests the method of selection for the person to be cut from the force. b. One or more other keypunch operators get sick or quit after Tom is let go. c. The agency policy points to an employee other than Tom as the most likely candidate. Additional problems: d. The work load is not reduced as anticipated. e. The agency revises its directive after Tom is cut. f. Employees slow down for fear that their number will be reduced if they get too productive.

Key to Self-Check 2
1. d
2. b
3. b
4. b
5. b
6. T
7. T
8. F
9. T
10. T
11. F
12. T
13. T
14. T
15. T
16. T
17. F
18. T
19. T
20. F

Problem: D, time; C, material; C, material; A, quantity; E, cost; B, quality.

Key to Self-Check 3
1. F
2. T
3. F
4. F
5. F
6. T
7. F
8. T
9. F
10. F
11. T
12. T
13. T
14. T
15. T
16. F
17. F
18. T
19. T
20. T
21. F
22. T
23. T
24. T
25. F
26. d
27. b
28. a
29. b
30. c

Key to Self-Check 4
1. T
2. F
3. F
4. T
5. T
6. F
7. T
8. T
9. T
10. T
11. b
12. c
13. a
14. b
15. d
16. d
17. a
18. b
19. c
20. c

Key to Self-Check 5
1. F
2. T
3. T
4. T
5. T
6. T
7. T
8. F
9. T
10. T
11. T
12. F
13. F
14. T
15. T
16. d
17. b
18. d
19. b
20. a

RANKINGS FOR ANSWERS TO CASES IN POINT

Index

Abboud, Michael J., 19
ABC analysis, 28–29
Absenteeism, 191–193
Acceptance theory of authority, 76
Accident-prone employees, 190
Accountability, 76
Adjustment, emotional, 184–185
Agenda, hidden, 134–135
Alcoholics Anonymous, 193
Alcoholism, 193–195
American College Testing Program (ACT), 13
American Telephone and Telegraph Company, 10
Anthony, Ted F., 19
Anxiety, 189
Appraisal, performance, 232–247
  bias in, 241–243
  checklist, 246–247
  and compensation, 236–237
  consistency in, 236
  discrimination charges, 237–238
  follow-up, 243
  halo effect, 241–242
  interviews, 239–241
  and job evaluation, 233–234
  and Management by Objectives (MBO), 243
  objective factors, 235
  purpose of, 233
  rating factors, 234
  reasons for poor performance, 243–244
  sandwich technique, 240–241
  saving face, 241
  subjective factors, 235
Apprenticeship training, 248–259
Attitude(s):
  changing, 137–138
  definition of, 135
  group, 124
  positive, 136
  sensitivity toward, 136–137
  survey, 139–140
Authority, 74–77
  acceptance theory of, 76
  accountability, 76
  chain of command, 77
  channels of, 77–78
  degrees of, 76–77
  delegation of, 77, 79–81
  institutional, 76
  and responsibility, 76
    (See also Responsibility)
  sources of, 75
Autocratic leadership, 37, 38, 40

Behavioral sciences [(see Groups); Human Relations; Motivation]

Benson, Carl A., 18
Blake, Robert R., 43–45
Body language, 155
Budgets, 56, 58, 93–94
Bulletin boards, 160
Byham, William C., 18

Canadian Department of National Revenue, 194
Carroll, Archie B., 19
Centralization, 73–74
Certification of managers, 13–14
Chain of command, 77
Channels, organization, 77–78
Collins, Ralph, 184
Commands, 165
Communications, 148–163
  action, 154
  ambiguity in, 172
  body language, 155
  bulletin boards, 160
  checklist, 162–163
  conferences, 160
  conflict situations, 136
  credibility, 152–153
  defined, 148
  disciplinary policy, 223
  employee counseling (see Counseling, employee)
  face-to-face, 157–158
  grapevine, 150–151
  group, 170
  instructions, 164–176
  letters, 159
  listening, 156–157, 170–171
  manner in, 155
  meanings, 155
  meetings, 160
  open, 150
  order-giving, 164–176
  organization channels, 77–78
  overcommunication, 153
  person-to-person, 158–159
  and personalities, 156
  and policy, 63–64
  reports, 159
  restricted, 150
  satellite, 149
  spoken, 158–160
  style, 169
  systems, 149–150
  taboos, 153
  telephone, 158
  three-dimensional, 151–152
  upward, 156–157
  visual aids, 161
  web, 150
  wheel, 150
  written, 159–161, 167–168

Compensation:
  and cooperation, 141
  exempt employees, 4
  and performance appraisal, 236–237
Complaints, employee (see Grievances)
Comprehensive Employment and Training Act (CETA) of 1973, 256–257
Conferences, 160
Conflict:
  attitudes of, 136–141
  communications, 136
  confrontations, 136
  handling of, 132–134
  hidden agendas, 134–135
  laboratory training, 134
  management checklist, 146–147
  sensitivity, 134–136
  sources of, 132
  (See also Cooperation)
Contingency leadership, 37
Continuum of leadership, 38–39
Control(s), 87–101
  automatic, 92
  budgetary, 93–94
    (See also Budgets)
  checklist, 100–101
  cost, 93
  cost variance report, 93–94
  employee response to, 96–97
  management-by-exception chart, 95
  Management by Objectives (MBO), 98
  material, 93
  and plans, 59
  quality, 92–93
  quantity, 92
  standards, 88–91, 96
  system, 93–94
  time, 93
  (See also Controlling)
Controlling, 11, 87–101
  checklist, 100–101
  measurements, 90–91
  people, 96–97
  and planning, 88–89
  process, 91–92
  purpose of, 87–88
  self-control, 97
  span of control, 74
  standards, 88–91, 96
  tolerance, 88
  [See also Control(s)]
Cooperation, 140–145
  appreciation of, 146–147
  with associates, 142–143
  avoiding misunderstanding, 144

277

Cooperation (*Cont.*):
   checklist, 146–147
   and compensation, 141
   with staff people, 143
   Transactional Analysis (TA), 143–144
   (*See also* Conflict)
Correspondence training, 256
Cost-benefit analysis, 26
Cost control, 93–94
Cost variance report, 93–94
Counseling, employee, 182–199
   absentees, 191–193
   accident-prone employees, 190
   adjustment, 184–185
   alcoholic employees, 193–195
   anxiety, 189
   breakdown, 189
   checklist, 197–199
   drug addiction, 195
   emotional problems, 183–186
   neurosis, 184
   nondirective counseling, 187
   objectivity in, 188
   process, 186–188
   professional, 190, 196
   psychosis, 184
   referral, 189–190
   results, 186–187
   schizophrenia, 184
   symptoms of problems, 185–186, 188–189
   techniques, 186–199
   workaholics, 195–196
Cover, William H., 18
Cowin, Ronald M., 18
Credibility, 152–153

Dallas Cowboys, 69
Davis, Keith, 6, 18
Decentralization, 73–74
Decision makers, 27–28
Decision making, 20–33
   ABC analysis, 28–29
   checklist, 32–33
   cost-benefit analysis, 26
   group, 29–30
   and intuition, 26–27
   mathematical, 25–26
   need for, 23
   and problem solving, 22–23
   systematic, 25
   trade-offs, 26
   (*See also* Problem solving)
Delegation:
   acceptance of, 80–81
   and accountability, 76
   and authority, 77
   methods, 79
   and responsibility, 77
   Supervisor's Task and Delegation Chart, 80
   timing of, 79
Democratic leadership, 37, 38

Development, employee (*see* Training, employee)
Directing, 11
   communications (*see* Communications)
   order-giving, 164–176
Discipline, employee, 214–226
   absenteeism, 191–193
   alcoholism, 193–195
   in anger, 219
   checklist, 225–226
   communicating policy, 223
   drug usage, 195
   evidence, 222
   hot-stove rule, 217–218
   and labor unions, 218, 220
   negative, 216
   policy, 60, 223
   positive, 216–217
   prejudices, 222
   progressive, 217, 222–223
   purpose of, 214–215
   records, 222
   rule breaking, 215–216
   suspension versus discharge, 220–221
   warnings, 220, 222
Discrimination in appraisals, 237–238, 241–243
Dissatisfaction, 112–113
Drug usage, 195
Du Pont Company, 190

Eastman Kodak Company, 184
Employee communications (*see* Communications)
Employee counseling (*see* Counseling, employee)
Employees:
   absentee, 191–193
   accident-prone, 190
   alcoholic, 193–195
   drug-using, 195
   problem, 185–189

Fair Labor Standards Act of 1938, 4
Fiedler, Fred, 37
Foch, Marshal, 35
Followership, 40
Ford Motor Company, 5
Free-rein leadership, 37, 38
Fulmer, William E., 18, 19

Gellerman, Saul W., 18
General Electric Company, 10
Georgopolous, Basil S., 19
Goals, supervisory, 55, 56, 64–65
Gordon, Gerald, 190
Grievances, 200–213
   arbitration, 208
   bargaining on, 203–204
   checklist, 212–213

Grievances (*Cont.*):
   common, 209–210
   handling process, 203
   imagined, 202
   loopholes, 205
   prevention of, 208–211
   procedure, 207
   saving face in, 206–207
   settlement of, 201, 205
   sources of, 208–209
   unsettled, 207–208
Group(s):
   attitudes, 124
   behavior in, 118–119
   checklist, 128–129
   decision making, 29–30
   dynamics, 119
   goals, 121–123
   individuality within, 120, 126–127
   informal, 119–120
   loyalties, 120–121
   orders, 170
   participation, 122–123
   popularity with, 124
   training for, 256–257
   week and strong, 124–125
   (*See also* Human relations; Motivation)

Halo effect, 241–242
Herzberg, Frederick, 112–113
Hierarchy of needs, 109–111
Hot-stove rule, 217–218
Human relations:
   and control process, 96–97
   counseling (*see* Counseling, employee)
   group behavior, 118–130
   motivation, 106–117
   [*See also* Group(s); Motivation]
Human resources development (*see* Training, employee)
Hygiene factors, 113

I'm okay, you're okay, 143–144
Induction training, 250
Institute of Certified Professional Managers (ICPM), 13
Instructions, checklist, 175–176
   (*See also* Communications; Order giving)
Insubordination, 167
International Management Council (IMC), 13
Interview, appraisal, 239–241
Intuition, 26–27

Job breakdown, 252–253
Job evaluation, 233
Job Instruction Training (JIT), 255

Key point in training, 252–254

Koppers Company, Inc., 45

Laboratory training, 134
Lasorda, Tom, 41
Leadership, 34–42
  autocratic, 37, 38, 40
  and behavioral sciences, 41–42
  characteristics, 35–36
  checklist, 47–49
  contingency, 37
  continuum, 38–39
  defined, 35
  democratic, 37, 38
  followership, 39
  free-rein, 37, 38
  integrative, 37
  and loyalty, 41
  and management, 34
  Managerial Grid, 43–45
  participative, 37–38, 40–45
  personality, 38–39
  and popularity, 35
  results-centered, 37
  situational, 37
  styles, 36–38
  tips on, 45–46
  traits, 35–36
  University of Michigan studies, 40
  (*See also* Motivation)
Levinson, Harry, 188–190
Likert, Rensis, 12, 19, 40
Line and staff, 71–72, 78
Listening, 156–157
  active, 170–171
  and attitudinal changes, 138
  passive, 171
  (*See also* Communications)
Loyalty, 41
  in groups, 120–121

McGregor, Douglas, 42–43, 97
Maintenance factors, 113
Management:
  and leadership, 34
  process, 10–11
Management by Exception, 94–96
Management by Objectives (MBO), 98, 243
Managerial Grid, 43–45
Mann, Floyd C., 19
Manual, supervisor's, 63
Maslow, A. H., 109, 110
Matrix organization, 73
Measurement, 88–91
Meetings, 160
Merit rating (*see* Appraisal, performance)
Mikado, 216
Minimum Wage Law, 4
Motivation:
  and anthropology, 107
  checklist, 116–117
  and dissatisfaction, 112–113

Motivation (*Cont.*):
  group, 118–130
  Herzberg, Frederick, 112–113
  and human relations, 107–108
  hygiene factors, 113
  individual, 106–117
  individuality, 108–109
  interaction, 108
  maintenance factors, 113
  Maslow, A. H., 109, 110
  needs hierarchy, 109–111
  personality, 109
  and psychiatry, 107
  and psychology, 107
  satisfaction, 111–114
  and sociology, 107
  for training, 259–260
  [*See also* Group(s); Human relations; Leadership]
Mouton, Jane S., 44–45

National Management Association (NMA), 13, 14
Neurosis, 184
Newport, M. Gene, 18
Northrup, Herbert R., 18

O'Donnell, Laurence, 18
Order giving, 164–176
  ambiguity, 172
  in anger, 169
  checklist, 175–176
  commands, 165
  group, 170
  guidelines for, 173–174
  insubordination, 167
  listening, 170–171
  repeating, 165
  requests, 165
  resistance to, 172
  tone of voice, 169
  written orders, 167–168
Organization(s):
  centralized, 73–74
  charts, 70–71
  checklist, 85–86
  customer, 72
  decentralized, 73–74
  departmental, 81–83
  divisional, 72
  functional, 72
  geographical, 72
  informal, 69, 119–120
  line-and-staff, 71–72
  matrix, 73
  project, 72
  task force, 72
  (*See also* Organizing)
Organizing, 11, 68–86
  authority, 74–77
  centralization versus decentralization, 73–74
  charts, 70–71

Organizing (*Cont.*):
  checklist, 85–86
  delegation, 77, 79–81
    (*See also* Delegation)
  departmental, 81–83
  line-and-staff, 71–72, 78–79
  principles, 81
  purpose of, 69–70
  responsibility, 74–77
  span of control, 74
  (*See also* Organization)
Orientation training, 249–250

Participation with groups, 122–124
Participative leadership, 37–38, 40–45
Patton, General George, 36
Performance appraisal (*see* Appraisal, performance)
Personality, 38–40, 109
Planning, 10–11, 54–67
  budgets, 56, 58
  checklist, 66–67
  and controls, 59
  definitions, 55
  five-point planning check chart, 59
  frequency, 58
  goals, standards, and objectives, 55, 56
  plans, types of, 57–58
    (*See also* Plans)
  and policy, 55, 60–64
    (*See also* Policy, company)
  premises, 57
  procedures, 56
  process, 55–57
  programs, 57
  rules and regulations, 55
  schedules, 56
  supervisory goals, 64–65
  targets, 58–59
  (*See also* Plans)
Plans, 55–58
  long-range, 57
  short-range, 57
  single-use, 58
  standing, 57
  (*See also* Planning)
Policy, company, 55, 60–64
  communicating, 63–64
  defined, 60
  disciplinary, 223
  interpretation, 62
  manual, 63
  scope, 60–61
  and supervisors, 61–62
  written, 61
Problem(s):
  definition of, 21
  potential, 21–22, 25
  recognition of, 21–22
  types of, 21
  (*See also* Decision making; Problem solving)

Problem solving, 20–33
  checklist, 32–33
  cutoff point, 27
  and decision making, 22–23
  gap, 21–22
  procedure, 23–25
  (*See also* Decision making)
Procedures, 56
Professionalism, 190, 196
  in supervision, 13–14
Programmed instruction, 257
  branching, 257
  linear, 257
  teaching machines, 257
Programs, 57
Project management, 72–73
Psychiatry, 107
Psychology, 107
Psychosis, 184

Quality control, 92–93

Reports, 159
Research Institute of America, 258
Responsibility, 74–77
Richardson, Homer L., 19
Rules and regulations, 215–216, 221–223

St. Louis, Ann, 194
Sandwich technique in appraisal, 240–241
Satisfaction, 111–114
Schappe, Robert H., 18
Schmidt, Warren H., 39
Sensitivity, 134–136
Shell (UK) Ltd., 191
Shop steward:
  and discipline, 220
  and grievances, 204–207
Situational leadership, 37
Skills inventory, 255
Sociology, 107
Somervell, Brehon, 45
Span of control, 74
Staff, cooperating with, 143

Staffing, 11
Standards, control, 88–91, 96
Supervision:
  balance in, 11–12
  certification of, 13
  characteristics of, 5
  checklist, 16–18
  definition of, 3–4
  drawbacks in, 13
  exempt classification, 4
  failings of, 14
  history of, 2–3
  as keystone in management, 6
  legal definition of, 4
  performance measures for, 7–9
  professionalism in, 13
  responsibilities of, 2–18
  source of, 4–5
  task difficulty, 9
Supervisor's manual, 63
Suspension versus discharge, 220–221
System 4, 40
System controls, 93–94

Taft-Hartley Act of 1947, 4
Tannenbaum, Robert, 39
Task and Delegation chart, 80
Task force, 72–73
Taylor, P. J., 191
Teaching machines, 257
Telephone usage, 158–159
Theory X and Theory Y, 42–43
Thorndike, Edward L., 257
Time standards, 93
  (*See also* Standards, control)
Tolerance, control, 88
Trade-offs, 26
Training, employee, 248–263
  apprenticeship, 258–259
  checklist, 262–263
  Comprehensive Employment and Training Act (CETA) of 1973, 256–257
  correspondence, 256
  four-step method, 251
  individual versus group, 256–257
  induction, 250

Training, employee (*Cont.*):
  job, 250–255
  job breakdown, 252–253
  Job Instruction Training (JIT), 251, 255
  key point, 252–254
  learning plateaus, 260
  learning retention, 258
  manuals, 256
  motivation, 259–260
  needs, 249
  older workers, 259
  orientation, 250
  outside reading, 256
  programmed instruction, 257
  sequence, 253
  skills inventory, 255
  teaching machines, 257
  timetable, 253, 255
  and training departments, 260
  vestibule, 259
  visual aids, 258
Transactional Analysis (TA), 143–144
Trice, Harrison M., 193
Trivial many, 29
20/80 syndrome, 28

Unions, labor, 7
  and supervisors, 4
  (*See also* Discipline, employee, Shop steward)
U.S. Bureau of Labor Statistics, 208
U.S. Department of Health, Education, and Welfare, 194
U.S. Department of Labor, 257
University of Michigan studies, 40
Uris, Auren, 39, 40

Vestibule training, 259
Visual aids, 161, 258
Vital few, 29

Workaholic, 195–196

Young Men's Christian Association (YMCA), 13